GENDER TRIALS

GENDER TRIALS

Emotional Lives in Contemporary Law Firms

JENNIFER L. PIERCE

UNIVERSITY OF CALIFORNIA PRESS
BERKELEY   LOS ANGELES   LONDON

University of California Press
Berkeley and Los Angeles, California

University of California Press, Ltd.
London, England

Library of Congress Cataloging-in-Publication Data

Pierce, Jennifer L., 1958–
    Gender trials : emotional lives in contemporary law firms /
Jennifer L. Pierce.
        p.   cm.
    Includes bibliographical references and index.
    ISBN 0–520–20107–8 (alk. paper).—ISBN 0–520–20108–6
(pbk. : alk. paper)
    1. Law firms—Social aspects—United States.   2. Practice
of law—Social aspects—United States.   3. Sex role in the work
environment—United States.   I. Title.
    KF300.P53   1995
    331.7´6134´973—dc20   94–24940

Printed in the United States of America
9 8 7 6 5 4 3 2 1
The paper used in this publication meets the minimum
requirements of American National Standard for Information
Sciences—Permanence of Paper for Printed Library Materials,
ANSI Z39.48–1984.

*For my parents, Judith Pierce and Robert Pierce,
and for Clayton, Dair, and Ann*

Contents

Preface and Acknowledgments

In 1980, I began working as a litigation paralegal in one of the largest law firms in San Francisco's financial district. Although I had worked previously in many different kinds of jobs, I was struck by the oppressiveness of this work environment. Hours were incredibly long for legal workers. Young lawyers, along with paralegals and legal secretaries, sometimes worked sixty and seventy hours a week. Work was typically routine, monotonous, and dull. Turnover was high, yet firm management did not appear to regard turnover as a problem at all. A young lawyer once characterized management's attitude toward legal workers with a chewing-gum analogy: "They just pop us in, chew us up, and spit us out when they're done." Like many other litigation paralegals, I left after several years for more promising horizons.

Almost ten years later I came back to work inside large law firms to do research for my dissertation. After spending fifteen months as a fieldworker in two different law offices and interviewing over sixty legal workers, I could see that many of the problems were the same. Hours continue to be long, especially for young associates. And turnover rates are still high for legal workers across job categories. This time, however, I found myself most attentive to sex segregation in law firms. The vast majority of lawyers in these offices are men, and support-staff workers such as paralegals and secretaries are predominantly female. Further, I was struck by the strong socio-emotional component in legal workers' jobs. Lawyers and paralegals not only performed mental tasks researching case law and writing legal

documents, but they also performed what sociologist Arlie Hochschild has termed "emotional labor." Whereas litigators are trained to
be alternately intimidating and strategically friendly, paralegals are
required to be nurturing and deferential. The more time I spent in
the field, the more I wondered why sex segregation persisted, especially as the number of women entering the legal profession grew so
dramatically. Further, I wondered what role emotional labor played
in law firms. This book is an attempt to formulate a sociological
framework to answer these questions.

Both the research and the writing of this book depended on the
support and encouragement of many people. Like many books, this
one began as a doctoral dissertation, when I was a graduate student
at the University of California at Berkeley. The chair of my dissertation committee, Arlie Hochschild, deeply influenced my thinking
early in this project and provided generous support through many
early drafts. Bob Bellah and Nancy Chodorow proved to be excellent
second committee members. Bellah encouraged me to consider the
moral implications of my work, while Chodorow's sharp analytical
comments pushed me to clarify my ideas. I also owe thanks to Eli
Sagan and Jorge Arditti, who read my dissertation and assured me it
would be worth rewriting, and I am grateful to Bob Freeland for his
encouragement at this project's inception and for his incisive comments on early chapter drafts. Finally, as a graduate student I was
fortunate to be a part of a dissertation group with a bright and lively
group of people. Gloria Cuadraz, Mary Beth Kelsey, and Anders
Schneiderman proved to be all one would want in an intellectual
study group: critical and tough-minded, yet encouraging and supportive.

Composing this book as an assistant professor at a public institu-
tion that values feminist research has made a difference. This project
would not have taken the direction it did without the two years I
have been affiliated with the Center for Advanced Feminist Studies
at the University of Minnesota or without my work on the editorial
board of *Signs*. Barbara Laslett was one of the first people to review
the revised manuscript from cover to cover, and Lisa Disch has read
and commented on almost all my revisions. The conversations as
well as the editorial board meetings we have shared have been a

constant source of intellectual challenge and stimulation. For reading and responding to various pieces of this project, I thank Ron Aminzade, Lisa Bower, Dair Gillespie, Susanna Ferlito, Alberto Pulido, Leola Johnson, Mary Jo Kane, Ann Leffler, Jane McLeod, Carmen Sirianni, and Deborah Smith. I was also fortunate to have excellent critical comments from the external reviewers for the University of California Press. Vicki Smith, in particular, provided pages and pages of single-spaced comments pushing me to strengthen and refine my theoretical argument. For assistance in the production stage of this book, I am grateful to Erika Büky and Ellen Stein with the University of California Press. Finally, I thank Clayton Gillespie, whose patience, confidence, and optimism have sustained me throughout this work.

In addition, I would like to thank Laurence Rose, Lou Natali, and the National Institute for Trial Advocacy for allowing me to attend and observe NITA's special three-week training seminar on trial advocacy, though of course all my discussion of the training sessions reflects my own interpretations and is not intended to represent NITA's goals or perspectives. I also want to thank all the people who took me into their work lives and spent hours in interviews or casual conversation sharing their views about stress and litigation.

This book was made possible by a number of institutional forms of support, including a University of California, Berkeley, Regents Fellowship; the Tomasina and Abigal Bellah Memorial Fellowship; the Sagan Fellowship; a Newhouse grant for dissertation research, and dissertation research grants provided by the Department of Sociology. In addition, I wish to thank the sociology department at the University of Minnesota for helping to create the optimal conditions for completing this book.

Chapter One

Gendering Occupations and Emotions in Law Firms

At the Bar: Rambos Invade the Courtroom
New York Times

I hate playing mom, but to [the attorney]
it's very important that you be that way.
Woman paralegal

In the United States, law firms, like many other workplaces, are sex-segregated.[1] Despite the increasing number of women entering the legal profession, most attorneys are still men, and most support-staff workers, such as legal secretaries and paralegals, are women (Epstein 1993; Murphree 1984; Johnstone and Wenglinsky 1985). Because of the proportions of men and women found in these occupations, we tend to construe them as gendered; in other words, we regard trial law as "men's work" because men do it and clerical work as "women's work" because women do it. The gendered nature of these jobs is expressed and reinforced by the idioms "Rambo litigator," which emphasizes the hypermasculinity associated with trial lawyers (Margolick 1988), and "mothering paralegal," which ties this occupation to the practice of mothering—something women, and not men, typically do in our culture.

The gendering of occupations not only contributes to an understanding of particular positions within law firms as appropriate for women or men, but it also constructs gendered expectations about the emotional dimensions of these jobs. Like Rambo, trial lawyers

1

are expected to be tough, aggressive, and intimidating, whereas
paralegals, on the other hand, are expected to be supportive and
nurturing mothers. Although this division of labor may seem natural,
or even unproblematic, the gendering of occupations and emotions
is not a neutral process. Naturalizing the division of labor conceals
the extent to which the gendered assignment of work creates and reproduces the asymmetrical distribution of power and resources between women and men. Compared to men, women are paid less for
their work—even when they both work in the same job (Reskin and
Roos 1990; Acker 1989). In addition, what is defined as women's
work carries less status and prestige than men's work and offers few
opportunities for advancement (Epstein 1970; Bridges 1982). Finally, even women's feelings are given less consideration on the job
than men's (Hochschild 1983).

This book contributes to the growing research on gender, emotions and occupations by exploring how sex segregation is maintained and reproduced through case studies of two law offices: a private law firm and an in-house corporate legal department. In each of
these offices, I study litigation paralegals and trial lawyers: two legal
occupations that are highly interdependent, yet clearly demarcated
by gender. As with other studies on sex segregation, my interest lies
in explaining how this gendered division of labor is maintained and
why it persists. However, this book differs from previous studies on
sex segregation in two important ways.

First, this ethnography aims to bridge the gap between two com-
peting sociological explanations for occupational sex segregation:
macro-level accounts that emphasize structural characteristics and
micro-level studies that focus on social actors to explain the gendered division of labor.[2] Studies emphasizing structural factors in the
reproduction of gender asymmetry examine formal and informal organizational practices, personnel policies, the labor process, and firm
and industry structure. Those that utilize actor-oriented approaches
examine the gendered meanings that women and men attach to the
work they do. Rather than adopting either a structural account or an
actor oriented-approach, this book examines the dynamic and reciprocal relationship between these two levels of analysis. My central
thesis is that the gendered structure of law firms shapes legal work-

ers' practices at the same time that legal workers participate—wittingly or not—in the reproduction of gender relations. To make this argument, I reconceptualize Marxist theories of the labor process by integrating feminist theories of organizations and psychoanalytic sociology to explain the gendering of organizations, occupations, and emotions.

Second, this study considers not only the structural characteristics of law firms and the role of legal workers but also emotions, or "emotional labor" (Hochschild 1983), as a site for the reproduction of gender.[3] In contemporary law firms, emotional labor takes the form of caretaking and deference for female paralegals. When trial attorneys lose their tempers, blow hot and cold, and yell or scream, their paralegals are expected to stay calm, and be comforting and deferential in the face of such outbursts. By playing this emotional role, women paralegals unwittingly reproduce their subordinate position in the law firm hierarchy. On the other hand, women who violate these emotional norms are harshly criticized for their "unprofessional behavior," sanctioned through a reduction in an annual raise or, in the most extreme case, faced with termination (see Chapters 4 and 6). These non-reciprocal and gendered emotional exchanges also take place when men and women work in the same job. Male paralegals, for example, are not held to the same norms as women. Although they encounter restrictions about the expression of anger, they do not have to "play mom." They can get away with being distant and polite, rather than nurturing or nice. In this way, gendering occupations constructs asymmetrical emotional relations between men and women not only when they work in different occupations but even when they hold the same type of job.

Emotional labor, despite its seemingly invisible attachment to job descriptions, poses both social and psychological consequences for legal workers. Socially, the systematic attribution of emotional tasks to particular jobs—the Rambo litigator, the mothering paralegal—imposes fixed and static conceptions of masculinity and femininity on men and women. For individuals whose personal feelings do not fit these prescribed roles and expectations, emotional labor is highly stressful for lawyers and for legal assistants and, as this book shows, can be most stressful of all for women workers in either category.

Theories of Occupational Sex Segregation

The process by which occupations and emotions become gendered in law firms, and the social and psychological consequences of this process for legal workers are central concerns of this book. Although the study of emotions as labor in the workplace is relatively new,[4] there is a considerable sociological and feminist literature on sex segregation, including macro-level accounts, which emphasize structural factors, and micro-level approaches, which focus on social actors. Perhaps most influential among the early macro-level studies on women and work is Rosabeth Moss Kanter's *Men and Women of the Corporation* (1977), in which she argues that one's position within organizational structure determines behavior. Comparing secretaries and managers, she argues that observed differences between groups with respect to such matters as personal aspirations and degree of acquiescence have been misleadingly attributed to sex differences when they actually reflect differential locations within the organizational structure—notably, different access to job mobility. More recent macro-level accounts of occupational sex segregation focus on industry structure; the economic, technical and organizational arrangements of firms; discrimination by employers; social control; the labor process and men's control over women's labor power (Reskin and Roos 1990; Jacobs 1989; Milkman 1987; Baron and Bielby 1987; Lyson 1982; Bridges 1982; Hartmann 1976; 1987).

Micro-level approaches privilege the role of individual actors in the reproduction of gender. Drawing from psychoanalytic feminist theory, Christine Williams (1989) argues that men in non-traditional jobs such as nursing maintain and reproduce gender difference by adopting a non-nurturing bedside manner, taking on the few positions of authority within the occupation, and socializing only with male doctors to emphasize their masculinity. Robin Leidner (1993) makes a similar argument about the reproduction of gender in service work from a symbolic interactionist perspective. In her study, men in sales frame their interactions with customers as "contests of will," where success is determined by persistence, aggression, and toughness, requirements "that allowed the agents to interpret their work as manly" (Leidner 1993: 201). Other micro-level studies explore the gendered meanings workers attach to jobs such as department-store sales, the printing trades, and waiting tables (Benson 1984; Cockburn 1983; Hall 1993) or emphasize individual choice and attributes rather than meaning in creating a gendered division of labor. For instance, Marini and Brinton (1984) argue that socialization leads to women's choices of sex-typed occupations, while human-capital theorists link level of education and other individual attributes to women's position in the labor market (Becker 1991).

Although both structural and micro-level accounts have made important contributions to our understanding of sex segregation, both types of studies have their limitations. By shifting focus from individual women to the structure of the workplace, macro-level approaches have helped document the nature of discrimination against women, wage differentials between women and men, and sexual harassment on the job. But structural accounts are limited theoretically because they neglect the role of human agency. They tend to treat workers' behavior as derivative of structural locations, an assumption that treats women, as well as other workers, as dupes who passively and unreflexively submit to the demands of the corporation. Furthermore, studies that look only at structural characteristics do not reveal the micro-level processes that often generate and sustain sex segregation. Micro-level accounts, on the other hand, help remind us that women workers actively participate in the construction of meaning of their work and resist degradation on the job (Rollins 1985; Glenn 1988; Diamond 1988; Statham 1988). Although these studies address some of the limitations of structural approaches, they tend to neglect the way micro-level interactions are tied to larger social institutions and embedded within historically specific contexts. Furthermore, because such approaches fail to recognize the historically contingent nature of the sexual division of labor, they often treat gender as universal and unchanging.

These criticisms resurrect a longstanding debate in social theory concerning the merits of structural approaches versus those that highlight actors (Bourdieu 1977a; Giddens 1979; Abrams 1982). Addressing the limitations of this debate, Anthony Giddens insists that structure and agency be understood in relational terms. He writes: "Even the most autonomous agent is in some degree dependent, and

the most dependent actor . . . retains some autonomy" (1979: 93).
His notion of the "duality of structure"—that is, "structure as both
the medium and the outcome of practice"—is an attempt to address
this problem (1979: 69). Like Giddens, I am also concerned with
moving beyond the structure-agency debate. In particular, I am interested in developing a historically specific account of sex segregation by theorizing the "duality of structure." To develop this theoretical framework, I draw from Marxist theories of the labor process,
particularly Michael Burawoy's (1979) argument that the organization
of work relations "manufactures consent" at the site of production.
For Burawoy, the labor process is at once relational—the organization of relations between people in a workplace—and practical—the
actual work that people perform. Thus, in his account of social reproduction, structure is the medium as well as the outcome of practice.
Further, Burawoy insists that these processes be located in their historically specific context, that of monopoly capitalism.

While Burawoy's contention can be extended to argue that the
structure of law firms shapes legal workers' practices at the same
time that these practices constitute and reproduce the hierarchical
structure of these organizations, it contains a number of limitations.
In my argument, the labor process in law firms is reproduced not
only through mental and physical labor, but through emotional labor
as well. Emotional labor, then, is a lens through which I explore the
complex patterns of work relations that give rise to consent and resistance among women and men legal workers. I argue that the
workplace is also a site for the reproduction of gender relations. For
instance, the fact that male and female paralegals work in a female-
dominated occupation that serves predominantly male attorneys
poses divergent consequences for the ways women and men are
treated by their employers and for the degree to which they consent
to or resist organizational practices.

Reconstructing Social Theory

In *Manufacturing Consent,* Burawoy (1979) argues that industrial
workers conform to production norms not because they are forced to

but rather because they choose to do so: "The labor process can be understood in terms of a specific combination of force and consent that elicits cooperation in the pursuit of profit" (1979: 30). More specifically, Burawoy argues that under monopoly capitalism with the development of unionization, a hegemonic form of work emerges in which coercion of workers has been replaced by limited autonomy granted them through collective bargaining. This creates a paradox, for in accepting this limited autonomy workers consent to the restrictions of the labor process. How does this come about?

In Burawoy's formulation, consent is elicited through a "game" workers enact on the shop floor: the rules of the game are defined in terms of "making out," that is, maximizing bonus pay-out for piece work. In his study, Burawoy finds that workers work as fast as they can to meet the piece rate and then spend the rest of their shift "goldbricking," simply hanging around. By participating in the game, men gain psychological rewards (e.g., the satisfaction derived from doing a tough job). Further, by choosing to work at their own pace, workers resist the time-clock regime of the factory. At the same time, however, their participation in the game fulfills the designated piece rate, thereby reproducing the labor process and procuring surplus value for the owners of the company.

In Burawoy's argument, the labor process is reproduced through manual labor. In my reconceptualization of Burawoy's theory, it is also reproduced through emotional labor. In Arlie Hochschild's influential conception of the term, emotional labor requires workers "to induce or suppress feeling in order to sustain the outward countenance that produces the proper state of mind in others" (1983: 7). Just as the flight attendants in Hochschild's study are expected to hide their irritation with difficult passengers and instead display concern for their welfare, factory workers must suppress the resentment associated with their subordinate status. Playing the game helps to suppress these emotions by giving workers feelings of competence and control and a sense of being "one up" on management. Thus, not only does the process of "making out" include an emotional dimension providing psychological rewards for workers but this dimension plays a role in the reproduction of the labor process.

Emotional labor is also part of the labor process in law firms. Paralegals, for example, are expected not only to do mental tasks, such as analyzing documents and completing legal research, but also to be deferential to trial lawyers and to provide emotional support for them. Similarly, the work of trial lawyers involves not only the research and writing of legal pleadings but also an emotional presentation of self as intimidating or strategically friendly. Emotional labor is crucial to understanding the paradox of limited autonomy and consent in law firms. As semi-professionals, paralegals also have limited autonomy in the law firm. While their job informally requires them to do emotional caretaking of the attorneys for whom they work, legal assistants select different strategies in performing this task. Some personalize relationships with lawyers (e.g., attempting to characterize their relationships with lawyers as friendships rather than exploitative work relations), whereas others regard this relationship cynically as an exercise in "babysitting." Whether paralegals choose to engage themselves fully in working relationships or to distance themselves, their strategies reinforce the attorney as the authority and themselves as subordinates, thereby reproducing the labor process within the law firm.

Expanding Burawoy's theory of the labor process to include emotional labor is useful in helping us to understand the reproduction of hierarchical relations within law firms. However, his analysis contains another limitation: it does not conceptualize the ways in which labor processes are gendered. In law firms, male attorneys are superordinate and women paralegals subordinate. Feminist theories of organizations help us to conceptualize the restrictions in the labor process as gendered (Acker 1990; Cockburn 1985; Game and Pringle 1983; Knights and Willmott 1986; Phillips and Taylor 1986). Rosemary Pringle (1988), for example, studies waged work by viewing organizations as gendered and the workplace as one of the many sites of the reproduction of gender and class relations. Similarly, Joan Acker argues that organizations are gendered, meaning "that advantage and disadvantage, exploitation and control, action and emotion, meaning and identity, are patterned through and in terms of a distinction between male and female, masculine and feminine. Gender is not an addition to ongoing processes, conceived of as gender neutral. Rather it is an integral part of those processes, which cannot be understood without an analysis of gender" (1990: 146). For these feminist theorists, gender is not simply a social category, but a "primary way of signifying relationships of power" (Scott 1986: 1067).

By reconceptualizing Burawoy's argument to incorporate the insights of these feminist thinkers, I argue that the restrictions of the labor process within law firms are gendered. The reproduction of the labor process means that men are affirmed as the authority and women as subordinates. Because gender is not simply a social category but a signifier for power relations, the gendering of law firms is not a neutral process; rather, these structures have a differential impact on women and men. Gendering law firms also has consequences for the amount of space one occupies and the possibilities for mobility within the firm. Men occupy a greater proportion of office space (see Chapter 2). Moreover, for the minority of men in paralegal positions, chances for mobility are greater because male lawyers encourage them professionally. Finally, even when men are in female-dominated jobs such as paralegals, they have more latitude to resist or ignore the feminized socio-emotional requirements than women do (see Chapters 4 and 6).

In this way, the gendering of organizations extends from the level of occupational structure to the performance of emotional labor. Indeed, Candace West and Don Zimmerman suggest that emotional labor is also a way of "doing gender" (1987: 144). Like Acker and other feminist scholars, they conceptualize "doing gender" in the context of male domination, so that "in doing gender, men are also doing dominance and women are doing deference" (1987: 146). As West and Zimmerman observe, deference and caretaking are consistent with our culturally held notions of female appropriate behavior. When women behave this way, they "produce enactments of their 'essential' femininity" (1987: 144). On the other hand, aggression and intimidation constitute gender-appropriate behavior for men, so doing gender enhances men's status as men. Within law firms, doing gender serves to reproduce the gendered occupational structure. By being deferential and providing emotional services, women paralegals simultaneously reinforce their status as subordinate and as female and affirm the status of attorneys as superordinate and as male.

The gendering of organizations and occupations also extends to the level of meaning and identity (Acker 1990). Burawoy's study, though it examines consent, does so only in behavioral terms and tends to overlook the subjective dimension of work. As David Knights writes: "Burawoy fails to theorise subjectivity or identity sufficiently to account for the workers' preoccupation with production output at Allied Corporation. His analysis of the game of making-out is not so much wrong as it is incomplete" (1990: 311).[5] In Knights's view, part of the explanation for men's behavior on the shop floor "must lie with the men's concern with their own masculine identity" (1990: 312). Their consent is obtained not only through their participation in the game (behavior), but through the simultaneous affirmation of their identities as men (gendered subjectivity).

Knights suggests that incorporating an understanding of gendered subjectivity would strengthen Burawoy's argument. Within sociology, sex-role socialization theories provide one explanation for the acquisition of a gendered sense of self. These perspectives argue that girls and boys learn to conform to cultural norms for sex appropriate roles and behavior through socialization processes such as the family, peer group, schooling, media, and other factors (Weitzman 1975). These approaches deny agency to social actors, however.[6] They tend to assume behavioral conformity and, as a result, cannot explain why some women conform and others do not. In these explanations, behavior is the result of conscious decisions and choices. Yet feelings and behavior are not always available to conscious thought. Many women paralegals I interviewed reported that they hated "playing mom" to trial lawyers for whom they worked, yet found themselves compelled to do so. Conceiving of feelings and motivations as unconscious—in the psychoanalytic sense of the term—helps to explain the tenacity of women paralegals' commitment to the organization of sex and gender. It helps to explain why they continue to behave as traditional female caretakers even when they may not want to do so. As Nancy Chodorow writes, "We do not just react to our contemporary situation and conscious wishes, nor can we easily change values, feelings and behavior simply if we have an encouraging social setting. . . . [P]sychoanalysis explains our commitment to this past, which arose at a time of huge feelings of helplessness and dependency, a commitment which is now repressed, unconscious. . . . It is who we are, and changing that is very difficult" (1989b: 171).

This does not mean that change is not possible or that people are not agents in their own lives. Psychoanalytic theory, particularly an object-relations approach,[7] assumes that if we become conscious of our unconscious actions and feelings, then we can make choices about how to act upon them. This is the meaning of Freud's famous dictum—"where id was, there shall ego be," and it is what makes psychoanalysis a potentially dynamic and emancipatory social theory.[8] Its central assumption is that people are creative subjects. Thus, socialization is not a one-way process. Instead of simply conforming to a predetermined set of roles and attitudes, individuals bring their own interests and identities to bear upon social interaction, often redefining them in the process.

Psychoanalytic sociology,[9] particularly feminist theories of gender personality, provides the final conceptual piece I introduce to my theoretical framework. These theories attempt an understanding of subjectivity which is gendered and active as well as conscious and unconscious (Chodorow 1978; Benjamin 1988; Johnson 1988). The earliest and most influential of these writers is Nancy Chodorow, who wrote *The Reproduction of Mothering*. Rejecting the instinctual determinism of the classic Freudian account in favor of a more nuanced, social psychological approach that incorporates recent developments in object relations theory,[10] Chodorow argues that the development of masculine and feminine personalities or gender identities is the consequence of a specific family form in which women, and not men, are exclusively responsible for the nurturing of children. Because the early social environment differs and is experienced differently by male and female children, she argues that boys and girls develop gender-specific personalities. Mothers tend "to experience their daughters as more like, and more continuous with themselves" (1978: 50). Girls experience themselves as like their mothers, thus fusing their gender identity formation with attachment and relationship to others. The mother treats her son quite differently by emphasizing his masculinity in opposition to herself and by pushing him to assume a sexually toned relation to her. Boys begin to separate themselves from their mothers after infancy, thus curtailing "their primary love and sense of empathic tie" (1978: 166). As a result, heterosexual male development involves a "more emphatic individuation and a more defensive firming of ego boundaries" as well as a sense of self as not female (1978: 166).

Differing object-relational capacities are the psychological consequence for girls and boys of these early asymmetrical relationships with mother. Each capacity entails a continuing preoccupation with a different set of psychical issues. For men, gender identity is the central issue: they experience a constant need to prove their masculinity. Unlike girls, boys must define themselves as not like their mothers and actively strive to acquire the characteristics of their different gender identity. The repression of their early identification with their mothers engenders a highly ambivalent stance toward women, one characterized by longing and disdain. Heterosexual men display this ambivalence by seeking out exclusive emotional relationships with women (marriage) and at the same time participating in the denigration of women (male domination).

Girls, in Chodorow's formulation, continue to be preoccupied with relational issues. Chodorow contends that women fulfill their relational needs by becoming mothers. For heterosexual women, the baby creates a new emotional triangle of mother/father/baby that parallels the woman's inner object-relational constellation of daughter/mother/father. Heterosexual women seek men to fulfill their desire for physical and emotional union. Because men cannot satisfy women's emotional needs, women turn to children to recreate the emotional triangle they once experienced as children themselves. Thus, women and men have differing but equally strong unconscious motivations to reproduce the family, gender, male domination, and mothering. For Chodorow, the only way out of this cycle is shared parenting, wherein women and men actively participate in early child care.

Chodorow's work has been criticized on a number of grounds.[11] Here I focus only on those related to women's experiences in the paid labor force, the most serious being that this psychoanalytic framework overstates the influence of a particular family structure on the development of personality and downplays the effects of other social factors, such as education, work, racial and ethnic background, and religious affiliation. In her second book, *Feminism and Psychoanalytic Theory,* Chodorow (1989a) responds to these criticisms, acknowledging the limitations of her argument in *The Reproduction of Mothering.* However, she cautions that feminist scholars should not dispense with psychoanalytic theory altogether:

People everywhere form a psyche, self and identity. . . . Historically, this method and theory [psychoanalysis] have not often been applied in a social or culturally specific manner, but there is not a basic antagonism between psychoanalytic thinking and social specificity. . . . As factors of race, class, culture or history enter into a labeled (conscious or unconscious) identity, or as they shape the particular early object-relational and family patterns and forms of subjectivity, psychoanalytic tools should be able to analyze these. (1989b: 4; emphasis added)

In her more recent work, Chodorow emphasizes the link between psychoanalytic thinking and "social specificity" and encourages feminist scholars to show how social identities vary in different social and historical contexts.[12]

One purpose of my book is to show how gender identity varies within and between occupational contexts. For example, I have found that women paralegals and some women lawyers attempt to affirm a relational identity through behavior such as being nice, nurturing, and personalizing work relationships. However, some women attorneys adopt the aggressive, male-defined adversarial role. Chodorow's earlier formulation cannot address these variations because it does not theorize the influence the workplace may have on gender personality. Here, my intent is to critique and extend Burawoy's argument about the reproduction of the labor process by integrating with it Chodorow's psychoanalytic theory of gender identity. In this way, psychoanalytic thinking is linked to a particular context—the workplace. Such an attempt adds the subjective dimension missing in Burawoy's account at the same time that it theorizes a socially and historically specific context for Chodorow's psychoanalytic gendered model.[13]

By drawing from the theoretical and conceptual insights of Burawoy's account of the labor process, Hochschild's concept of emotional labor, feminist theories of organizations, and psychoanalytic sociology, I have reconstructed existing social theory to explain the reproduction of sex segregation in contemporary law firms. My revised theoretical account is a dynamic theory that examines the interplay of gender at both the macro and micro levels of analysis. At the level of structure, gender shapes legal workers' practices, at the same time that their practices constitute and reproduce gendered relations.

This theory does not assume a simple one-to-one relationship between social structure and behavior. In law firms, some women who are trial lawyers challenge the adversarial model by adopting a more relational practice of law, while others strictly adhere to the role of the "zealous advocate." Their varied behavior emerges from a particular context, that of marginalized women in a male-dominated profession. However, their behavior is not simply determined by that context. A psychodynamic theory of agency presupposes an active and creative subject who brings unconscious feelings and identities to bear in social interaction, feelings and identities that can change in practice. Some women consent to the male-defined norms, while others resist. Such a dynamic understanding also suggests that gender identity does not automatically determine a specific type of behavior. Social identities are constantly negotiated and renegotiated through historically specific situations. In contemporary law firms, female litigators navigate between the limits of professional behavior and their feelings about being women, finding a variety of ways to do gender.

Selection of Cases

To address the gendering of occupations and emotions I chose to study litigation paralegals and trial attorneys because these occupations are strongly sex-typed by the proportion of men and women found in each and by the gendered idioms used to describe them. In addition, each job requires—formally or not—a substantial amount of emotional labor. Finally, that both jobs are considered extremely stressful suggests that their emotional demands are high. In examining these sex-segregated jobs, my intent is to highlight the processes that simultaneously gender occupations and emotions and render them so psychologically costly.

Paralegals or legal assistants are a relatively new occupational category. With the exponential growth of large law firms within the last twenty-five years and the competitive pressures to cut costs, firms have expanded their division of labor to include new legal workers who save money for the firm by performing many tasks previously assigned only to lawyers but actually accomplishable by workers who do not have law degrees (Nelson 1988; Johnstone and Wenglinsky 1985). Like other semi-professional occupations, this one is female-dominated: 85 percent of all paralegals are women (Johnstone and Wenglinsky 1985). Though paralegals are a step above secretaries in the law-firm hierarchy and perform slightly different tasks, the supportive and emotional dimension of their job is quite similar. Just as "good" secretaries are expected to be nice and sensitive to the feelings of others (Murphree 1984; Kanter 1977), so too are paralegals.

In addition to the proportion of women found in this occupation, the idioms used to describe it—particularly its emotional dimension—are strongly gendered. The image of the "mothering paralegal" and a related set of practices (caretaking and deference) emerge again and again in my fieldwork and interviews (see Chapters 4 and 6). Many lawyers and personnel directors participate in the construction of these idioms stating a preference for women in this kind of job, explaining that women were "nicer" and "friendlier" than their male counterparts, and hence, "more suited" for the position (see Chapter 4).

Legal assistants work in a variety of specialties within the legal profession, including probate, tax, corporate, real estate, patents, and litigation. The paralegals I studied worked in large law firms for litigators. Litigation is a male-dominated occupation: in fact, it has the highest percentage of men—88 percent—of all specialties within law (Menkel-Meadow 1989; Epstein 1983). Trial lawyers differ from other lawyers in that they are "people persuaders" rather than "symbol manipulators" (Heinz and Laumann 1982). Unlike probate lawyers or tax attorneys, who spend most of their time doing legal research and writing, litigators have ongoing face-to-face interaction with clients, judges, juries, and opposing counsel. As a consequence, emotional labor is a substantial part of their job. Psychologist Isaiah Zimmerman (1983) observes that what is most stressful for litigators is keeping their own feelings in check while trying to manipulate the feelings of others in the courtroom. The central metaphor for this specialty of law is that of battle, with the lawyer playing the role of the modern-day gladiator.

The idioms associated with this specialty within the legal profession—gladiator, Rambo litigator—are strongly male. As Cynthia Fuchs Epstein observes (1983), the emotional qualities associated with a good litigator—being tough-minded, hard-hitting, and aggressive—are also those associated with maleness in American culture. Trial attorneys participate in the construction of this gendered idiom by describing their courtroom battles as "macho" or as "something men get into." In addition, their discussions about why women do not make good litigators—"They're not tough enough"—underscore the exclusionary nature of this gendered idiom (see Chapters 3 and 5).

Of course, many other occupations and professions also are sex-typed in these ways and require emotional labor. What makes these two occupations unique, however, is the high level of stress associated with the work. Psychologists, lawyers, and other legal workers regard litigation as the most stressful area of law (Zimmerman 1983; Gould 1984a, 1984b). Many studies show that trial lawyers have much higher rates of job dissatisfaction, marital problems, alcoholism, drug abuse, and "burn-out" than do workers in other occupations (Holmes 1988; Frank 1985; Gillette 1982).[14] In addition, litigation paralegals have higher rates of job dissatisfaction and turnover than do legal assistants in other areas of specialization (Johnstone and Wenglinsky 1985). Studying these extreme cases of job dissatisfaction best illuminates the working conditions that render jobs so stressful and psychologically costly.

Looking at women and men in these two occupations also provides several important bases for comparison. First, it allows me to study paralegals and trial attorneys in relation to one another. Studies on legal workers tend to focus on one occupation as if it existed in isolation from the others. For example, Epstein (1983) and Nelson (1988) study lawyers, Johnstone and Wenglinsky (1985) study paralegals, and Murphree (1981, 1984) examines only legal secretaries. These occupational strata have an important interdependent and asymmetrical relationship to one another. Paralegal work is a satellite occupation whose very existence is determined by the needs of attorneys. By the same token, lawyers depend on paralegals for emotional support and to do much of their own work at less cost to the client. Studying these two occupations in relation to one another highlights not only their interdependence but the reproduction of gender asymmetry in law firms.

Second, this study allows me to compare the experiences of women and men within a masculinized occupation. Some sociologists have suggested that the demands of a male-dominated profession such as law conflict with traditional expectations of women's interests (Podomore and Spencer 1987; Epstein 1983). For example, Epstein (1983) argues that young women lawyers often experience a "double-bind" situation in trying to be good lawyers because there is a basic incongruity between their personal identity as female and their membership in a profession that is strongly masculine. A male lawyer who is tough is considered to be a good litigator, but a woman who is equally tough is considered difficult to get along with. One of my interests lies in how women and men negotiate these emotional expectations on the job.

Finally, I compare women and men in a feminized occupation such as paralegal work. Do male legal assistants as the statistical minority in this occupation experience a "double-bind?" Kanter (1977), for example, suggests that tokens face "performance pressures" from members of the dominant group. Do male paralegals feel compelled to perform the same socio-emotional tasks associated with their position that women do? Here, I am concerned with how women and men negotiate the feminized emotional demands associated with this occupation.

An Ethnographer in Law Firms

Participant observation and in-depth interviewing provide the methodological framework for my research. As a fieldworker, I spent six months as a paralegal in a San Francisco law firm and nine months in the legal department of a large corporation in the Bay

Area. The private firm and the legal department were of comparable size—approximately 150 lawyers, 40 paralegals, and 40 secretaries. I also spent three weeks in Boulder, Colorado, at the National Institute of Trial Advocacy observing training sessions in which lawyers learn how to present cases in trials. In addition, I conducted a total of sixty interviews with a random sample of attorneys, paralegals, and secretaries from each site and eight interviews with personnel directors from leading firms in the Bay area.

Interviews provide insight into the subjective experiences of workers that simple observations do not, while fieldwork allows the participant a chance to see how people's self-understanding is translated into action in a social setting. Fieldwork is also compatible with psychoanalytic methods of investigation (Hunt 1989). Much like traditional analysts, fieldworkers have prolonged contact with the people they study, providing the opportunity for observing patterns and themes in individual behavior as well as patterns of behavior between groups. And much like an analyst, the researcher's self is the primary instrument for gathering data. Because everything the fieldworker observes is mediated though the relationships she develops in the field, constant reflection about the varied roles the researcher adopts is essential to understanding one's role in the construction of knowledge. These reflexive issues are explored in detail in Appendix 1.

Participant observation raises an immediate question for the ethnographer in the field—will she be primarily a participant or an observer? Originally, I had planned to be more of an observer. When I contacted personnel directors and managing partners, they expressed interest in and enthusiasm for my project and agreed to allow me access to their employees for interviews. However, when I said I also planned to observe the field site and record my observations of interactions between coworkers, they denied my request. One cited the risks my research would pose to their clients' confidentiality. Another worried that my research would be potentially disruptive to an already busy and overworked department. My promise of confidentiality and my stated intent to be as unobtrusive as possible did little to assuage their fears. After several rejections, I realized that overt fieldwork was simply not possible.

By necessity, and after much thought, I became a participant observer, or more accurately, a covert fieldworker. Despite making this choice, my research was not entirely covert. After obtaining a position as a legal assistant in the litigation department of the private firm, I made no secret of the fact that I was also a graduate student in sociology doing a dissertation on occupational stress among legal workers. I also requested and obtained formal permission from the managing partner at each site to do interviews. As I was to discover, litigation and stress was a popular topic. Legal workers volunteered their views both formally in interviews and informally in private conversations.

Although I "came out" to my subjects as a sociologist and an interviewer, I did not reveal that I was a fieldworker. Doing research in this way raises an important ethical question about the deception of one's subjects. Although legal workers at both sites knew I was a graduate student, they did not know I worked at the firm to observe and document their behavior, their interactions, and the details of their work life. The ethics of deceiving subjects through covert research has been debated at length in the methodological literature (Bulmer 1982; Warwick 1982; Douglas 1979). Martin Bulmer (1982), for example, argues that deception is completely unacceptable. By contrast, Jack Douglas (1979) argues that because all social science research is deceptive, the issue of covert research is a moot point. Still others adopt a "situational ethics" (Punch 1986).

In my own research, I often felt uncomfortable with deception because people confided in me about personal troubles I doubted they would have revealed had they known my actual status. On the other hand, the very problems they revealed shed light on the emotional dimension of lawyering and paralegal work. What I learned through participant observation was often much richer and more nuanced than what people told me in interviews. For example, trial lawyers were much more likely to talk candidly about their work difficulties when they were working in the office than when they were being formally interviewed (see Appendix 1). Despite my misgivings, I eventually concluded—as did sociologist Judith Rollins (1985), who had worked covertly as a domestic worker—that there was more to be gained than lost from a study of this kind. There are no ethnographic studies on lawyers and paralegals,[15] and I could not conceive of a better method for uncovering the core of emotional labor in these jobs. However, like Rollins, I believe that academics should not regard deception in research lightly, and I join her in urging social scientists to evaluate research situations carefully before making such a decision and to keep ethical questions under discussion.

The firms I chose to study had to meet two criteria associated with stressful working conditions. The first concerns the size of the firm. Large firms, that is, firms employing one hundred lawyers or more,[16] are often described as impersonal and hierarchical, with few avenues for personal or professional advancement and autonomy (Holmes 1988). Further, large law firms are considered to be on the cutting edge of the practice of law. Their experiences and their conceptions of the organization of work inform our ideas of what lawyering is (Nelson 1985). The second criterion for selection lay in obtaining a position in litigation. As mentioned above, litigation is considered the most stressful area of law. My several years' previous experience as a litigation paralegal made entry into my first field site quite simple. Several firms offered me litigation positions, and the firm I call Lyman, Lyman and Portia[17] best met the criteria—it employed more than one hundred fifty lawyers, and its largest department was litigation.

I worked in the litigation department at Lyman, Lyman and Portia for six months in the winter and spring of 1988. I began working part-time (thirty hours per week), then full-time (forty hours per week), and later, fifty-plus hours a week when I assisted in trial preparation. During those months I worked with lawyers individually as well as on teams. (A team is a work group composed of several lawyers, paralegals, and secretaries working together on a large case.) These work relationships provided the opportunity for one-on-one observations of lawyers as well as comparisons between different groups of legal workers. In addition, I socialized with paralegals and secretaries in the break room, at lunch, and after hours and attended firmwide functions such as the annual picnic and the secretary's day luncheon.

Finding my second field site proved more difficult. I had hoped to find a large firm that closely matched the first. I was offered several jobs, but they were either at smaller firms or in departments other than litigation at large firms. Eventually, I was offered and accepted a litigation position in the legal department of a large corporation. Although in-house legal departments differ from private law firms, structurally they bear many similarities (Spangler 1986). Unlike lawyers in private firms, who spend a good deal of time and energy courting and impressing new clients in an effort to bring more business into the firm, in-house lawyers work for the corporation, and the corporation in turn is their client. As a consequence, there is no need for these lawyers to find clients because the client is always there. But in many large corporations, legal departments are considered law firms within corporations (Bellis and Morrison 1989; Roy 1989), which appears to be the case with respect to the legal department I studied. It was the same size as the private firm—approximately one hundred fifty lawyers. It also contained about the same number of paralegals (forty) and legal secretaries (forty). In addition, both firms comprised similar departments, such as litigation, labor, tax, telecommunications, and patents. (Chapter 2 provides a more detailed description of the organizational structure of each field site.)

I worked in the litigation department at a company I call Bonhomie Corporation for nine months, from the fall of 1988 to the spring of 1989. I began working full-time and continued to do so through my entire stint with the company, except for an eight-week period when I worked fifty-plus hours a week on a trial. Again, I worked with lawyers individually as well as on teams. In addition, I attended biweekly litigation meetings with lawyers and paralegals, socialized with paralegals and secretaries on breaks and at lunch, and attended the legal department's Christmas party, as well as two special internal legal-department conferences for paralegals.

In the third site for my fieldwork, the National Institute of Trial Advocacy (NITA), I was an overt fieldworker. NITA is an organization whose main purpose is to train litigators to prepare and perform cases for trial. I obtained permission from the director of NITA to attend and observe their three-week summer training session in Boulder, Colorado, in 1988. I attended sessions, talked informally with many of the participants, and interviewed some of the teachers. I also helped lawyers prepare their cases and participated in some of the mock trials as a witness. Initially, many of the lawyers expressed interest in my project and sought me out to give me their point of view. By the end of the three weeks, I had worked closely with a number of lawyers. On the last day, several departing attorneys asked for my law office address, suggesting not only that they recognized my legal expertise but that they had forgotten that I was not a lawyer.

In addition to fieldwork, I conducted sixty-eight interviews with twenty lawyers, twenty paralegals, twenty legal secretaries, and eight personnel directors. Interviews with secretaries and personnel directors were done to supplement the paralegal and attorney interviews.[18] I drew a random sample of paralegals, secretaries, and lawyers in the litigation department of each field site. Because I wanted to interview a comparable number of men and women in each category, I overinterviewed the statistical minority in each group. For example, there were only four male secretaries at the private firm. If I had utilized a truly random sample of this job category, I would have interviewed only one or possibly no male legal secretaries at all. To achieve comparability, I interviewed all the male secretaries and a random sample of the women. I followed the same procedure for each occupation.

Interviews lasted approximately one-and-a-half to two-and-a-half hours. Interviews with attorneys, legal assistants, and secretaries all followed roughly the same format, beginning with questions about family background and education and then moving to a discussion of work experiences. At the conclusion, subjects often asked questions about my research and my own experiences as a legal assistant. The informal discussions that followed often yielded interesting data. Interviews with personnel directors were more formal discussions about law-firm hiring practices, salaries, raises, and turnover.

Overview of Book

Chapter 2 describes the gendered organizational structure of the two firms studied in this book and provides a brief history of changes in the structure and composition of law firms from the turn of the century to the present in the United States. In contrast to other studies, which depict contemporary law firms as gender-neutral, bureaucratic structures, I argue that these organizations are male-dominated workplaces. My focus in this chapter on the process through which these organizations become gendered highlights the systematic differences in the types of jobs women and men hold and the consequences such differences have, for legal workers' access to power, prestige, and good salaries, and for other aspects of their working lives. Furthermore, as I argue, this structure must be understood in its social and historical context. With changes in such factors as the organization of work, technology, educational requirements, federal regulations, and the market for legal services, the all-male guildlike structure of the late nineteenth century has gradually emerged as the sex-segregated law "factory" of today.

In Chapters 3 and 4, my analysis moves from the gendering of organizations to the gendering of occupations and emotions. Here, my focus is on the predominant norms and expectations of gender appropriate emotional labor for trial lawyers and for legal assistants. In litigation, the form and idioms of emotional labor are construed as masculine. *Gamesmanship*—my term for the emotional labor associated with this job—entails the utilization of legal strategy through an emotional presentation of self designed to influence the feelings and judgment of a particular legal audience: the judge, the jury, the witness or opposing counsel. The rules governing gamesmanship derive from the adversarial model that underlies the basic structure of our legal system. Within this system the attorney's main objective is to win the client's case by whatever means within the letter of the law. In contrast to the popular image of the tough, aggressive litigator, intimidation is only one component of gamesmanship. Lawyers also make use of strategic friendliness, that is, the use of charm or flattery to manipulate others. In spite of the apparent differences between these two types of emotional labor, both share an emphasis on the manipulation of others toward a specific end, that is, winning a case. Domination through intimidation or strategic friendliness is also a way for men to "do gender." Thus, the attempt to dominate and control judges, juries, and opposing counsel not only serves the goals of effective advocacy but also serves as a way for trial lawyers to construe their work as "manly."

Chapter 4 examines the gendered norms of emotional labor in a feminized occupation—paralegal work. The two main components of emotional labor that legal workers are called upon to perform in this job are deference and caretaking. In contrast to gamesmanship, the forms this emotional labor takes and the idioms—i. e., the mothering paralegal—used to describe it are feminized. Paralegal work is feminized not simply because women do it but because taking care of others is construed as something that women are well suited to do. Additionally, this seemingly invisible aspect of work has significant consequences for the reproduction of the labor process in the large bureaucratic firm. Through deference and caretaking, paralegals function to support and maintain the emotional stability of the lawyers for whom they work. By affirming the status of lawyers, they also reproduce gender relations in law firms. Most attorneys who receive their caretaking and support are men, and the majority of legal assistants who provide these emotional services are women.

Chapters 5 and 6 present the findings that support my central argument about the reproduction of gender asymmetry in law firms. In the legal profession and in paralegal work, gender is organized and reproduced by the reciprocal interaction between the macro and micro levels of social relations. I argue that doing gender is the mediating link between these two levels of analysis. In Chapter 5, I begin by examining the different structural constraints women and men face in the legal profession. Women, as the numerical minority in the profession, are less likely than men to be located in positions of power within the firm and are likely to make less money than men. In addition, they encounter more difficulty in creating new business contacts, experience sexual harassment, and face serious obstacles to balancing work and family. Moreover, women face a double bind that men do not in displaying occupationally appropriate emotional labor. Whereas men are praised for using intimidation and strategic friendliness, women who are aggressive are censured for being difficult to get along with, and women who are nice are considered "not tough enough" to be good litigators. Women lawyers do not respond passively to these constraints, however. Instead, they actively and creatively devise a variety of ways to do gender. Some practice an ethic of care to resolve legal disputes, others adopt an adversarial role for the courtroom and a more relational stance for working in the office, and finally, a small minority conform to the male-defined role.

Chapter 6 begins by examining how gender influences the occupational positioning of paralegals, as workers treated in certain ways by their employers and subject to particular expectations with regard to the emotional division of labor. The focus then shifts to the paralegals themselves, who do gender through their interactions with others and by performing emotional labor. I argue that gender shapes the experiences of paralegals in law firms at the same time that paralegals reproduce gender through their interactions with lawyers. Finally, I explore the strategies paralegals utilize to resist emotional degradation on the job. Even when paralegals resist the feeling rules implicit in their occupational life, the individualized coping strategies they choose often serve to reproduce the gendering of the labor process. The concluding chapter draws out the implications of my findings for sociological theorizing about sex segregation, the labor process, and the construction of gender identity in the workplace. In addition, it raises questions for future research on women and emotional labor. Finally, I discuss possible solutions to the problems sex segregation creates for women legal workers in both feminized and non-traditional occupations.

Chapter Two

The Gendered Organizational Structure of Large Law Firms

Let me put it this way: I think Clarence Darrow once said women are too nice to be lawyers. I think he was right. It's not that I don't think women are bright or competent—they just don't have that *killer instinct*.

Male attorney

I don't know if it's discriminating to say that men can't [work as paralegals], but I think a lot of what's involved in being a paralegal is dealing with people and using social skills. In terms of supportive skills, men aren't socialized to be that way.

Personnel director, San Francisco law firm

The contemporary large law firm and the in-house legal department are sex-segregated workplaces: most lawyers are male, and the majority of non-professional employees, such as paralegals, secretaries, library assistants, file clerks, and word-processing operators are female. Gender ideology tends to support the notion of such a division of labor as natural—women do not possess the "killer instinct" necessary to be lawyers, and men do not have the requisite "social skills" for paralegal work. History, however, demonstrates that this conception of a gendered division of labor is far from static or natural, but is fluid, changing, and socially malleable. Before the turn of the century, the traditional law firm was an entirely male office, with a handful of lawyers, "gentlemen clerks," and copyists (Auerbach 1976; Lockwood 1958). In the last eighty years, firms have not only increased greatly in size—the "large" firm today has more than one hundred lawyers—but the all-male office has been transformed into a sex-segregated organizational structure, increasingly feminized on the bottom tiers, while remaining predominantly male at the top.

The organizational structure of the two law firms in this study—Lyman, Lyman and Portia and the legal department in Bonhomie Corporation—is gendered. Far from being gender-neutral, these contemporary bureaucratic structures are male-dominated workplaces. Most men are located in the most powerful, prestigious, and well-paying positions within these organizations, while most women work in support staff positions designed to serve those higher-status men. By spelling out the process through which these organizations become gendered, the first section of this chapter highlights the systematic differences in the types of jobs women and men hold and the consequences such differences have for legal workers' access to power, prestige, good salaries, office space, and prospects for intrafirm mobility.

The second part of this chapter examines the historical emergence of the gendered bureaucratic law firm. The transformation of the law firm from an all-male enclave at the turn of the century to today's large bureaucratic structure is a complex process. The few historical and sociological studies on the development of the large law firm[1] focus on the impact bureaucratization has had on the profession. Little attention has been given to how the process of bureaucratization has been accompanied by the development of a sex-segregated organizational structure. My account differs from previous studies by demonstrating how the gendered structure of the law firm has changed from the turn of the century to the present.[2] This historical account is not intended to be comprehensive or exhaustive in its focus—that task I leave to historians—but is meant to provide a context for the emergence of the types of firms where I did my fieldwork and to show how the structure of firms has changed over time.

The Large Law Firm
as a Gendered Bureaucracy

Despite the differences between in-house legal departments and large law firms—the most important being their relationship to the client—the two field sites for this study can be best described as bureaucratic.[3] In making this characterization, I draw from Nelson's

(1988) influential study of large law firms. Nelson defines bureaucratic law firm management by specific criteria, including (1) a central policy-making committee that does strategic planning; (2) an administrative component consisting of a managing partner and a
financial tracking mechanism for collecting and analyzing data on
lawyers' work performance; and (3) well-defined departments "with
recognized heads who supervise the department and report back to
the central policy-making committee" (Nelson 1988: 91–92).

The field sites for this study both fit these criteria. Lyman, Lyman
and Portia and the legal department in Bonhomie Corporation are
each run by a central planning committee that does all the strategic
planning and consists only of senior counsel. Managing partners at
both firms are responsible for collecting and analyzing monthly sum-
maries of billable hours[4] for individual lawyers and for paralegals.
(*Billable hours* is a term referring to the time attorneys bill to clients
for their work on a case.) At the next level, lawyers who head departments, such as litigation, labor, tax, and corporate practice, supervise the work groups or "teams," which in turn are made up of
partners, associates, paralegals, and secretaries. Department heads
are responsible for issuing monthly reports to the central planning
committee.

While Nelson's term is useful for distinguishing bureaucratic
firms from other types of law-firm management, his gender-neutral
definition does not tell us *who controls* the bureaucratic firm, *who
fills the positions* within the firm, or *whose interests* strategic planning may serve. Job titles such as managing partner, partner, and associate obscure the fact that most of these positions are held by men,
while most clerical and support positions are held by women. This
description of organizational structure and job titles conceals how
law firms, like most organizations and the positions within them, are
deeply structured by gender (Mills and Tancred 1992; Acker 1990;
Pringle 1988).[5]

In her book on clerical workers, Pringle (1988) argues that "gender and sexuality are not only central in the boss-secretary relationship, but in all workplace relations" (1988: 84). She regards the division of labor between these two categories of workers as a gendered
division between reason and emotion: secretaries are supposed to be

more emotional, while their bosses are expected to be logical and rational. Women secretaries are sexualized in the workplace in ways that men are not. They are objectified as well as verbally and sexually harassed. Finally, being female fosters stereotyped perceptions and rationales about lower salaries and status as well as limited authority and opportunities.

Indeed, the gendering of organizations has serious consequences for the nature of work and for the individual worker. "Men's work" is well paid and prestigious in our culture, while "women's work" is not. As Kanter's (1977) research suggests, once jobs have been gendered as masculine, they are very difficult for women workers to break into. Given the power differentials between men and women—men accrue greater benefits from the gendered division of labor than women do—it is crucial to understand the processes through which organizations are gendered.

In what ways are law firms gendered? In the United States, the contemporary large firm is a pyramid structure with a professional stratum resting on top of a non-professional or support-staff tier. The top comprises lawyers—partners and associates—most of whom are male. The bottom tier contains librarians and their assistants, personnel employees, paralegals, secretaries, receptionists, case clerks, and duplicating operators—most of whom are female.[6] As a consequence, the firm is stratified by occupational status and by gender. The feminization of the bottom tier is also accomplished through its dependent relationship to the legal profession. The fact that women serve men is one of the central features in these work environments. Another characteristic of this organizational structure is the complete lack of mobility between tiers. Secretaries and paralegals rarely move up the organizational hierarchy; lawyers do not move down. Furthermore, there are strict, though unwritten, rules about social interaction. Workers socialize with one another within tiers, but infrequently between them.

By incorporating gender into our analysis, we can reconceptualize Nelson's bureaucratic firm as a male-dominated bureaucracy with a professional, predominantly male tier on top and a non-professional, predominantly female, tier below whose primary service is to support members above. Feminist scholars have only recently begun to theorize the process by which large organizations become gendered (Mills and Tancred 1992; Acker 1990; Pringle 1988). Sociologist Joan Acker, for example, describes this process as the means by which "advantage and disadvantage, exploitation and control, action and emotion, meaning and identity are patterned through and in terms of a distinction between male and female, masculine and feminine" (1990: 146). Empirically, she suggests examining the way distinctions are constructed along the lines of gender in areas such as the "division of labor, allowed behavior and locations in physical space" (1990: 149). At both field sites for my study, these facets of organizational life are all associated with distinctions by occupational status and gender.

At the private firm and in the legal department, each stratum is strongly associated with gender. The attorney or superior stratum in the private firm is predominantly white (99 percent) and male (88 percent), consisting of 150 attorneys, 102 associates and 48 partners. Similarly, the legal department at the Bonhomie Corporation is also largely white (95 percent) and male (80 percent) with approximately 150 lawyers, with 114 associates and 36 senior counsel.[7]

Lawyers within each firm can be further differentiated by specialty. The greatest number of lawyers at the private firm, one third (50), worked in the litigation department, where I did my fieldwork. In addition to litigation, other specialties include labor, real estate, tax, securities, telecommunications, bankruptcy, corporate, and estate planning. At Bonhomie Corporation, litigation was also the largest department (43 lawyers). Other departments include labor, telecommunications, patents and trademarks, corporate, and tax. As Epstein (1983) and Podomore and Spencer (1986) argue, specializations within the legal profession are also gendered. Women tend to be concentrated in probate, tax, family law, and securities work. On the other hand, litigation is a predominantly male specialty. Fifty-six percent of probate lawyers are female, compared with 16 percent of litigators. At Bonhomie Corporation, the litigation department had the smallest number of women (18 percent), and patents the highest (66 percent).

By contrast, the non-attorney stratum at each firm is predominantly female. The top end of the stratum includes personnel workers, librarians and their assistants. Beneath them in rank order are paralegals, legal secretaries, receptionists, case clerks and duplicating operators. Of these workers, 91 percent are white and 85 percent are female. The two largest groups of non-attorneys are paralegals and secretaries. There are 37 paralegals at the private firm and 34 at Bonhomie Corporation. At the private firm, 95 percent of the legal assistants are white,[8] and 86 percent are female; in the legal department, 88 percent are white,[9] and 82 percent are female. The percentage of women workers is even higher among legal secretaries: the private firm has 43 secretaries, 93 percent of whom are female, and at Bonhomie Corporation, 98 percent of the 51 legal secretaries are women.

The division of labor between attorneys, paralegals, and secretaries reflects not only occupational status and differential gender composition, but sex-stereotyping. Epstein (1970) observes that female occupations such as teaching and nursing are so called not only because of the high proportion of women found within them, but because they involve tasks judged to be "expressive and person-centered, helping, nurturing and empathizing." Occupations believed to require "coolness, detachment, analytic objectivity, or object-orientation such as law . . . are male occupations" (1970: 155). In my study, not only are most lawyers men, but lawyers do the intellectual, analytic, prestigious, and well-paid work—work that is commonly referred to as "men's work." By contrast, female paralegals and secretaries supposedly do the routine, semi-skilled, low status, and low-paid clerical or "women's work." As Chapters 3 and 4 show, the distinction between men's and women's work also extends to emotional labor. Women as paralegals are expected to provide emotional services such as nurturance and deference to the lawyers for whom they work, whereas men as attorneys are required to be aggressive and manipulative. Despite the dichotomous construction of these tasks, there is actually a great deal of overlap between them. Like attorneys, paralegals also do legal research and writing. Moreover, these positions are highly interdependent. Just as paralegal work is dependent upon the needs and demands of lawyers, much of lawyers' work in large law firms could not be accomplished without the extensive support staff. Sex-stereotyping these positions masks the similarities between them and obscures their interdependent relationship.

Sex-stereotyping is also reflected in income differentials between strata. As in many other occupations and professions, men's work in law firms is more highly paid than women's work. In 1989, associates at Lyman, Lyman and Portia started at $58,000. This is almost three times the salary of the lowest paid secretary ($20,000) and the lowest paid paralegal ($22,000) and twice as much as the average secretary ($29,000) and paralegal ($30,000). The average senior partner's salary ($250,000) was twelve times the lowest secretarial salary, ten times the average, and eight times the highest. (These figures do not include profit sharing.) At Bonhomie Corporation salary differentials were not as great, but they followed a similar pattern. In 1989, associates started at $40,000, compared to starting secretaries at $18,000 and paralegals at $25,000. In 1989, the average salary for senior counsel was $100,000.[10]

Gender differences between tiers are also apparent in office space assignments. Goffman (1956) has suggested that one way of measuring differences in status is by looking at who is granted more physical space in social situations or what he calls "spatial deference." Following Goffman, Henley (1977) found that just as subordinates have less space than superordinates, women in our society are allowed less space than men. My research supports Henley's findings. At the private firm and in the legal department, workers occupying the predominantly male or attorney strata have more office space and privacy than those workers occupying the predominantly female tier.

At Lyman, Lyman and Portia, the offices of senior partners are located in large corner offices with unencumbered views of the San Francisco Bay. Each partner's office is carefully decorated and furnished according to personal taste: in one office, we find a Southwest motif; in another, art deco designs; and in still another, an original, brightly colored Rothko on the wall. Associates are assigned to smaller and simpler offices, ranging from modest offices with windows to those without. Though more functional furnishings and office size distinguish the junior attorneys from their superiors, the privacy of their surroundings elevates them from the great majority of the non-legal staff and marks them as professionals.

The size and location of offices is also a measure of status at Bon-homie Corporation. Senior counsel are housed in large corner of-fices, though one is more likely to find diplomas from local Bay area night law schools hanging on their walls than original artwork. The view from their offices overlooks not the San Francisco Bay but a warehouse district, with the Bay Bridge far in the distance. Associ-ates are located in smaller offices along the main corridor, with win-dows looking out over the street.

By contrast, in the female-dominated strata of paralegals and legal secretaries, office space and decor are determined primarily by func-tional requirements, and privacy is minimal. Most of these workers are housed in interior space devoid of either natural light or privacy. At Lyman, Lyman and Portia, paralegals are housed in closet-sized offices on the inside of the corridor, without windows to the out-side.[11] Identical, imitation wood-grain desks are found in all the of-fices. Each is furnished with a desk, a secretary's chair, and an addi-tional chair next to the desk. Posters and family photographs are displayed on the walls. At Bonhomie Corporation, two paralegals share an associate-size office. A beige room-divider cuts the office in half, giving the illusion of separate space and privacy. Each paralegal has a beige desk and secretary chair. Here, too, legal assistants hang their children's artwork, posters, and family photos on their office walls.

Bordering the attorneys' offices at the private firm are fluores-cent-lit corridors, which serve as secretarial areas. In this maze of corridors far beyond the reception area at the private firm and at Bonhomie Corporation, the work environment for these women workers is also considerably different from the surroundings of lawyers. At Lyman, Lyman and Portia, two to three identical black metal desks are lined up back to back. Each is furnished with an up-holstered secretary chair, a telephone, and a computer terminal. At the private firm, personal decorations are expected to be minimal. An announcement in the firm's daily newsletter decreed personal decorations in secretarial cubicles "unprofessional." Nevertheless, legal secretaries, like paralegals, attempt to place a personal stamp on their working environment. Many display photos of family, part-ners, and children on their desks. One secretarial cubicle bears the sign: "Lack of Organization on Your Part Does Not Constitute an Emergency on Mine." In the legal department of Bonhomie Corporation, secretarial areas are quite similar to those found at the private firm, except that the furniture is beige rather than black. Personal decorations are minimal: the most common are family photos and other personal mementos, such as company awards, postcards, and small potted plants.

Lacking their own offices, secretaries have even less privacy than paralegals do. Much like Foucault's (1977) description of the panopticon designed to allow maximum surveillance of prisoners in their cells, the layout of secretarial areas places secretaries on constant display.[12] Attorneys, clients, the personnel director, paralegals, and even other secretaries all have the opportunity to observe these women at work. Secretaries dislike the surveillance. As one secretary said, "You can't even blow your nose in private. Everyone watches what you do." What they like even less is the fact that the surveillance requires them always to appear busy: "I hate that I'm supposed to look busy even when I am not." By denying secretaries privacy, management has more control not only over the labor process but also over the personal appearance of secretaries. At the private firm, their personal appearance is closely monitored. In my field notes, I frequently recorded observations of the personnel director "patrolling the halls looking secretaries up and down." She told women who wore pants they were "unprofessional." Women who wore casual clothes or mini-skirts were sent home to change. The personnel director often said, "What would the client think?"

Some male attorneys also participated in surveillance, although theirs was typically more sexual in nature. Daniel, for example, complimented the personal appearance of his secretary Janice *only* when she was wearing a short skirt. Another secretary once overheard her boss tell a client, "Ask Jody to get you a cup of coffee. When she gets up, you'll see what great legs she has." Others reported more blatant occurrences of unwanted and uninvited remarks about their personal appearance, as well as intrusions into their physical space. Dana, a secretary, was physically cornered against her desk by a partner (not her boss), who told her that if she did not have sex with him he would see to it that she never got another secretarial position.[13] Although such physical and sexual harassment was unusual, the fact that it could happen set a tone of intimidation. Of all the occupational space in the two offices, secretarial areas are the most feminized, not only in terms of how little space the workers have and how little privacy, but also in terms of the sexualized nature of the control over their working space and their bodies.[14]

Both sites demonstrate a lack of mobility and social interaction between the predominantly male and predominantly female, professional and semi-professional strata.[15] A law degree is required for entry into the professional strata. At Lyman, Lyman and Portia, degrees from prestigious law schools such as Boalt, Stanford, Yale, and Harvard are strongly preferred. Over 60 percent of the firm's lawyers come from these elite or prestige schools.[16] In the legal department at Bonhomie Corporation, lawyers are more likely to come from local second-tier schools, such as Golden Gate University, University of San Francisco, and the University of Santa Clara.

In theory, a secretary or paralegal could leave the firm, obtain a law degree and apply for an attorney position at the firm. However, this rarely occurs. Although several people I interviewed knew one paralegal or secretary who had gone to night law school, no one could name any individuals who returned to the firm. When I asked the personnel director at Bonhomie Corporation about this, she said, "Of course, the company supports the career development of its employees, but you often find that *those* people aren't very bright or motivated" (emphasis in original). At the private firm, the managing partner espoused a more egalitarian ideology. "Anyone who is bright, motivated, and competent can be a lawyer." When I pointed out that I knew of only one lawyer who had been a paralegal before going to law school, he added, "Well, few people in those positions are very ambitious. After all, who would take such a dead-end job if they had big plans for their future?"

Though legal assistants rarely moved up to attorney positions within firms, men were more likely than women to receive encouragement from lawyers to go to law school or to professional school (see Chapter 6). These findings suggest that although mobility is rare within firms, opportunities and advice for such movement vary by gender. Female paralegals and secretaries received little support or encouragement for advancement.

There are also rigid norms prohibiting social interaction. Smigel (1969) observed this phenomenon in his classic study of Wall Street law firms in the late fifties:

> Except for their office contacts, the lives of the members in the various castes (professional, non-professional) seldom cross. It is, for instance, not considered nice to socialize with a secretary. One associate was seen lunching with a male secretary and was told professional people do not eat with secretaries. When lawyers were asked about this taboo, they would point out . . . a member of the firm who was married to a secretary. Still, most would admit it was not considered smart to go out with one. (1969: 228)

In the private firm and the in-house legal department, restrictions on social intercourse are accomplished in a number of ways. For example, although the firms include paralegals and secretaries in the few, formal firm-wide social occasions, these legal workers rarely interacted with attorneys during such events. At both firm Christmas parties, most of the associates stood together in groups, the partners in another group with clients, and the majority of the support-staff workers in several other small groups. Although intermingling occurred, it was not typical, and if it occurred at all, it was usually initiated by attorneys. Secretaries and paralegals who ignored this unwritten rule found themselves to be quickly snubbed by the lawyers for whom they worked. One female legal assistant described her experiences at the Christmas party:

> I was getting ready to leave the party, and so, I went up to my boss to say merry Christmas and good bye. He was talking to a bunch of other partners. I kept saying, "Daniel, excuse me" and he kept ignoring me. I kept standing there waiting. Just as I turned to go, he looked at me and said, "Oh, Mary, I'll talk to you later."

A female legal secretary who worked for her boss for ten years said:

> I recently remarried, so when I came to the Christmas party, I brought my new husband along and [my boss] Harold didn't even say hello. I kept trying to catch his eye. He was busy talking to the client. I remember thinking, "I've worked for this man for ten years, I have filed every important brief of

his career, I have babysat him through his divorce, and on Christmas Eve, he can't even say hello to my new husband!"

Secretaries and paralegals are seldom invited to informal, social activities with lawyers, such as lunch, drinks after work, and sporting events. Typically, paralegals and secretaries form their own groups for lunch or a break in the cafeteria. Partners sometimes subtly reproach attorneys, especially associates, for socializing with female staff. This is usually accomplished in a joking manner. For example, one young lawyer told me he had been teased by his supervising attorney about "the deep intellectual conversations he was having" with a secretary he had gone to lunch with. Such teasing has dual implications. On the one hand, it suggests that lunch with a female secretary carries sexual rather than intellectual connotations. On the other, it serves to remind the young associate about whom it is appropriate to have lunch with. Another young lawyer who frequently talked to female secretaries and paralegals was told jokingly that "people were beginning to wonder." In contrast to the glamorized secretary-boss relationships depicted in the television show *L.A. Law*, office romances in this study are rare.[17]

The Historical Development of the Sex Segregated Firm

Changes in the organizational structure of the large law firm since the turn of the century can be viewed as occurring primarily during two eras. The first period, beginning around 1870 and extending through the 1920s, encompasses the early rise and development of the law firm as a new bureaucratic form of organization and the initial entry of women into firms as clerical workers. The contemporary post-industrial period, beginning roughly in the early 1960s, encompasses the emergence of the large firm as it exists today, the resurgence of corporate in-house counsel, the creation of additional feminized occupations within firms, such as paralegals, and the increase in the number of women lawyers.

With the formation of a powerful national economic elite in the late nineteenth century led by railroad, utility, and steel interests, the United States entered the age of corporate capitalism. This economic consolidation of power gave rise to a new legal elite based on Wall Street and substantially altered the scope and nature of legal practice (Mills 1951; Larson 1977; Murphree 1981). With big business growing and government regulations increasing, the resolution of legal disputes required skills, expertise, and specialization in entirely new areas of law. Furthermore, the demands of business corporations called for a rationalized, efficient organizational structure.

The patrimonial, guildlike structure and craftlike production of nineteenth century law firms did not meet these "modern" requirements. Traditional law offices, which lacked telephones, typewriters, and other modern office equipment, were all-male enclaves, employing several lawyers, a few "gentlemen clerks," and copyists (Auerbach 1976). The male clerks or "gentlemen apprentices" were often sons of "men of property," who worked for very little pay under an apprenticeship system in order to gain the experience necessary to become a lawyer (Lockwood 1958). While lawyers were away from the office, senior clerks acted as office bookkeeper, managing the office and supervising other clerks, whereas copyists spent their days under dim lamps laboriously copying legal documents with quill pens (Lockwood 1958). By the beginning of the twentieth century, these offices faced competition from a novel organizational structure, which incorporated a new technology and a new division of labor. These changes marked the beginning of both the Wall Street law firm and the entry of women workers into a male domain.

The emergence of these new firms was accompanied by changes in their structure and organization. The new organizational form, which was introduced at the turn of the century by the lawyer Paul D. Cravath, became the model for the organization of law firms on Wall Street and across the country (Hoffman 1973; Auerbach 1976; Larson 1977). Much like Frederick Taylor's "principles of scientific management," Cravath's system introduced efficiency into the law firm by rationalizing the labor process and streamlining the organization of work. According to Larson (1977), in early twentieth-century America, Frederick Taylor's "ideology of efficiency" went hand in hand with bureaucratization and rationalization of production under corporate capitalism. Law firms were no exception to this process.

When Cravath joined the Seward firm in 1899, he began to implement this new model (Swaine 1946: 573). Before Cravath came to Seward, the partners worked independently of one another with no apparent overall organization or supervision. Business decisions affecting the firm as a whole were made haphazardly at best. Much like decisions in Weber's pre-bureaucratic patrimonial structure, hiring decisions were made on the basis of personal ties rather than merit. The Seward partners' apparent disorganization and lack of business acumen led Cravath to restructure the firm into "a cohesive team containing men both with training and experience designed to give them a comprehensive view of the problem of the office client as well as the specialist highly trained through concentration in particular fields" (Swaine 1946: 575). As Robert Swaine, firm historian and former Cravath partner, writes in his three-volume history of the firm, "Cravath had a definite philosophy about the organization of the law firm, its partners, its practice and its relations to its associates" (Swaine 1946: 1). This philosophy became the Cravath System.

The Cravath System included recruitment based on merit, training, partnership, a rigorous division of labor, a specific scope of practice, and a new form of management (Swaine 1946: 1–12). From his previous employer, Walter Carter, Cravath learned the advantages of hiring recent law-school graduates. In 1901, Carter wrote, "I thought the best way to get a good lawyer was to make him to order, instead of getting him ready-made" (Carter 1901: 105). Social or personal connections no longer automatically qualified a young lawyer for firm membership. Under the Cravath model, criteria for new recruits became more universalistic and meritocratic and included a college degree, a degree from a prestigious law school, a good law school record and preferably law review experience, and great physical stamina and "warmth" and "force" of personality (Swaine 1946: 1–12).

In practice, these new hiring criteria still proved exclusionary. Auerbach (1976) and Carlin (1962) argue that Jews and recent immigrants were more likely to attend night school than the more expensive, prestigious law schools such as Harvard and Yale. As a result, they would not even be considered for positions at the big Wall Street firms. Moreover, early discrimination against Jews meant that even if they did attend Harvard or Columbia, Wall Street firms would not hire them. Neither did large firms hire white women or African Americans (Morello 1986; Segal 1983). Thus, the Cravath recruitment system continued to select primarily native-born, white, Protestant men from upper-middle-class backgrounds.

Once recruited to the firm, young Cravath lawyers began the arduous process of training. Cravath believed that neophyte lawyers should be trained first as generalists before learning the intricacies of specialty practice. According to the firm historian, they were "not thrown into deep water and told to swim; rather, they are taken into shallow water and carefully taught strokes" (Swaine 1946: 14). As young lawyers' abilities increased, so did their responsibilities and opportunities for specialization. By 1880, well-defined specialties in patents, industrial consolidation, real estate, insurance, bankruptcy, and taxation were becoming common in the legal profession throughout the United States (Mills 1956: 121–29; Larson 1977: 170).

Young lawyers who excelled in this environment were rewarded with more and more responsibility, and eventually, partnership. Cravath insisted upon selecting partners from within the firm. He believed strongly that the firm should have an "up or out" policy. Attorneys remained as long as they were "growing in responsibility." Under the Cravath System, lawyers were to be constantly recruited, move up, and become partners or leave (Swaine 1946). Furthermore, young Cravath lawyers were made to understand that the practice of law must be their primary interest, and that all business conducted in the office was Cravath business. The nature of this business was clear: "The practice of the office is essentially a civil business practice" (Swaine 1946: 10). Cravath desired a staff equipped to serve corporate and banking clients in many of their legal problems.

The Cravath model introduced a new division of labor and a pyramid structure of status and responsibility. Cravath believed that the firm should have a strong philosophy of organization. Partners were located at the top of the pyramid, and associates at the bottom. Further divisions existed within each tier. Young lawyers were ranked by their length of tenure, level of ability, and responsibility. Those who demonstrated increasing ability and responsibility moved into the next tier—partnership. Partners shared more or less equally in the share of profits, liability, management of the firm, and, within limits, permanent tenure. The managing partner and the senior partner stood at the top of this stratum. The entire firm was organized and managed by the managing partner; the senior partner, in turn, recruited and hired new attorneys. By 1910, the Cravath system, widely emulated, dominated the expanding world of law firms.[18]

Another important social change influencing the development of large firms was the development of new educational requirements for the practice of law. Until the end of the nineteenth century, formal apprenticeships in which male clerks were eventually promoted to lawyer were commonplace (Carlin 1962; Auerbach 1976). By 1920, formal training in law school replaced the apprenticeship system (Carlin 1962). For example, in 1870, 25 percent of those admitted to the bar were law-school graduates (Carlin 1962). In the decade from 1922 to 1931, over 99 percent of those who took the bar exam in New York state were law-school graduates (Wickser 1933). Because promotion within the firm was no longer possible without a law degree, clerking positions began to look less promising.

The traditional male preserve of the "gentlemen apprentices" also faced competition from the development of modern technology such as the telephone and the typewriter and from the increasing number of women entering clerical positions. By the late twenties, new technology had found its way into business offices across the United States. The telephone had become an important feature in the office by the end of World War I (Lockwood 1958). For attorneys, it facilitated communication with clients, colleagues, and adversaries. As a consequence, lawyers had less need to leave their offices to talk to clients or opposing counsel, and secretaries began to adopt the tasks of "telephone operator and receptionist" (Murphree 1981: 59). The telegraph also became a necessity for law firms whose practice had spread abroad. Of greatest importance, however, was the invention of the typewriter, or "mechanical writing machine." In combination with stenography, typing became a useful tool for standardizing and speeding up communication. It also made possible the growing volume of correspondence, document production, and record-keeping attendant on industrial expansion (Murphree 1981). By 1900, the typewriter was widely used in most American offices (Mills 1951: 193).

As new machines were introduced to big business, the proportion of women in clerical positions began to increase. In 1870, women accounted for 2.3 percent of the 95,000 office workers in the country (Davies 1982, table 4). By 1900, the total number of office workers had risen to 700,000, and the proportion of women to 25 percent (Davies 1982, table 4). By 1930, women made up 50 percent of the census category for clerical workers, thereby doubling their proportionate representation since the turn of the century (Hedstrom 1988). Murphree (1981) argues that the demographic shift of women into clerical positions also occurred in law firms. The increase in paperwork, the newly rationalized production, and the increasing usage of new technology led many firms to turn away from male clerks to the large and growing pool of female labor. The increase in routine filing and the usage of the typewriter did not so much create demand for female labor as reinforce an existing trend to hire women as less expensive forms of labor. By the end of World War I, "the society of gentlemen legal clerks and their craftlike production had almost been entirely replaced by an elite corps of women—each a legal secretary—trained to operate the typewriter, the telephone and other office equipment" (Murphree 1981: 57).

The feminization of clerical work in the law firm created a third tier beneath associates in the Cravath pyramid. The male preserve had been feminized, though only at the bottom. Women, rather than male clerks or copyists, worked as secretaries,[19] and men continued to work as lawyers.[20] Murphree (1981) describes the legal secretaries of this time period as "skilled generalists" who supervised the order of supplies for the office, kept the library up to date, maintained the court calendar, recorded and edited minutes and proceedings, drafted standard legal forms such as wills, and did legal research. In addition to these clerk-like tasks, legal secretaries were also expected to do typing and filing and to provide emotional support for their bosses. Although early secretarial work did not have the low status it does today (Davies 1982), its low pay contrasted sharply with the lawyers' better pay and higher status.

Unlike the traditional firm, where male clerks could gain experience to become lawyers themselves, the new Cravath model allowed female secretaries no mobility. The end of the apprenticeship system meant that a law degree was the only means of becoming a lawyer. Although it was possible for women to obtain law degrees at a handful of schools before World War I,[21] and in fact, 1.4 percent of lawyers were women in 1920,[22] they were still excluded from the Ivy League, one of the main criteria for entrance into a Wall Street firm. In response to suffragists' demands during World War I, law-school dean and Supreme Court Justice Harlan Stone predicted that if Columbia Law School admitted women, his school would be thriving with "freaks and cranks" (cited in Auerbach 1976: 295). Columbia reluctantly admitted women in 1928. Harvard Law School did not admit women until 1950 (Epstein 1983: 50). Despite their admission to Columbia in 1928, women were still barred from employment at large firms until their "token entry" in the late 1960s and early 1970s (Auerbach 1976: 29).

In the thirty years following the Great Crash, the sex-segregated structure of the large firm remained very much the same. Although the depression had an economic impact on the business of Wall Street's elite firms—some firms lost their big corporate retainers after 1929—bankruptcy, receiverships, and corporate reorganization continued to create work for many of the more prominent firms (Auerbach 1976). Those hurt most by the Great Crash were the young men and a handful of women lawyers seeking access to Wall Street firms (Auerbach 1976; Morello 1986). Many corporate firms sharply cut back on recruitment between 1931 and 1933, which meant that fewer or in some cases no new associates were hired. The depression also reinforced restrictions against hiring women as lawyers. Sadie Turak, a woman law-school graduate of the period, recalls that at every job interview she was asked how she

could possibly be expected to be considered when there were men out there with families to support. It was bad enough I wasn't going to get a job with any of those law firms—on top of it they insisted on making me feel guilty. (quoted in Morello 1986: 203)

While the top tier of the large firm remained largely inaccessible to women, the number of women workers at the bottom of the organizational hierarchy increased. Until World War II, the only women employed in the Wall Street firms—the major leagues of the legal profession—were "receptionists, switchboard operators, secretaries and cleaning women" (Morello 1986: 203).

During World War II a small number of women lawyers were employed by firms when men were called to service, but the innovation was temporary. For example, the lawyer Catherine Tilson credited the war with providing her with an opportunity to work for a prestigious firm. However, when the war was over, men resumed their careers as though they had never left, and women like Tilson never made partner (Morello 1986). At the same time, the feminization of secretarial work had increased. By 1950, the vast majority of all clerical workers were women (Reskin and Roos 1990).

The second historical period, which began roughly in the late fifties or early sixties, marked the next major change in the organizational structure of the large law firm. During this time, firms grew in size and number, newer and more sophisticated office technology was developed, jobs became more specialized, new feminized occupations were created, and women began to enter the legal profession in large numbers.

The growth of the law firm was dramatic. The law "factory" on Wall Street decried by former Supreme Court Justice Harlan Stone in 1934 had no more than twenty lawyers (Auerbach 1976); today, the largest law firm in the United States has over eight hundred (Abramson 1988). Erwin Smigel first documented this growth in 1969, when he observed that the size of firms had doubled between 1957 and 1967. More recently, Robert Nelson observes that the nation's fifty largest firms have increased sixfold since 1960, and by 70 percent since the first half of the 1980s (Nelson 1988). In 1968, when Smigel wrote the second edition of his classic study, *The Wall Street Lawyer*, there were only twenty firms that employed as many as one hundred lawyers (Smigel 1969: 358–59). Today, more than two hundred firms employ one hundred or more lawyers (Nelson 1988).

Nelson (1988) attributes the phenomenal growth of these new types of firms to the changing market for legal services. Just as the New Deal created entirely new areas of law in the 1930s, Lyndon Johnson's War on Poverty, the creation of the Equal Employment

Opportunity Commission, and other civil-rights legislation led to many significant changes in American law (Auerbach 1976). The increase in government support for representation of clients through legal-aid programs, the creation of new legal entitlements for minorities, and the liberalization of rules for class-action suits and the standing necessary to initiate litigation—all brought about a dramatic shift in scope and character of the involvement by lawyers and legal authorities in public and private organizations.[23] In addition, the scope of federal law and regulations greatly expanded during the 1960s and 1970s in new areas of law, such as the environment, occupational safety, health and product safety, public financing of medical care, and the production of energy (Krier and Stewart 1978; Bibby, Mann and Ornstein 1982). And, finally, private citizens have become more litigious than ever before (Galanter 1983b; Lieberman 1981).

The growth in size and number of legal departments within large corporations also increased dramatically during this period. In post–Civil War America, railroad general counsel was one of the most powerful and prestigious actors in the legal profession. This status declined at the turn of the century, when lawyers in private law firms gained professional dominance (Hurst 1950: 297–98 and 303–08). More recently, to control costs, many companies have created their own internal legal counsel.[24] This trend has made in-house legal departments one of the fastest growing segments of the profession in the last twenty years (Bellis and Morris 1989; Galanter 1983a). And it has made the market for legal services even more competitive.

Despite the expansion in scope of law and the rise of internal counsel, Nelson (1988) argues that the organization of firms still reflects Cravath's original philosophy. Firms have moved toward hiring lawyers on the basis of merit and continue to utilize an "up or out" policy for their associates. What has changed, however, is their "entrepreneurial agenda." At the turn of the century, the leading firms on Wall Street held a relatively secure position in the market based on longstanding social and commercial ties. Because the market is much more uncertain today, firms "must develop strategies to diversify their client base and deal with increasingly unpredictable demands for their services" (Nelson 1988: 74).

Along with changes brought about by economies of scale, the division of labor in our post-industrial era has also been affected by technological innovations and an unprecedented increase in the numbers of women entering the paid labor force. The percentage of women working outside the home rose from 31 percent in 1950 to 43 percent in 1970 and 51 percent in 1980. By 1986, this figure had risen to 55 percent (Reskin and Roos 1990, table 1.5). The combination of new technology and the increasing number of women entering the labor market, particularly in administrative support and service occupations, has had a profound effect on the growth and expansion of the division of labor in the large firm.

Murphree (1981) argues that by the early 1960s, most large firms rationalized production by using the latest legal and clerical technology and implementing bureaucratized control in every level of their organizations. Today, some of these technological developments include computerized legal research, computerized document retrieval, the word processor, Xerox machines, fax machines, voice mail, electronic mail and the speaker phone. One of the most significant technological developments has been the introduction of the word processor (Machung 1984). Since the development of the microchip in the 1970s, law firms have spent millions of dollars on operating systems. For example, one of the leading firms in San Francisco, Pillsbury, Madison and Sutro, spent eight million dollars in 1988 on a new state-of-the art operating system (Jensen 1989).

The implementation of word processors has brought about further changes in the division of labor. Because word processing increases productivity, legal secretaries now work for several lawyers instead of one. Routine typing is farmed out to large word-processing centers which operate on eight-hour shifts, sometimes twenty-four hours a day, to meet the overtime demands of large firms. Sex-segregation continues: over 90 percent of these legal workers are women (Murphree 1981; Machung 1984).Skilled jobs have been broken down into simpler and more routine tasks. New departments and categories of workers, such as word processors, and duplicating operators, have been created. While many lower-level service departments, such as the word processing center, the duplicating center and the central file room make the job for legal secretaries easier by relieving them of routine copying and filing, Murphree (1981) argues that this reorganization has also resulted in the "deskilling" of secretarial work and an increase in monotony. Intellectually challenging tasks such as drafting legal documents and doing legal research, which were done by the "skilled generalist" of the turn of the century, were taken over by a new category of workers called paralegals in the late 1960s (Shipp 1989). Paralegals or legal assistants play an intermediate role between secretaries and attorneys in the law-firm bureaucracy, performing many non-typing tasks, such as researching legal and factual questions, drafting discovery motions and other pleadings, summarizing depositions, reviewing and organizing document productions, and locating and preparing witnesses for trial and depositions (Manikas 1975; Johnstone and Wenglinsky 1985; Larbalestrier 1986). In large law firms, paralegals have become highly desirable as "lawyer adjuncts." A recent article in the *National Law Journal* reported that "competitive pressures" on law firms are forcing them to manage their "partner time" more strategically: "A law firm maximizes its financial performance by allocating a partner's legal skills to legal matters that can be priced at premium rates, and by delegating routine legal matters . . . to other law firm personnel such as paralegals" (Granat and Saewitz 1989). Thus, legal assistants can perform many of the tasks that lawyers do, but their services cost clients less money, making them more cost-effective for many projects than lawyers are.

Although legal assistants do work similar to that of attorneys, as members of a "satellite occupation" they must work under the supervision and control of lawyers (Johnstone and Wenglinsky 1985: 2). Like other semi-professional workers, such as nurses, paralegals lack exclusive control and autonomy over their own work.[25] In fact, the tasks performed by paralegals and other semi-professionals have a direct and dependent relationship on a profession. Semi-professionals often act in service of a profession. As sociologist Natalie Sokoloff (1980) observes, "the fact that it is women 'serving' men is of crucial importance to understanding why women work in these areas and why male professionals have accepted large-scale female employment in these areas" (1980: 57). Johnstone and Wenglinsky (1985) estimated that 85 to 95 percent of paralegals were women in

1980.[26] The feminized character of this semi-profession continues today.[27]

Although the growth in the size of large firms, the development of new technology, and the deskilling of clerical work has restructured the division of labor in the law firm by creating new job categories, the firm continues to be sex-segregated. Why do jobs at the bottom of the firm hierarchy, such as paralegals and legal secretaries, continue to be feminized? Oppenheimer (1970) argues that the transformation of the labor process often paves the way for ideas about which sex does what job. Technology alone does not explain why a particular job has been feminized rather than masculinized. The process is also fostered by the ideological notion that some jobs constitute women's work. The assumption that women are more dexterous, more detail-oriented, and more suited to menial and routine tasks than men continues to be used as a justification for a gendered division of labor (Hossfeld 1989; Fernandez-Kelly 1983; Davies 1982). For example, the personnel director at Lyman, Lyman and Portia explained the firm's division of labor in this way:

I know it's not popular to say these things, but in my years of experience in personnel I have found that women are just better at some jobs. Women are neater and more organized than men are. They pay more attention to details. . . . Unlike men, they don't mind being asked to do menial tasks. Attorneys tell me that they find it harder to ask male secretaries to do these kinds of things.

Johnstone and Wenglinsky (1985) found that lawyers provided similar explanations for their preferences of women as paralegals. In my interviews, attorneys expressing preferences for women in these job categories used similar rationales. These findings suggest that ideology, as well as changes in technology, is important in determining the feminization of occupations.

The sex-typing of this job as "women's work" is somewhat contradictory. In addition to routine clerical tasks, paralegals also perform tasks done by lawyers, such as drafting standard legal documents and doing legal research—so-called "men's work." Reskin and Roos argue that construing work as appropriate for either women or men is simple "because most jobs contain both stereotypical male and female elements" (1990: 51). For example, Milkman (1987) found that during World War II, women's war work was defined as an extension of domesticity, and then, after the war, reconstrued as men's work. The war mobilization demonstrates "how idioms of sex-typing can be flexibly applied to whatever jobs women and men happen to be doing" (1987: 50). Similarly, the creation of the paralegal job category shows how easily sex-typing can be applied. As Chapter 4 shows, lawyers have stated preferences for women doing this kind of work. And, as I will argue, legal assistants themselves participate in reproducing these idioms through the types of emotional labor they perform.[28]

At the same time that more feminized occupations have been created at the lower level of the law firm, more and more women have decided to go to law school. In 1968, women comprised 6 percent of students enrolled in law school. By 1973, the figure had risen to 16, and in 1980, 33 percent (Epstein 1983: 53). In 1988, 42 percent of the students nationwide who attended law school were women (Prokop 1989). While this last figure is reflected in the number of women hired in firms across the country (40 percent), it is not reflected in the percentage of women lawyers overall or among those who achieve partnership. Nineteen percent of all attorneys are women and only 8 percent of the partners in the nation's 247 largest firms are women (Epstein 1993; Abramson 1988). In spite of the fact that almost half of students entering law school classes are female, women are still found primarily in associate positions, and men predominate in the partnership tier. These employment trends are reflected in the proportion of women found in associate and partnership positions in the firm in this study. Approximately 20 percent of associates across all departments in both firms are women, and less than 10 percent of partners are women.

Chapter Three

Rambo Litigators

Emotional Labor in a Male Dominated Job

> Late in the afternoon, I was sitting with Ben and Stan. . . .
> They were complaining about being litigators, or as they
> put it, how "litigation turns people into bastards—you
> don't have any real choices." Stan said that if you don't fit
> in, you have to get out because you won't be successful.
> And Ben added, "To be a really good litigator, you have to
> be a jerk. Sure you can get by being a nice guy, but you'll
> never be really good or really successful."
>
> Field notes

The comments made by these two young lawyers suggest that the
legal profession often requires behavior that is offensive not only to
other people, but to oneself: "To be a really good litigator, you have
to be a jerk." In popular culture and everyday life, jokes and stories
abound that characterize lawyers as aggressive, manipulative, unreli-
able, and unethical.[1] This image is expressed in the joke about why
the lawyer who falls overboard in shark-infested waters is not eaten
alive—it's professional courtesy. Our popular wisdom is that lawyers
are ruthless con artists who are more concerned with making money
than they are with fairness (Post 1987; *National Law Journal* 1986).[2]
Few consider, as these two young men do, that the requirements of
the profession itself support and reinforce this behavior.

How does the legal profession support such behavior? Legal
scholar Carrie Menkel-Meadow suggests that the adversarial model,
with its emphasis on "zealous advocacy" and "winning," encourages a
"macho ethic" in the courtroom (1985: 51–54). Lawyers and teachers
of trial lawyers argue that the success of litigators depends on their
ability to manipulate people's emotions (Brazil 1978; Berg 1987;
Spence 1988; Turow 1987). Trial lawyers must persuade judges and

juries and must intimidate witnesses and opposing counsel in the courtroom, in deposition, and in negotiations. The National Institute of Trial Advocacy, for example, devotes a three-week training seminar to teaching lawyers to hone such emotional skills.[3] Furthermore, attorneys recognize that to attract and retain clients they must not only provide a competent professional service, but spend considerable energy wooing potential business as well as listening to current clients, reassuring them and impressing them with their professional competence and expertise (Zimmerman 1983; Stibelman 1988a).

This chapter examines this emotional dimension of legal work in a particular specialty of law—litigation. Sociological studies of the legal profession have yet to seriously examine the emotional dimension of lawyering.[4] Although a few studies make reference to it, they do not make it the central focus of their research. For example, in their classic book, *Lawyers and Their Work*, Johnstone and Hopson (1967) describe in detail the many tasks associated with the lawyering role, such as advising clients, negotiation, drafting, litigation, investigation of the facts, legal research, and "business getting" (1967: 78–121). In only two of these nineteen task descriptions do Johnstone and Hopson allude to the emotional dimension of lawyering— "emotional support to client" and "acting as a scapegoat" (1967: 119–20). My findings suggest that these tasks as well as litigation, negotiation and business getting all contain an emotional as well as an intellectual component. More recently, Nelson (1988) reduces these varied tasks to three roles, finders, minders, and grinders: finders are lawyers "who seem to bring in substantial clients"; minders are lawyers "who take care of the clients who are already here"; and grinders are the lawyers "who do the work" (senior partner quoted in Nelson 1988: 69). Nelson's reduction of these roles to their instrumental and intellectual dimensions neglects the extent to which instrumental tasks like "finding" and "minding" also contain emotional elements.

My study shows that this neglected dimension of lawyering is a significant part of the work. Litigators make use of their emotions to persuade juries, judges, and witnesses in the courtroom, in depositions, and in communications with opposing counsel and with clients. However, in contrast to the popular image, intimidation and aggression constitute only one component of the emotional labor of lawyering. Lawyers also make use of strategic friendliness, that is, charm or flattery to manipulate others. Despite apparent differences in these two types of emotional labor, both involve the manipulation of others for a specific end—winning a case. While other jobs require the use of manipulation to achieve specific ends, such labor may serve different purposes and be embedded in a different set of relationships. Flight attendants, for example, are trained to be friendly and reassuring to passengers to alleviate their anxiety about flying (Hochschild 1983). However, flight attendants' friendliness takes the form of deference: their relationship to passengers is supportive and subordinate. In litigation the goal of strategic friendliness is to "win over" or dominate another. As professionals who have a monopoly over specialized knowledge, attorneys hold a superordinate position with respect to clients, witnesses, and jurors, and they take a competitive position with other lawyers. To win their cases, trial lawyers must manipulate and ultimately dominate others for their professional ends.

By doing whatever it takes, within the letter of the law, to win a case, lawyers fulfill the goal of zealous advocacy: persuading a third party that the client's interests should prevail. In this way, intimidation and strategic friendliness serve to reproduce and maintain the adversarial model. By exercising dominance and control over others, trial lawyers also reproduce gender relations. The majority of litigators who "do dominance" are men, and those who defer are either women—such as secretaries and paralegals (see Chapter 4)—or men who become feminized in the process of losing. In addition to creating and maintaining a gendered hierarchy, the form such emotional labor takes is itself gendered. It is a masculinized form of emotional labor not only because men do it but because dominance is associated with masculinity in our culture. West and Zimmerman (1987) argue, for example, that displays of dominance are ways for men to do gender. Similarly, psychoanalytic feminists equate masculinity with men's need to dominate women (Benjamin 1988; Chodorow 1978). In the case of trial lawyers, the requirements of the profession deem it appropriate to dominate women as well as other men. Such "conquests" or achievements at once serve the goals of effective advocacy and become means for the trial lawyer to demonstrate his masculinity.

Of course, not all litigators are men. My usage of the masculine pronoun in this chapter is meant to reflect not only that this area of law is male-dominated but also that the norms and idioms of appropriate emotional labor are masculinized. Furthermore, use of *he* highlights the contradictions women trial attorneys face as women in this profession: how can a woman be a woman and a lawyer who strives to prove his masculinity? The double binds women litigators experience will be examined in Chapter 5. This chapter emphasizes the unexamined, masculinized emotional norms of litigation practice.

Gamesmanship and the Adversarial Model

Popular wisdom and lawyer folklore portray lawyering as a game, and the ability to play as gamesmanship (Fox 1978; Spence 1988). As one of the trial attorneys I interviewed said,

The logic of gamesmanship is very interesting to me. I like how you make someone appear to be a liar. You know, you take them down the merry path and before they know it, they've said something pretty stupid. The challenge is getting them to say it without violating the letter of the law.

Lawyering is based on gamesmanship—legal strategy, skill, and expertise. But trial lawyers are much more than chess players; their strategies are not simply cerebral, rational, and calculating moves, but highly emotional, dramatic, flamboyant, shocking presentations that evoke sympathy, distrust, or outrage. In litigation practice, gamesmanship involves the utilization of legal strategy through a presentation of an emotional self that is designed specifically to influence the feelings and judgment of a particular legal audience—the judge, the jury, the witness, or opposing counsel. Furthermore, in my definition, the choices litigators make about selecting a particular strategy are not simply individual; they are institutionally constrained by the structure of the legal profession, by formal and informal professional norms, such as the American Bar Association's Model Code of Professional Responsibility (1982), and by training in trial advocacy, through programs such as those sponsored by the National Institute of Trial Advocacy.

The rules governing gamesmanship derive from the adversarial model that underlies the basic structure of our legal system.[5] This is a method of adjudication in which two advocates (the attorneys) present their sides of the case to an impartial third party (the judge and the jury), who listens to evidence and argument and declares one party the winner (Luban 1988; Menkel-Meadow 1985). As Menkel-Meadow (1985) observes, the basic assumptions that underlie this set of arrangements are "advocacy, persuasion, hierarchy, competition and binary results (win/lose)." She writes: "The conduct of litigation is relatively similar . . . to a sporting event—there are rules, a referee, an object to the game, and a winner is declared after play is over" (1985: 51).

Within this system, the attorney's main objective is to persuade the impartial third party that his client's interests should prevail (American Bar Association 1982: 34). However, clients do not always have airtight, defensible cases. How then does the "zealous advocate" protect his client's interests and achieve the desired result? When persuasion by appeal to reason breaks down, an appeal to emotions becomes paramount (Cheatham 1955: 282–83). As legal scholar John Buchan writes, "the root of the talent is simply the power to persuade" (1939: 211–13). And in "Basic Rules of Pleading," Jerome Michael writes:

The decision of an issue of fact in a case of closely balanced probabilities therefore, must, in the nature of things, be an emotional rather than a rational act; and the rules regulating that stage of a trial which we call the stage of persuasion, the stage when lawyers sum up to the jury. . . . The point is beautifully made by an old Tennessee case in which the plaintiff's counsel, when summing up to the jury began to weep. . . . The lawyer for the defendant objected and asked the trial judge to stop him from weeping. Weeping is not a form of argument. . . . Well, the Supreme Court of Tennessee said: "It is not only counsel's privilege to weep for his client; it is his duty to weep for his client." (1950: 175)

By appealing to emotions, the lawyer becomes a con man.[6] He acts as if he has a defensible case; he puffs himself up; he bolsters his case. Thus, the successful advocate must not only be smart, but, as the famous turn-of-the-century trial lawyer Francis Wellman[7] observed, he must also be a good actor (1986 [1903]: 13). In *The Art of Cross-Examination,* first published in 1903 and reprinted to the present, Wellman describes how carefully the litigator must present himself to the judge and jury:

> The most cautious cross-examiner will often elicit a damaging answer. Now is the time for the greatest self-control. If you show by your face how the answer hurt, you may lose by that one point alone. How often one sees a cross-examiner fairly staggered by such an answer. He pauses, blushes, [but seldom regains] control of the witness. With the really experienced trial lawyer, such answers, instead of appearing to surprise or disconcert him, will seem to come as a matter of course, and will fall perfectly flat. He will proceed with the next question as if nothing happened, or else perhaps give the witness an incredulous smile, as if to say, "Who do you suppose would believe that for a minute." (1986 [1903]: 13–14)

More recently, teacher and lawyer David Berg (1987) advises lawyers to think of themselves as actors and the jury as an audience:[8]

> Decorum can make a difference, too. . . . Stride to the podium and exude confidence, even if there is a chance that the high school dropout on the stand is going to make you look like an idiot. Take command of the courtroom. Once you begin, do not grope for questions, shuffle through papers, or take breaks to confer with cocounsel. Let the jury know that you are prepared, that you do not need anyone's advice, and that you care about the case . . . because if you don't care, the jurors won't care. (1987: 28)

Wellman and Berg make a similar point: in the courtroom drama, attorneys are the leading actors. Appearance and demeanor are of utmost importance. The lawyer's manner, his tone of voice, and his facial expressions are all means to persuade the jury that his client is right. Outrageous behavior, as long as it remains within the letter of the law, is acceptable. Not only are trial lawyers expected to act, but they are expected to act with a specific purpose in mind: to favorably influence feelings of the judge and jurors.

This emphasis on acting is also evident in the courses taught by the National Institute for Trial Advocacy, where neophyte litigators learn the basics of presenting a case for trial. NITA's emphasis is on "learning by doing" (Kilpatrick quoted in Rice 1989). Attorneys do not simply read about cases but practice presenting them in a simulated courtroom with a judge, a jury, and witnesses. In this case, doing means acting. As one of the teachers/lawyers said on the first day of class, "Being a good trial lawyer means being a good actor. . . . Trial attorneys love to perform." Acting, in sociological terms, constitutes emotional labor, that is, inducing or suppressing feelings in order to produce an outward countenance that influences the emotions of others. The instructors discuss style, delivery, presentation of self, attitude, and professionalism. Participants, in turn, compare notes about the best way to "handle" judges, jurors, witnesses, clients, and opposing counsel. The efforts of these two groups constitute the teaching and observance of "feeling rules," or professional norms that govern appropriate lawyerly conduct in the courtroom.

The tone of the three-week course I attended in Boulder, Colorado, was set by one of the introductory speakers, a communications expert and actor. He began his lecture by describing his personal "presentation of self":

"Let's see, tall, blond, Scandinavian looking. Can't change that. But let's think about what I can change." He stands erect, imperious, and exclaims, "A Nordic Viking!" The class laughs. He doubles over, limps along the dais, and says in a shaky voice, "A bent, old man." There is more laughter. He stands erect again and begins making exaggerated faces—he smiles, grimaces, frowns; he looks sad, stern, angry. There is more laughter. "So you see, I do have something to work with! Now let's start with you. Everyone stand up." People stand. "Are you a sloucher, do you walk with a ramrod up your. . . . Let's practice by standing for awhile and try thinking confidence. You want to convey confidence in the courtroom! How do you do that?" He addresses one of the students: "No, you do not slouch!" There is more laughter. "Stand tall. . . . Stand tall." He looks around the room. "Have any of you ever heard of animation? Standing tall is great, but—" he pauses and looks significantly at a woman student— "standing tall and looking bored does not convey confidence! How do you convey confidence? It helps to look confident—but you also have to feel confident."

In his lecture, he provided a list of acting techniques that attorneys could use in the courtroom. He encouraged the litigators to practice facial expressions in front of a mirror for at least fifteen minutes a day. However, his lecture was not just a lesson in "surface acting," that is, the display of facial expressions, but in "deep acting," as well. Deep acting is similar to the Stanislavski method, in which the actor induces the actual feeling called upon by the role (Hochschild 1983: 35). NITA's communications expert, for example, encouraged students to visualize themselves in situations where they had felt confident, to "hold on to that feeling" and "project it" into the current situation.

The remainder of the three-week course took students through various phases of a hypothetical trial—jury selection, opening and closing statements, direct and cross-examination. In each stage of the trial the lawyer has a slightly different purpose. For example, the objective in jury selection is to uncover the biases and prejudices of the jurors and to develop rapport with them. The opening statement sets the theme for the case, whereas direct examination lays the foundation of evidence for the case. Cross-examination is intended to undermine the credibility of the opposition's witness, and closing represents the final argument. Despite the differing goals of each phase, the means to achieve the lawyer's goals is similar in each case, that is, to attempt to persuade a legal audience to be favorably disposed to one's client through a particular emotional presentation of self.

In their sessions on direct and cross-examination, students were given primarily stylistic rather than substantive responses to their presentations. They were given finer criticisms on the technicalities of their objections and the strength or weakness of their arguments. But in the content analysis of my field notes of each session I found that 50 to 80 percent of comments were directed toward the attorney's particular style. These comments fell into five categories: (1) personal appearance; (2) presentation of self (nice, aggressive, or sincere manner); (3) tone and level of voice; (4) eye contact and (5) rapport with others in the courtroom.

For example, in one of the sessions, Tom, a young student in the class, did a direct examination of a witness to a liquor-store robbery. He solemnly questioned the witness about his work, his special training in enforcing liquor laws, and his approach to determining whether someone was intoxicated. At one point, the witness provided a detail that Tom had not expected, but rather than expressing surprise, Tom appeared nonchalant and continued with his line of questions. At the end of his direct, the teacher provided the following feedback:

Good background development of witness. Your voice level was appropriate but try modulating it a bit more for emphasis. You also use too many thank you's to the judge. You should ingratiate yourself with the judge, but not overly so. You also made a good recovery when the witness said something unexpected.

When Patricia, a young woman attorney, proceeded nervously through the same direct examination, opposing counsel objected repeatedly to some of her questions, which flustered her. The teacher told her:

You talk too fast. And, you didn't make enough eye contact with the judge. Plus, you got bogged down in the objections and harassment from opposing counsel. Your recovery was too slow. You've got to be more forceful.

In both these examples, as in most of the sessions I observed, the focus of the comments is not on the questions asked but on how the questions are asked. Tom is told to modulate his voice; Patricia is told not to talk so fast. In addition, the teacher directs attention to rapport with others in the courtroom, particularly the judge. Moreover, the teacher commends Tom for his "recovery," that is, regaining self-composure and control of the witness. He criticizes Patricia, on the other hand, for not recovering well from an aggressive objection made by opposing counsel.

In my fieldwork at NITA and in the two law offices, I found two main types of emotional labor: intimidation and strategic friendliness. Intimidation entails the use of anger and aggression, whereas strategic friendliness utilizes politeness, friendliness, and/or playing dumb. Both types of emotional labor are related to gamesmanship.

Many jobs appear to require strategic friendliness and intimidation. Domestic workers, for example, sometimes "play dumb" so as not to alienate their white female employers (Rollins 1985). For domestic workers, however, this strategy offers a means for someone in a subordinate position to survive a degrading job. By contrast, for litigators strategic friendliness, like intimidation, allows an individual with professional status to control and dominate others in an effort to win one's case. Although both the litigator and the domestic worker may play dumb, their behavior serves different goals, which are indicative of their divergent positions in relationship to others.

Intimidation and strategic friendliness not only serve the goals of the adversarial model but also exemplify a masculine style of emotional labor. They become construed as masculine for several reasons. First, emotional labor in the male-dominated professional strata of the gendered law firm is interpreted as masculine simply because men do it.[9] Ruth Milkman, for example, suggests that "idioms of sex-typing can be applied to whatever women and men happen to be doing" (1987: 50). Male trial attorneys participate in shaping this idiom by describing their battles in the courtroom and with opposing counsel as "macho," "something men get into" and "a male thing." In addition, by treating women lawyers as outsiders and excluding them from professional networks, they further define their job as exclusively male (see Chapter 5).

The underlying purpose of gamesmanship itself, that is, the control and domination of others through manipulation, reflects a particular cultural conception of masculinity. Connell (1987), for example, describes a hegemonic form of masculinity which emphasizes the domination of a certain class of men—middle- to upper-middle-class—over other men and over women. Connell's cultural conception of masculinity dovetails neatly with feminist psychoanalytic accounts that interpret domination as a means of asserting one's masculinity (Chodorow 1978; Benjamin 1988). The lawyers I studied also employed a ritual of degradation and humiliation against other men and women who were witnesses, opposing counsel, and, in some cases, clients. The remainder of this chapter describes the main components and purposes of litigators' emotional labor and shows how these forms become construed as masculine.

Intimidation

Litigation is war. The lawyer is a gladiator
and the object is to wipe out the other side.

Cleveland lawyer quoted in the *New York Times*, August 5, 1988

The most common form of emotional labor associated with lawyers is intimidation. In popular culture, the tough, hard-hitting, and aggressive trial lawyer is portrayed in television shows such as *L.A. Law* and *Perry Mason* and in movies such as *The Firm, A Few Good Men*, and *Presumed Innocent*. The news media's focus on famous trial attorneys such as Arthur Liman, the prosecutor of Oliver North in the Iran-Contra trial, also reinforces this image. Law professor Wayne Brazil (1978) refers to this style of lawyering as the "professional combatant." Others have termed it the "Rambo litigator" (a reference to the highly stylized, super-masculine role Sylvester Stallone plays in his action movies), "legal terrorists," and "barbarians of the bar" (Margolick 1988; Sayler 1988; Miner 1988). Trial attorneys themselves call litigators from large law firms "hired guns" (Spangler 1986). And books on trial preparation, such as McElhaney's *Trial Notebook* (1987), endorse the litigator-as-gladiator metaphor by portraying the attorney on the book's dust jacket as a knight in a suit of armor ready to do battle (McElhaney 1987).

The recurring figure in these images is not only intimidating but strongly masculine. In the old West, hired guns were sharpshooters; men who were hired to kill other men. The strong, silent movie character Rambo is emblematic of a highly stylized, supermasculinity. The knight in shining armor preparing to do battle on the front cover of McElhaney's *Trial Notebook* is male, not female. Finally, most of the actors who play tough, hard-hitting lawyers in the television shows and movies mentioned above are men. Thus, intimidation is not simply a form of emotional labor associated with trial lawyers, it is a masculinized form of labor.

Intimidation is tied to cultural conceptions of masculinity in yet another way. In a review of the literature on occupations, Connell (1987) observes that the cult of masculinity in working-class jobs centers on physical prowess and sexual contempt for men in managerial or office positions (1987: 180). Like the men on the shop floor in Michael Burawoy's (1979) study who brag about how much they can lift or produce, lawyers in this study boast about "destroying witnesses," "playing hard-ball," and "taking no prisoners" and about the size and amount of their "win." In a middle-class job such as the legal profession, however, intimidation depends not on physical ability but on mental quickness and a highly developed set of social skills. Thus, masculinizing practices such as aggression and humiliation take on an emotional and intellectual tone in this occupation.

This stance is tied to the adversarial model's conception of the "zealous advocate" (American Bar Association 1982). The purpose of this strategy is to intimidate the witness or opposing counsel into submission. A destructive cross-examination is the best example.[10] The trial attorney is taught to intimidate the witness in cross-examination, "to control the witness by never asking a question to which he does not already know the answer and to regard the impeachment of the witness as a highly confrontational act" (Menkel-Meadow, 1985: 54). Wellman describes cross-examination in this way:

It requires the greatest ingenuity; a habit of logical thought; clearness of perception; infinite patience and self-control; the power to read men's minds intuitively, to judge of their characters by their faces, to appreciate their motives; ability to act with force and precision; a masterful knowledge of the subject-matter itself; an extreme caution; and, above all the instinct to discover the weak point in the witness under examination. . . . It is a mental duel between counsel and witness. (1986 [1903]: 8)

In his lecture on cross-examination, Berg echoes Wellman's words: "The common denominator for effective cross-examination is not genius, however. It's a combination of preparation and an instinct for the jugular" (1987: 27). Again, cross-examination involves not only acting mean but creating a specific impression on the witness. An article in the *National Law Journal*, "Testifying Can be Deadly, Witness Says," speaks to the intended effect of an aggressive cross-examination (Ziegler 1989: 6). The author describes a case in which cross-examination was so aggressive that the witness had a heart attack on the witness stand. Nevertheless, opposing counsel recalled the witness as soon as he got out of the hospital, suggesting not only the importance of the witness to the case but the persistence and ruthlessness of the lawyer in obtaining the desired result. The effect on the witness has been portrayed more humorously in popular culture. In a cartoon featured in the New Yorker magazine, a witness sitting in the witness box says to the judge in reference to the lawyer before him, "Your honor, I feel threatened by this gentleman's intensity." And in John Mortimer's *Rumpole of the Bailey*, Philida Trant, a fictional woman lawyer, compares the effect of a destructive cross-examination to "being hit by a steam roller at 90 miles an hour" (1978: 348).

In the sections on cross-examination at NITA, teachers trained lawyers to "act mean." The demonstration by the teachers on cross-examination best exemplified this point. Two male instructors reenacted an aggressive cross-examination in a burglary case. The prosecutor relentlessly hammered away until the witness couldn't remember any specific details about the burglar's appearance. At the end of his demonstration, the audience clapped vigorously. Three male students who had been asked to comment responded unanimously and enthusiastically that the prosecutor's approach had been excellent. One student commentator said, "He kept complete control of the witness." Another remarked, "He blasted the witness's testimony." And the third added, "He destroyed the witness's credibility." The fact that a destructive cross-examination served as the demonstration for the entire class underscores the desirability of aggressive behavior as a model for appropriate lawyer-like conduct in this situation. Furthermore, the students' praise for the attorney's tactics collectively reinforce the norm for such behavior.

Teachers emphasized the importance of using aggression to motivate oneself as well. Before a presentation on cross-examination, Tom, one of the students, stood in the hallway with one of the instructors trying to "psyche himself up to get mad." He repeated over and over to himself, "I hate it when witnesses lie to me. It makes me so mad!" The teacher coached him to concentrate on that thought until Tom could actually evoke the feeling of anger. He said later in an interview, "I really felt mad at the witness when I walked into the courtroom." In the actual cross-examination, each time the witness made an inconsistent statement, Tom became more and more angry: "First, you told us you could see the burglar, now you say your vision was obstructed! So, which is it, Mr. Jones?" The more irate he became, the more he intimidated and confused the witness, who at last completely backed down and said, "I don't know" in response to every question. The teacher characterized Tom's performance as "the best in the class" because it was "the most forceful" and "the most intimidating." Students remarked that he deserved to "win the case."

NITA's teachers also utilized mistakes to train students in the rigors of cross-examination. For example, when Laura cross-examined the same witness in the liquor store case, a teacher commented on her performance:

Too many words. You're asking the witness for information. Don't do that in cross-examination. You tell them what the information is. You want to be destructive in cross-examination. When the other side objects to an answer, you were too nice. Don't be so nice! Next time, ask to talk to the judge, tell him, "This is crucial to my case." You also asked for information when you didn't know the answer. Bad news. You lost control of the witness.

By being nice and losing control of the witness, Laura violated two norms underlying the classic confrontational cross-examination. A destructive cross-examination is meant to impeach the witness's credibility, thereby demonstrating to the jury the weakness in opposing counsel's case. In situations that call for such an aggressive cross-examination, being nice implies that the lawyer likes the witness and agrees with her testimony. By not being aggressive, Laura created the wrong impression for the jury. Second, Laura lost control of the witness. Rather than guiding the witness through the cross with leading questions[11] that were damaging to opposing counsel's case, she allowed the witness to make his own points. As we will see in the next section of the chapter, being nice can also be used as a strategy for controlling a witness; however, such a strategy is not effective in a destructive cross-examination.

Laura's violation of these norms also serves to highlight the implicitly masculine practices utilized in cross-examination. The repeated phrase, "keeping complete control of the witness," clearly signals the importance of dominating other women and men. Further, the language used to describe obtaining submission—"blasting the witness," "destroying his credibility," pushing him to "back down"—is quite violent. In addition, the successful control of the witness often takes on the character of a sexual conquest. One brutal phrase used repeatedly in this way is "raping the witness." Within this discursive field, men who "control," "destroy," or "rape" the witness are seen as "manly," while those who lose control are feminized as "sissies" and "wimps," or in Laura's case as "too nice."

The combative aspect of emotional labor carries over from the courtroom to other lawyering tasks, such as depositions, negotiations, communications with opposing counsel, and discovery. Attorneys "shred" witnesses not only in the courtroom but in depositions as well. When I worked at the private firm, Daniel, one of the partners, employed what he called his "cat and mouse game" with one of the key witnesses, Jim, in a deposition I attended. During the deposition, Daniel aggressively cross-examined Jim. "When did you do this?" "You were lying, weren't you?" Jim lost his temper in response to Daniel's hostile form of interrogation—"You hassle me, man! You make me mad!" Daniel smiled and said, "I'm only trying to get to the truth of the situation." Then he became aggressive again and said, "You lied to the IRS about how much profit you made, didn't you, Jim!" Jim lost his temper again and started calling Daniel a liar. A heated interchange between Daniel and opposing counsel followed, in which opposing counsel objected to Daniel's "badgering the witness." The attorneys decided to take a brief recess.

When the deposition resumed, Daniel began by pointing his index finger at John, the other attorney, and accusing him of withholding crucial documents. Opposing counsel stood up and started yelling in a high-pitched voice—"Don't you ever point your finger at me! Don't you ever do that to me! This deposition is over. . . . I'm leaving." With that he stood up and began to cram papers into his briefcase in preparation to leave. Daniel immediately backed down, apologized, and said, "Sit down John, I promise, I won't point my finger again." He went on to smooth the situation over and proceeded to tell John in a very calm and controlled voice what his objections were. John made some protesting noises, but he didn't leave. The deposition continued.

In this instance, the deposition, rather than the courtroom, became the "stage" and Daniel took the leading role. His cross-examination was confrontational, and his behavior with the witness and opposing counsel was meant to intimidate. After the deposition Daniel boasted to me and several associates about how mad he had made the witness and how he had "destroyed his credibility." He then proceeded to reenact the final confrontation by imitating John standing up and yelling at him in a falsetto voice. In the discussion that followed, Daniel and his associates gave the effects of his behavior on the "audience" utmost consideration. Hadn't Daniel done a good job forcing the witness to lose control? Hadn't he controlled the situation well? Didn't he make opposing counsel look like a "simpering fool?"

The reenactment and ensuing discussion reveal several underlying purposes of the deposition. First, they suggest that for the attorney the deposition was not only a fact-finding mission but a show designed to influence a particular audience—the witness. Daniel effectively flustered and intimidated the witness. Second, Daniel's imitation of John with a falsetto voice "as if" he were a woman serves as a sort of "degradation ceremony" (Garfinkel 1956). By reenacting the drama, he ridicules the man on the other side before an audience of peers, further denigrating him by inviting collective criticism and laughter from colleagues. Third, the discussion of the strategy builds up and elevates Daniel's status as an attorney for his aggressive, yet rational control of the witness and the situation. Thus, the discussion creates an opportunity for collectively reinforcing Daniel's intimidation strategy.

In addition to highlighting the use of intimidation in depositions, this example also illustrates the way in which aggression as legal strategy, or rule-governed aggression (Lyman 1987; Benjamin 1988), becomes conflated with masculinity, whereas aggression that is not rule-governed is ridiculed as feminine. John shows anger, but it is deemed inappropriate because he loses control of the situation. Such a display of hostility does not serve the interests of the legal profession because it does not achieve the desired result—a win for the case. As a result, Daniel and his associate regard John's behavior—his lack of control, his seeming hysteria, his high voice—with contempt. This contempt takes on a specific sexual character. Just as the working-class "lads" in Paul Willis's (1977) book *Learning to Labor* denigrate the "earholes" or sissies for their feminine attributes, Daniel and his colleagues ridicule John for his female-like behavior. Aggression as legal strategy or maleness is celebrated; contempt is reserved for aggression (or behavior) which is not rule-governed, behavior which is also associated with the opposite sex.

Attorneys also used the confrontational approach in depositions at Bonhomie Corporation. In a deposition I sat in on, Mack, a litigator, utilized an aggressive cross-examination of the key witness.

Q: What were the names of the people that have mi-
        grated from one of the violators, as you call it, to
        Bonhomie Corporation?

A: I don't remember as of now.

Q: Do you have their names written down?

A: No.

Q: Well, if you don't remember their names and
        they're not written down, how can you follow their
        migration from one company to another?

A: You can consider it in the process of discovery that I
        will make some enquiring phone calls.

Q: Did you call anyone to follow their migration?

A: Well, I was unsuccessful as of yet to reach other
        people.

Q: Who have you attempted to call?

A: I can't tell you at this time. I have a list of processes
        in my mind to follow.

Q: Do you recall who you called and were not able to
        reach?

A: No.

Q: What's the list of processes in your mind to follow?

A: It's hard to describe.

Q: In other words, you don't have a list?

A: [quietly] Not really.

Q: Mr. Jensen, instead of wasting everyone's time and
        money, answer the question yes or no!

Opposing Counsel: Don't badger the witness.

Q: Answer the question, Mr. Jensen, Yes or No!

Opposing counsel: I said, don't badger the witness.

Q: Mr. Jensen, you are still required to answer the
        question!

A: [quietly] No.

In this case, Mack persists in badgering the witness, who provides
incoherent and vague answers. As the witness becomes more eva-

sive, the attorney becomes more confrontational. By using this approach, the lawyer succeeds in making the witness appear uncooperative and eventually pushes him to admit that he doesn't have a list.

Later, in the same deposition, the attorney's confrontational tactics extend to opposing counsel.

Q:	Let's change the subject. Mr. Jensen, can you tell me what representations were made to you about the reliability of the Bonhomie Corporation's spider system?
A:	Nancy, the saleslady, said they use it widely in the United States, and could not be but very reliable. And, as we allege, fraudulent, and as somebody referred to it, was the, they wanted to give us the embrace of death to provide us more dependency, and then to go on and control our operation totally.
Q:	Who said that?
A:	My attorney.
Q:	When was that?
Opposing Counsel:	Well, I . . .
Mack:	I think he's already waived it. All I want to know is when it was supposedly said.
A:	Well . . .
Opposing Counsel:	I do use some great metaphors.
Mack:	Yes, I know, I have read your complaint.
Opposing Counsel:	Sorry?
Mack:	I have read your complaint. That will be all for today, Mr. Jensen.

Here, the attorney does not stop with badgering the witness. When the witness makes the statement about the "embrace of death," Mack is quick to find out who said it. And when opposing counsel brags about his "great metaphors," Mack parries back with a sarcastic retort. Having had the final word, he abruptly ends the deposition. Like the other deposition, this one is an arena not only for intimidating the witness, but for ridiculing the attorney on the other side. In this way, intimidation is used to control the witness, and sar-

casm to dominate opposing counsel. In doing so, Mack has achieved
the desired result—the witness's submission to his line of questioning and a victory over the other side. Furthermore, in his replay of
the deposition to his colleagues, he characterizes his victory as a
"macho blast against the other side," thereby underscoring the masculine character of his intimidation tactics.

Even phone calls to opposing counsel become an opportunity for
intimidation. One of the lawyers at the private firm described gear-
ing himself up for the next phone call with the plaintiff's lawyer:

> Sometimes, I spend the whole day mentally preparing myself for the
> next phone call with the plaintiff's lawyer.
> *What do you do?*
> I think about how much he pisses me off. By the time I call him, I'm
> ready for a fight.
> *Then what happens?*
> Well, today he said he didn't have the documents for the production
> ready yet. I told him that we needed them and reminded him about the
> rules of discovery. He said something insulting like, "I guess you should
> know, since you're a Harvard boy." Then I said, "I'll get sanctions from the
> judge." By the end of the conversation, we were yelling at each other on the
> phone. [He laughs and looks embarrassed.] It's a male thing.
> *Male thing?*
> It's a competition. Men beating each other up, trying to show one an-
> other up. Only these aren't fist fights, they're verbal assaults.

Other lawyers, both at the private firm and Bonhomie Corporation, described similar telephone interactions. "I get into yelling
matches with opposing counsel over the phone at least once a week."
And another, "On one case I was on the phone every day with the
other side." "Opposing counsel play hardball all the time—even on
the telephone. It's another way to intimidate you. It's part of the
game." In these instances, the phone conversation itself becomes an
arena for competition. The lawyer works to build up emotional
readiness. Then each side works to insult and bully the other. The
masculine character of the "verbal assault" is underscored by the attorney himself when he describes it as "a male thing."

Attorneys rarely use intimidation to manipulate their clients.
Clients are the bread-and-butter for these professionals. Lawyers

want to please their clients, win repeat business, maintain their business, and create future business contacts through them. Alienating a client is usually the last thing they want to do. However, in extreme circumstances, lawyers will resort to such a strategy. In an article questioning the ethics of the manipulative strategies used by trial lawyers in their daily practice, Wayne Brazil (1978) describes how an attorney emotionally bullied a client to achieve the desired result in a trial. In preparation for the trial, the attorney warned his client that expressing certain feelings during the trial itself would be detrimental to their case. The client promised to keep these feelings to himself; however, when he got on the witness stand, he began to say the very things he had been warned not to say. A lunch recess intervened before too much damage had been done. Brazil describes how the attorney handled this situation:

> At lunch the attorney was silent and cold for a few minutes, then he threw a tantrum over the testimony the client was giving. The lawyer shouted that though the rules of professional responsibility forced him to continue as counsel in this case, he had no obligation to spend any social time with the client. The attorney then threw his napkin on the table and stormed out of the room. He neither spoke nor saw his client again until that afternoon, when the badly shaken client followed the attorney's pretrial instruction to the letter and suppressed all feelings he wanted to air. (1978: 109)

As Brazil observes, the tantrum by the lawyer had been "completely contrived." Because the attorney "had failed to control the client's behavior through an appeal to self-interest and reason, he had used all the emotional power accessible to him" (1978: 110). In this way, the litigator disguised his own feelings in an effort to manipulate his client and to achieve the goals of zealous advocacy: obtaining the best result at trial without violating the letter of the law.

At the private firm, trial lawyers did not use intimidation with clients; they utilized strategic friendliness. Certainly, litigators grumbled about trying to please difficult clients behind the scenes, but no one complained personally to a client. At Bonhomie Corporation the attorney-client relationship was different because the company itself was the client. It was often difficult to get other departments to cooperate with the legal department because lawyers were regarded as "watchdogs" or people who created more work for their unit.[12] As a consequence, relations between departments were often strained. Tension typically began when the client from another department refused to cooperate. In one instance, the lack of cooperation escalated until the attorney personally visited the client in the other department to scream at the offending party. Eleanor said:

> The final straw came when Judy from [department X] told me that she didn't feel like doing any overtime to work on the case. At that time, I had been putting in sixty-hour weeks for two months to prepare for this trial. So, I just let her have it. I told her I worked my tail off for the company. And that we were all in this together, a team, and it was just too bad if she didn't feel like it because she was going to do it anyway!
> *What happened then?*
> I called her supervisor and yelled at him. "Why aren't you doing your job? Don't you know how to manage your employees? Why aren't you cooperating with us, after all this is a lawsuit against the Company."
> *What did he say?*
> He didn't say a thing. In fact, he still ignores me when he sees me in the elevator. But he must have done something because Judy did the overtime.

Other lawyers at the Bonhomie Corporation reported similar incidents. For example, one lawyer told me that one client was so uncooperative—never returning phone calls, canceling appointments—that he and his paralegal finally camped outside his office door early one morning.

> [When he saw us] the client was furious. I told him if he didn't start to cooperate with us right this minute, we'd sue his ass all the way to Kalamazoo and he'd never work for the company again.
> *What did he do?*
> He unlocked his office door and invited us in.

Masculine images of violence and warfare—destroying, blasting, shredding, slaying, burying—are used repeatedly to characterize the attorney's relationship to legal audiences. They are also used to describe discovery tactics and filing briefs. Discovery tactics such as enormous document requests are referred to as "dropping bombs" or "sending missiles" to the other side. And at the private firm, when a lawyer filed fourteen pretrial motions the week before trial, over three hundred pages of written material, he referred to it as "dumping an avalanche" on the other side.

Strategic Friendliness

> *Mr. Choate's appeal to the jury began long before final argument. . . . His manner to the jury was that of a friend, a friend solicitous to help them through their tedious investigation; never an expert combatant, intent on victory, and looking upon them as only instruments for its attainment.*
>
> (Wellman 1986 [1903]: 16–17)

The lesson implicit in Wellman's anecdote about famous nineteenth century lawyer Rufus Choate's trial tactics is that friendliness is another important strategy the litigator must learn and use to be successful in the courtroom. Like aggression, the strategic use of friendliness is a feature of gamesmanship, and hence, a component of emotional labor. As Richard, one of the attorney/teachers, at NITA stated, "Lawyers have to be able to vary their styles; they have to be able to have multiple speeds, personalities, and style." In his view, intimidation did not always work, and he proposed an alternative strategy, what he called "the toe-in-the-sand, aw-shucks routine." Rather than adopting an intimidating stance toward the witness, he advocated "playing dumb and innocent": "Say to the witness, 'Gee, I don't know what you mean. Can you explain it again?' until you catch the witness in a mistake or an inconsistent statement." Other litigators such as Leonard Ring (1987) call this the "low-key approach." Ring describes how opposing counsel delicately handled the cross-examination of a child witness:

The lawyer for the defendant . . . stood to cross-examine. Did he attack the details of her story to show inconsistencies? Did he set her up for impeachment by attempting to reveal mistakes, uncertainties and confusion? I sat there praying that he would. But no, he did none of the things a competent defense lawyer is supposed to do. He was old enough to be the girl's grandfather [and] the image came through. He asked her very softly and politely: "Honey, could you tell us again what you saw?" She told it exactly as she had on my direct. I felt relieved. He still wasn't satisfied. "Honey, would you mind telling us again what you saw?" She did again exactly as she had before. He still wasn't satisfied. "Would you do it once more?" She did. She repeated, again, the same story—the same way, in the same words. By that time I got the message. The child had been rehearsed by her mother the same way she had been taught "Mary Had a Little Lamb." I won the case, but it was a very small verdict. (1987: 35–36)

Ring concludes that a low-key approach is necessary in some situations and advises against adhering rigidly to the prototypical combative style.

Similarly, Scott Turow (1987), the lawyer and novelist, advises trying a variety of approaches when cross-examining the star witness. He cautions against adopting a "guerrilla warfare mentality" in cross-examination and suggests that the attorney may want to create another impression with the jury:

Behaving courteously can keep you from getting hurt and, in the process, smooth the path for a win. [In one case I worked on] the cross examination was conducted with a politesse appropriate to a drawing room. I smiled to show that I was not mean-spirited. The chief executive officer smiled to show that he was not beaten. The commissioners smiled to show their gratitude that everybody was being so nice. And my client won big (1987: 40–42).

Being nice, polite, welcoming, playing dumb, or behaving courteously are all ways that a trial lawyer can manipulate the witness in order to create a particular impression for the jury. I term this form of gamesmanship strategic friendliness. Rather than bully or scare the witness into submission, this tactic employs friendliness, politeness and tact. Yet it is simply another form of emotional manipulation of another person for a strategic end—winning one's case. For instance, the attorney in Ring's account is gentle and considerate of the child witness for two strategic reasons. First, by making the child feel comfortable, he brings to light the fact that her testimony has been rehearsed. Second, by playing the polite, gentle grandfatherly role, he has made a favorable impression on the jury. In this way, he improves his chances for winning. As, in fact, he did. Although he didn't win the case, the verdict for the other side was "small."

Although strategic friendliness may appear to be a softer approach than intimidation, it carries with it a strongly manipulative element. Consider the reasoning behind this particular approach. Ring's attorney is nice to the child witness not because he's altruistically concerned for her welfare, but to achieve the desired result, as simply a means to an end. This end is best summed up by litigator Mark Dombroff: "So long as you don't violate the law, including the rules of procedure and evidence or do violence to the canons of ethics, winning is the only thing that matters" (1989: 13).

This emphasis on winning is tied to traditional conceptions of masculinity and competition. Sociologist Mike Messner (1989) argues that achievement in sporting competitions such as football, baseball, and basketball serve as a measure of men's self-worth and their masculinity. This can also be carried over into the workplace. For example, as I have suggested, by redefining production on the shop floor as a "game," Burawoy's factory workers maintain their sense of control over the labor process, and hence, their identity as men. In her research on men in sales, Leidner (1991) finds that defining the jobs as competition becomes a means for construing the work as masculine:

The element of competition, the battle of wills implicit in their interactions with customers, seemed to be a major factor which allowed agents to interpret their work as manly. Virtually every step of the interaction was understood as a challenge to be met—getting in the door, making the prospect relax and warm up, being allowed to start the presentation . . . making the sale, and perhaps even increasing the size of the sale. (1991: 168)

For litigators, keeping score of wins in the courtroom and the dollar amount of damages or settlement awards allows them to interpret their work as manly. At Bonhomie Corporation and at Lyman, Lyman and Portia, the first question lawyers often asked others after a trial or settlement conference was "Who won the case?" or "How big were the damages?" Note that both Ring and Turow also conclude their pieces with descriptions of their win—"I won the case, but the verdict was small" and "I won big." Trial attorneys who did not "win big" were described as "having no balls," or as being "geeks" or "wimps." The fact that losing is associated with being less than a man suggests that the constant focus on competition and winning is an arena for proving one's masculinity.

One important area that calls for strategic friendliness and focuses on winning is jury selection or voir dire. The main purpose of voir dire is to obtain personal information about prospective jurors in order to determine whether they will be "favorably disposed to you, your client, and your case, and will ultimately return a favorable verdict" (Mauet 1980: 31). Once an attorney has made that assessment, biased jurors can be eliminated through challenges for cause and peremptory challenges.[13] In an article on jury selection, attorney Peter Perlman maintains that the best way to uncover the prejudices of the jury "is to conduct voir dire in an atmosphere which makes prospective jurors comfortable about disclosing their true feelings" (1988: 5). He provides a checklist of strategies for lawyers to utilize which enable jurors to feel more comfortable. Some of these include:

Given the initial intimidation which jurors feel, try to make them feel as comfortable as possible; approach them in a natural, unpretentious and clear manner.

Since jurors don't relate to "litigants" or "litigation," humanize the client and the dispute.

Demonstrate the sincere desire to learn of the jurors' feelings.

The lawyer's presentation to the jury should be positive and radiate sincerity. (1988: 5–9)

Perlman's account reveals that the underlying goal of jury selection is to encourage the jury to open up so that the lawyer can eliminate the jurors he doesn't want and develop a positive rapport with the ones who appear favorable to his case.

This goal is supported not only by other writings on jury selection (Blinder 1978; Cartwright 1977; Mauet 1980; Ring 1983; Wagner 1981) but also through the training offered by NITA. As one teacher, a judge, said after the class demonstration on jury selection, "Sell your personality to the jury. Try to get liked by the jury. You're not working for a fair jury, but one favorable to your side." This fact is also recognized by a judge in Clifford Irving's best-selling novel

Trial: "Assuming his case has some merit, if a lawyer gets a jury to like him and then trust him more than the son of a bitch who's arguing against him, he's home free" (1990: 64).

At NITA, teachers emphasized this point on the individual level. In their sessions on voir dire, students had to select a jury for a case which involved an employee who fell down the steps at work and severely injured herself. (Jurors for the case were classmates, including me.) Mike, one of the students, began his presentation by explaining that he was representing the woman's employer. He then went on to tell the jury a little bit about himself: "I grew up in a small town in Indiana." Then he began to ask each of the jurors where they were from, whether they knew the witness or the experts, whether they played sports, had back problems, suffered any physical injuries, and had ever had physical therapy. The instructor gave him the following comments:

The personal comments about yourself seem forced. Good folksy approach, but you went overboard with it. You threw stuff out and let the jury nibble and you got a lot of information. But the main problem is that you didn't find out how people feel about the case or about their relatives and friends.

Another set of comments:

Nice folksy approach, but a bit overdone. Listen to what jurors say, don't draw conclusions. Don't get so close to them, it makes them feel uncomfortable. Use body language to give people a good feeling about you. Good personality, but don't cross certain lines. Never ask someone about their ancestry. It's too loaded a question to ask. Good sense of humor, but don't call one of your prospective jurors a "money man." And don't tell the jury jokes! You don't win them over that way.

The sporting element to voir dire becomes "winning over the jury." This theme also became evident in discussions student lawyers had before and after jury selection. They discussed at length how best "to handle the jurors," "how to get personal information out of them," "how to please them," "how to make them like you," and "how to seduce them to your side." The element of sexual seduction is apparent in the often used phrase "getting in bed with the jury." The direct reference to sexual seduction and conquest suggests, as did the intimidation strategy used in cross-examination, that "winning over the jury" is also a way to prove one's masculinity. Moreover, the desired result in both strategic friendliness and intimidation is similar: obtaining the juror's submission, and winning.

Strategic friendliness is also utilized in the cross-examination of sympathetic witnesses.[14] In one of NITA's hypothetical cases, a woman dies of an illness related to her employment. Her husband sues his deceased wife's employer for her medical bills, lost wages, and "lost companionship." One of the damaging facts in the case, which could hurt his claim for "lost companionship," was the fact that he had a girlfriend long before his wife died. In typical combative, adversarial style, some of the student lawyers tried to bring this fact out in cross-examination to discredit his claims about his relationship with his wife. The teacher told one lawyer who presented such an aggressive cross-examination:

It's too risky to go after him. Don't be so confrontational. And don't ask the judge to reprimand him for not answering the question. This witness is too sensitive. Go easy on him.

The same teacher gave the following comments to another student who had "come on too strong":

Too stern. Hasn't this guy been through enough already! Handle him with kid gloves. And, don't cut him off. It generates sympathy for him from the jury when you do that. It's difficult to control a sympathetic witness. It's best to use another witness's testimony to impeach him.

And to yet another student:

Slow down! This is a dramatic witness. Don't lead so much. He's a sympathetic witness—the widower—let him do the talking. Otherwise you look like an insensitive jerk to the jury.

In the cross-examination of a sympathetic witness, teachers advised students to be gentle. Their concern, however, is not for the witness's feelings but for how their treatment of the witness appears to the jury. The jury is already sympathetic to the witness because he is a widower. As a result, the lawyers were advised not to do anything which would make the witness appear more sympathetic and them less so. The one student who did well on this presentation demonstrated great concern for the witness. She gently asked him about his job, his marriage, his wife's job and her illness. Continuing with this gentle approach, she softly asked him whether anyone had been able to provide him comfort during this difficult time, and thus was able to elicit the testimony about the girlfriend in a sensitive manner. By extracting the testimony about the girlfriend, she decreased the jury's sympathy for the bereaved widower. How much companionship did he lose, if he was having an affair? At the same time, because she treated the witness gently, she increased the jury's regard for herself. Her approach is similar to Laura's in utilizing "niceness" as a strategy. However, in Laura's case, being nice was not appropriate to a destructive cross-examination. In the case of cross-examining a sympathetic witness, such an approach is effective.

The non-confrontational approach is also advantageous in opening statements. NITA provided a hypothetical case called *BMI v. Minicom*, involving a large corporation that sues a small business for its failure to pay on a contract. Minicom signed a contract for a $20,000 order of computer parts from BMI. BMI shipped the computer parts through UPS to Minicom, but they never arrived. According to the law in the case, the buyer bears the loss, typically through insurance, when the equipment is lost in mail. Mark gave an opening statement that portrayed Minicom as a small business started by ambitious, hardworking college friends "on their way to the big league in business." He played up the difficulties small businesses face in trying to compete with giant corporations. And at a dramatic moment in the opening, he asked the jury to "imagine a world where cruel giants didn't squeeze out small companies like Minicom." The teacher provided the following comments:

Good use of evocative imagery. BMI as cruel giant. Minicom squeezing in between the cracks. Great highlighting of the injustice of the situation.

In his attempt to counter this image, Robert, the lawyer for BMI, utilized a courteous opening statement. He attempted to present himself as a nice guy. He took off his jacket, loosened his tie, smiled at the jury, and spoke in a friendly conversational tone: "This case is about a broken contract. BMI fulfilled their side of the contract. Mr. Blakey, my client, worked round the clock to get the shipment ready for Minicom. He made phone call after phone call to inventory to make sure the parts got out on time. He checked and rechecked the package before he sent it to Minicom." He pauses for dramatic emphasis and says, looking sincere and concerned, "It's too bad UPS lost the shipment, but that's not BMI's fault. And now, BMI is out $20,000." He received the following comments from the teacher:

Great use of gestures and eye contact. Good use of voice. You made the case sound simple, but important. You humanized yourself and the people at BMI. Good building of sequence.

Here, the attorney for BMI tried to play down his client's impersonal, corporate image by presenting himself as a nice guy and by personalizing the events at issue with a story about concerned, hardworking Mr. Blakey. Before he began his opening statement, he took off his jacket and loosened his tie to suggest a more casual and ostensibly less corporate image. He smiled at the jury to let them know that he is friendly—not the cruel giant depicted by opposing counsel. He used a friendly conversational tone in his opening statement. And he even admitted that it wasn't fair that the other side didn't get their computer parts. As the teacher's comments suggest, this strategy was most effective for this particular kind of case.

Lawyers working at Bonhomie Corporation also used strategic friendliness. In a mock trial, a litigator representing the company made an effort to "play down the corporate-giant image" by presenting himself as a nice guy. He smiled at the jury, used a conversational tone of voice, maintained eye contact with the jury and the witness. He said afterwards: "These jury studies show that people don't like big corporations. You've got to work extra hard to cancel out that image when you're defending Bonhomie."

This approach can also be used in closing statements. In a hypothetical case where an insurance company alleged that the claimant set fire to his own business, the lawyer for the store owner tried to defuse the insurance company's strategy with a highly dramatic closing statement:

Visualize Elmwood Street in 1952. The day Tony Rubino came home from the navy. His father took him outside to show him a new sign he had made for the family business. It read "Rubino & Son." Standing under the sign

"Rubino and Son" with his father was the happiest day of his life. [Pause] The insurance company wants you to believe, ladies and gentlemen of the jury, that Tony set fire to this family jewel. "I'll carry on," he told his father, and he did. . . . [With tears in her eyes, the lawyer concludes] You don't set fire to your father's dream.

The teacher's comments for Janine's closing statement were effusive:

Great! Well-thought out, sounded natural. Good use of details and organization. I especially liked "I don't know what it's like to have a son, but I know what it's like to have a father." And, you had tears in your eyes! Gave me the closing-argument goose bumps. Pitched emotion felt real, not phoney.

Janine's use of sentimental and nostalgic imagery, the son returning home from the navy, the beginning of a father-and-son business, the business as the "family jewel," is reminiscent of a Norman Rockwell painting. It also serves to counter the insurance company's allegation that Tony Rubino set fire to his own store. With the portrait the lawyer paints and the concluding line, "You don't set fire to your father's dream," she rallies the jury's sympathy for Tony Rubino and their antipathy to the insurance company's malicious claim against them. Moreover, her emotional presentation of the story is so effective that the instructor thought it "sounded natural" and "felt real, not phoney." The great irony here is that this is not a real case—it is a hypothetical case with hypothetical characters. There is no Tony Rubino, no family store, and no fire. Yet Janine's "deep acting" was so convincing that the teacher believed it was true—it gave him "the closing-argument goose bumps."

Strategic friendliness carries over from the courtroom to depositions. Before deposing a particularly sensitive or sympathetic witness, Joe, one of the attorneys in the private firm, asked me whether "there is anything personal to start the interview with—a sort of warm-up question to start things off on a personal note?" I had previously interviewed the woman over the phone, so I knew something about her background. I told him that she was a young mother who had recently had a very difficult delivery of her first child. I added that she was worried about the baby's health because he had been born prematurely. At the beginning of the deposition later that afternoon, Joe said in a concerned voice that he understood the witness had recently had a baby and was concerned about its health. She appeared slightly embarrassed by the question, but with a slow smile and lots of encouragement from him, she began to tell him all about the baby and its health problems. By the time Joe began the formal part of the deposition, the witness had warmed up and gave her complete cooperation. Later, the attorney bragged to me and one of the associates that he had the witness "eating out of his hand."

After recording these events in my field notes, I wrote the following impressions:

On the surface, it looks like social etiquette to ask the witness these questions because it puts her at ease. It lets her know he takes her seriously. But the "personal touch" is completely artificial. He doesn't care about the witness as a person. Or, I should say, only insofar as she's useful to him. Moreover, he doesn't even bother to ask the witness these questions himself the first time around. He asks me to do it. I'm to find the "personal hook" that he can use to manipulate her to his own ends.

Thus an innocuous personal remark becomes another way to create the desired impression with a witness and thereby manipulate him or her. Perhaps what is most ironic about strategic friendliness is that it requires a peculiar combination of sensitivity to other people and, at the same time, ruthlessness.[15] The lawyer wants to appear kind and understanding, but that is merely a cover for the ulterior motive—winning. Although the outward presentation of self for this form of emotional labor differs from intimidation, the underlying goal is the same: the emotional manipulation of the witness for a favorable result.

Attorneys also employed strategic friendliness when dealing with clients. As I mentioned in the previous section, intimidation is rarely used with clients, particularly at the private firm, who are typically treated with a politesse, courtesy, and reassurance. The sensitivity to the client's needs and interests does not reflect genuine concern, however, but rather serves as a means to an end—obtaining and maintaining the client's current and future business. The importance of clients to lawyers can be gauged by one of the criterion for determining partnership at private law firms: the ability to attract and maintain a client base (Nelson 1988; Smigel 1969). In this light, clients become another important legal audience for whom the lawyer performs and obtaining a client's business is construed as another form of "winning."

Articles in legal newspapers such as the *National Law Journal* address the importance of lawyers' efforts to attract new clients (O'Neil 1989; Foster and Raider 1988). These articles underscore the importance not only of obtaining business but of appealing to clients through "communication," "cultural sensitivity," and "creating good first impressions." Thus, "finding" new clients is not simply an instrumental role as Nelson (1988) suggests, it also carries with it an emotional dimension.

"Wooing clients" to the firm, or "making rain," as lawyers call it, is a common practice at the private firm. Partners were rewarded in annual bonuses for their ability to bring in new business. In informal conversations, partners often discussed the competition between firms for the clients' business. For example, when one of the partners procured a case from a large San Francisco bank that typically did business with another large firm in the city, he described it as a "coup." Attorneys boasted not only about bringing clients into the firm but about how much revenue "their client" brought into the firm's coffers. The constant focus on capturing clients, "making rain," and making big money betrays male lawyers' need to prove themselves through accomplishments and achievements. Further, those who lost big clients were considered "weak," "impotent," and no longer "in with the good old boys." In this way, winning clients' business is also associated with manly behavior.

In addition to finding new clients for the firm, lawyers must also "mind" clients. This is accomplished not only by providing competent professional service, but through displaying confidence, reassurance, and courtesy. For example, how does a layperson know whether her attorney is doing a good job? In response to this question, a partner, in Susan Wolf's novel about a California law firm, advises a young and socially inept associate:

You tell him. You remind him every day that he's lucky to have you. I don't give a damn if you don't listen to him. He's a boring bastard. But you gotta make him think you're listening all the time. Make him think he's got the most interesting legal problem you can think of. . . . You've got to dance with the client, you've got to show him that you're right there with him all the time. (1989: 42)

Minding clients can also take the form of reassurance. Zimmerman (1983) observes that the clients made constant emotional demands of the attorneys he interviewed. As one of the lawyers he interviewed said, "We are, for a while, the most important person in the client's life [and] sometimes it's just the sound of my voice they need to hear . . . to know I am available" (1983: 7). And another said, "Many clients have to be reassured, told the same thing over and over again. Clients seldom want to face reality" (1983: 7). Although attorneys in this study engaged in reassuring clients, it is not in the sense one typically thinks of reassurance. Rather than telling the client everything will be okay—something female paralegals and secretaries often do—the attorney reassures the client through an appeal to his own competence, expertise, and skill as a professional. "I've handled lots of cases like this in the past." "I know antitrust law inside and out. They [the other side] can't trip us up." "Don't worry about a thing, this is something for a lawyer to handle." To generate confidence and, hence, reassure the client, the lawyer builds himself up and projects an image of competence, self-assurance. Through such appeals to professional expertise, he underscores his superordinate position in relation to the client. By contrast, paralegals reassure attorneys by being supportive and deferential, thereby reinforcing their subordinate position in relation to lawyers (see Chapter 4). Thus, for attorneys reassuring clients is a way of "doing dominance," whereas for paralegals, it is a way of doing deference.

Chapter Four

Mothering Paralegals

Emotional Labor in a Feminized Occupation

Sarah is regarded by her boss, Richard, as an excellent litigation paralegal. Richard, who is a highly successful and influential senior partner in the legal department at Bonhomie Corporation, describes her as "highly organized, efficient, hardworking, and possessing a terrific mind for details." But more importantly, he thinks she's one of the most intuitive people he's ever known: "She anticipates my every move. It's almost as though she reads my mind." Sarah does not share the glowing evaluation of herself: "I always feel like I'm in over my head, constantly playing catch-up, putting out one fire after another." Part of what makes her job so difficult is that in addition to the mental tasks she must accomplish, such as summarizing deposition transcripts and analyzing documents, she must also expend energy taking care of people at the office. She described a typical day at the office:

I got back to my office just in time to pick up my ringing phone. It turned out to be two of the witnesses I had been trying to contact—they conference-called me. Neither had any idea why I had been trying to contact them. They had received the notification letter I'd sent, but neither one knew anything about the case or the plaintiff. So, I had to explain who the plaintiff was, why he initiated the lawsuit, the nature of the lawsuit and why we wanted them to be witnesses. I had the whole routine memorized. They both expressed concern about the trial, about testifying, about remembering the details of an incident which occurred three years ago and, of course, about missing their vacation. So, I reassured away. I explained that we [paralegals and attorneys] would prepare them for their day in court, make sure they had relevant materials to read, and so on. And, I reassured them that they had room to move in terms of vacation plans, just keep us posted. My first reassuring words were about how likely it would be for the trial to be continued [rescheduled]. It was hard for me to listen to the conference call. They kept interrupting each other. And since I'd never spoken to them before, I couldn't tell who was who when one of them would start talking. . . . Anyway, I bet I was on the phone for half an hour or so just reassuring these clowns about what was going on. Oi!

[Later] I sailed into Richard's office and said, "I just wanted to drop off your weekend reading material." When he looked up at the accordion file, he groaned and said, "What's this! More weekend reading material, I just got a repeat request on another case, and I have all this other stuff to read. . . ." So, I went into my reassuring routine: "It's really not so bad as it looks—most of the materials are charts, graphs, and tables. There's very little actual text." I flipped through the charts for emphasis. He said, "Thanks for the reassurance!" I spent the rest of the morning working on a document production. [This involves going through boxes of written material to locate material responsive to the plaintiff's legal request for documents relevant to the case.] . . . It's the most boring and exhausting kind of work legal assistants do. And predictably, twenty minutes before her court appearance, Dianne [another lawyer] called me asking for a copy of a report from the documents to support a legal argument she wanted to make. . . . I hate these last-minute rushes—it always makes me nervous. I found a report and ran upstairs, but it turned out to be the wrong one. Dianne was furious with me. She started grilling me. "What kind of reports do we have? What's in the correspondence? Was there anything damaging?" I started panicking about whether I'd ever find the right report, but I said I'd take care of it and ran back downstairs to continue my search.

The minute I hit the document room, the phone rang. It was Dianne telling me to drop the search and call Greg [the client] and ask him what he knew about the report. Greg had been less than cooperative in previous attempts to gather information. [So, I called him and]. . . I told him it was an emergency request for Dianne and convinced him that we were desperate. He responded immediately to the request. Then I ran back upstairs to tell Dianne. As I explained the contents of the report to her, she filled her briefcase and shut it. She barraged me with questions as we walked down the hall to the bathroom. Inside she stood looking in the mirror, making last-minute adjustments to her hair and suit and mumbling about how her suit looked, while I carefully tried to answer all her questions, told her she

looked fine, and reminded her that it was time to go. She walked out the
door, and I went back downstairs to try and finish reviewing the documents.
The phone rang again. This time it was Richard, who wanted another report from the documents that I hadn't placed in the accordion file. He was
completely vague about what was in the report, when it had been written,
but he knew that I would find it as soon as possible. I started looking again
with that sinking feeling. Suddenly, I felt completely exhausted. . . . [To the
interviewer:] Are you sure you want me to keep going? That was only ten
o'clock.

Sarah's description highlights not only the frenetic pace and the
variety of tasks associated with paralegal work but its socio-emotional
dimension as well. Sarah reassures witnesses for the upcoming trial
and attorneys about their work—"I reassured away" and "I went into
my reassuring routine." While working on a document production,
she allays the panic of the attorney, convinces the client of the desperate need for information, relays information between client and
attorney, and props up the attorney's sense of self, all while quelling
her own panic beneath a cheerful exterior. In addition, she must
contend with a constant barrage of questions and interruptions.

Sarah's emotional role as a paralegal is not unique. My fifteen
months of fieldwork at Lyman, Lyman and Portia and in the legal
department at Bonhomie Corporation provide a daily record of the
variety of socio-emotional tasks found in paralegal work. The in-
depth interviews I conducted with litigation legal assistants further
corroborate these findings. Surprisingly, the one major sociological
study on paralegals (Quintin Johnstone and Martin Wenglinsky
1985) overlooks the emotional requirements of the job. Johnstone
and Wenglinsky surveyed paralegals in various law practice settings
in New York City, describing where paralegals work, what they do,
who they are, and where they come from, but not addressing this
seemingly hidden dimension of labor. Despite the invisibility of
emotional labor, this unexamined aspect of paralegal work has significant consequences for the reproduction of the labor process in the
large bureaucratic law firm and for the psychological well-being of
legal assistants.[1] These legal workers function to support and maintain the emotional stability of the lawyers they work for, through deferential treatment and caretaking. By affirming the status of the

lawyers, paralegals also reproduce gender relations in the law-firm hierarchy. Most attorneys who receive the caretaking and support are men, and the majority of legal assistants who provide these emotional services are women. While gamesmanship as emotional labor supports and reinforces the adversarial model, the emotional labor required of legal assistants serves to reproduce the gendered structure of the law firm.

The emotional labor paralegals perform not only reproduces a gendered hierarchy, but the form it takes is also gendered. In contrast to the masculinized form of gamesmanship, the emotional labor that paralegals perform is feminized, not only because women do it but because such work is dependent upon the legal profession. Structurally, paralegal positions are specifically designed for women to support higher-status men, and the content of paralegal work is consistent with our cultural conceptions of appropriate behavior for traditional wives and mothers. Rosabeth Moss Kanter (1977) was the first sociologist to utilize the "marriage metaphor" to characterize the working relationship between secretary and boss. In her view, secretaries are much like wives and mothers because their status derives from the person for whom they work and because the relationship is particularistic, with expectations of personal service and loyalty. In addition, it is characterized by "an emotional division of labor in which the woman plays the emotional role and the man the providing role" (1977: 89). Much like the traditional wife and mother who defers to the wishes of her husband and children and attends to their psychological needs, the paralegals and the legal secretaries in the firms I studied were expected to show deference for the attorneys for whom they work and to take care of their emotional needs.

Paralegals and Emotional Labor

As a semi-profession, the content of paralegal work is determined primarily by the needs and demands of lawyers. For example, when a new case comes into the office, the supervising attorney overseeing the "team" will divide tasks among paralegals, associates, and secretaries. There is more to this routinization of tasks than a simple bureaucratic relationship, however. In contrast to Weber's (Girth and

Mills 1946 [1922]) classic conception of a rationalized, depersonalized bureaucracy, the paralegal-attorney relationship is highly personal.[2] This fact is supported by the numerous statements lawyers made emphasizing the importance of personality traits over work-performance skills in hiring decisions. Sarah's boss, for example, highlights her "intuitive qualities" as most important to him. Personnel directors discussed the importance of being "pleasant" and being able to work with "difficult" attorneys, and attorneys invariably ranked personal characteristics such as being "pleasant" or "unflappable" above task-related skills such as being a "good organizer" or "detail-oriented."

These findings suggest that there is a significant socio-emotional dimension to paralegal work. This element is largely missing from most formal job descriptions. For example, in the legal department at Bonhomie Corporation, a job listing for a legal-assistant position read:

To provide analytical support, legal research and writing and data management to Art Fulton [attorney]. General areas of involvement are: litigation, intellectual property, and federal contracts. This position involves managing legal projects including: analyzing, reviewing, drafting and administering contracts; performing legal and factual research; interviewing clients and witnesses and organizing and synthesizing complex issues and data.

Similarly, a typical want ad in *The Recorder,* one of the Bay Area's legal newspapers, lists a job as:

Opening for paralegal with two years experience in general litigation. Must possess excellent writing and organization and communication skills. Able to work independently. Salary commensurate with experience (June 13, 1988: 39).

Nevertheless, interpersonal tasks are a crucial, if not overriding, feature of the actual relationship between trial lawyers and paralegals.[3]

Data from several sources highlight the socio-emotional side of the job, including evaluation forms used by law firms to determine the job performance of paralegals, paralegal training seminars, and finally, the observations and data I obtained through my fieldwork and interviews.

Evaluation forms are commonly used by lawyers to evaluate a

given paralegal's job performance for annual salary reviews. In the legal department at Bonhomie Corporation, the standardized form had nine parts, including (1) writing, (2) oral presentation, (3) legal research, (4) legal knowledge, (5) technical and operational knowledge, (6) judgment and problem solving, (7) relationship to clients or professionalism, (8) work habits and relationship to others, and (9) managerial ability. The last three often include substantial amounts of emotional labor.

These forms were taken quite seriously by management at Bonhomie Corporation in determining "salary treatment." One of the paralegals I worked with at Bonhomie, Diana, was unhappy with her evaluation. Whereas she had received a 5 on a scale of 1 to 5 for her technical expertise, the first six categories of the evaluation form, she received 3s for her ability to get along with other people. She was told that she didn't work well with attorneys, caused friction with the client, and needled secretaries and support staff people unnecessarily. Although the supervising attorney agreed with Diana's assessment of the situation—that she had criticized attorneys, secretaries and clients when such comments were in fact warranted—he told her that she had to learn how to give criticism in a positive manner that wouldn't offend people and added that she needed to "work on her interpersonal skills." As a result, the overall average for her performance evaluation was pulled down to a 4, and she did not receive the raise she would have gotten had she done better on her "people skills."

Training seminars also suggest that the position as a paralegal involves emotional labor. Paralegal conferences often hold special sections on "stress and the paralegal," which underscore the emotional demands of the job and provide lessons on such coping strategies as deep breathing, visualization, exercise, and so forth. For example, at Bonhomie Corporations's paralegal conference, a psychologist suggested that after a paralegal was yelled at by an attorney, she could alleviate stress by jumping rope for ten minutes.[4]

Just as gamesmanship is gendered, so too is the emotional labor legal assistants perform. Despite the fact that many elements of paralegal work, such as legal research and writing, overlap with lawyer-like tasks or so-called men's work, paralegal work is construed as women's work. Attorneys and personnel directors stated an explicit preference for hiring women for the job. One male attorney said:

I actually prefer working with women. They just have less testosterone going through their system, less of an ego battle with them. They don't work out their needs through dominance and conflict, but through conflict resolution.

And another commented:

I'd just rather work with the gals—they're a lot nicer and they know how to listen.

Other lawyers also suggested that women were "nicer," "friendlier," and "easier to get along with" than their male counterparts. Personnel directors said they believed women were "more suited" than men to paralegal work.

The employers' argument for women's supposed suitability for the job links the presumed match between women's "innate" emotional skills and the demands of the job. Paralegals are expected to be deferential and concerned for the well-being of attorneys for whom they work, just as women in the traditional roles of wife and mother are supposed to be good at these tasks.[5] The feminization of this occupation, then, is created not only by employer preference for women, but by the fact that the occupation itself—formally or not—calls for women to cater to men's emotional needs.

Deference

> *There is always the underlying assumption*
> *that the term* wife *implies husband, and wife*
> *is the subordinate term in the relationship.*
> (Johnson 1988: 39)

Sociologist Miriam Johnson argues that the word "wife" carries with it the implication of subordinate status. In traditional white working-class and middle-class marriages, women as wives defer to their husbands' authority (Hochschild 1989). Women may also play such roles in the office by affirming and enhancing the status of their male boss

(Benet 1973; Kanter 1977; Pringle 1988). Such deferential behavior characterizes the first component of emotional behavior expected of paralegals.[6] In his article, "The Nature of Deference and Demeanor," Erving Goffman defines deference as a type of ceremonial activity that "functions as symbolic means by which appreciation is regularly conveyed to the recipient" (1956: 477). For Goffman, what is important about deference behavior between subordinate and superordinate is that it reproduces the hierarchical nature of the relationship by confirming each person's position within it. Deference as emotional labor, then, is the means by which paralegals reproduce the attorney's position as well as their own in the law-firm hierarchy.

What Goffman's account often neglects is the extent to which deference is raced and gendered.[7] In the racist caricature of Uncle Tom, a Black man shows deference to a white man by bowing his head, averting his eyes while speaking, "playing dumb," and emphasizing his superiors' status through repeated use of phrases such as "Yes sir." White men, on the other hand, do not show deference to Black men. Similarly, women defer to men, but not the reverse. Advice on dating or finding a husband in popular books and magazines often cautions women against seeming too competent or knowledgeable in the presence of men. In fact, West and Zimmerman (1987) argue that for women, doing gender means doing deference. Deference, then, implies not only a relationship between subordinate and superior, but a power relationship with a gendered and racialized character. In corporate law firms, displays of deference take on a distinctly gendered character.[8]

The first and perhaps most fundamental aspect of deference reflects the nature of the legal profession itself: it requires that paralegals be treated as if they were adversaries by attorneys. Just as opposing counsel, clients, and witnesses are interrogated, intimidated, grilled, and regarded with great suspicion and distrust, so too are paralegals. Marguerite, a twenty-six-year-old legal assistant, describes her discussions with Eric, an attorney, in this way:

I feel like I am on the witness stand when I'm talking to him about the trial. After I give him detail after detail to his questions, he says: "Anything else? Anything else?" in this aggressive way. . . . I think what's weird about Eric is how he can't turn off this adversarial style. . . . He just persists in cross-examining me.

A male paralegal characterized the pretrial behavior of Mark, an attorney:

Mark asks question after question like a rapid-fire machine gun . . . and he stares intently at you while he's asking questions. I think it's one of those strategies they teach lawyers to intimidate witnesses . . . and [I feel like] he's just practicing on me.

Janice, another legal assistant, commented bitterly:

I hate the adversarial relationship. You can never have a normal discussion about a case. It's always an argument, and I just get pushed to the other side. Sometimes I want to say, "Hey, I'm on your side, remember!"

Although paralegals are subjected to adversarial practices, they are not allowed to respond in a like manner. As subordinates, they are not true adversaries. Like the traditional wife in relation to her husband, legal assistants must recognize the attorney as the authority, not challenge him as an equal. Thus, they affirm the attorney's status by enduring the humiliation of being treated as if they were opposing counsel.

By treating paralegals in this way, attorneys objectify legal assistants, a masculinizing practice. On the other hand, being objectified exemplifies a feminized stance. Simone de Beauvoir (1958) argues that woman functions as man's Other, object to his subject. This insight is confirmed by the purpose of male lawyers' denigration of opposing counsel. Male attorneys often consider those whom they have "conquered" or "destroyed" as "weak," "sissies," and hence, feminine. Thus, by the very structure of their relationship with trial attorneys, paralegals become feminized objects.

To cope with being treated as the objects of attorneys' hostility, paralegals must manage anger—their own and that of the attorneys. Whenever a lawyer is angry about X, Y, or Z, the paralegal is liable to suffer the consequences—even when it was not her fault. For example, Greg, a paralegal, had brought a client into his office to wait until the attorney, Chris (a woman), got off the phone. Greg had been specifically instructed to sit with the client rather than leaving him out in the lobby to wait. While they were waiting, Greg received an important and long-awaited call about the client's case. Rather than discuss the business in front of the client, he forwarded the call to a more private line and retreated to a nearby, empty conference room. In his absence, the impatient client began to wander the halls and happened into the attorney's office. The attorney immediately got off the phone, welcomed the client, and commenced their business. After the client left, Chris yelled at the paralegal for leaving the client by himself. Greg explained what had happened. Rather than apologizing for her outburst, the attorney angrily replied: "Well, I just had to yell at someone, and you were there." The implication is that the attorney has the right to yell at Greg, and Greg's job is to submit to the outburst.

Not only did I see many such incidences in my fieldwork, but I found that legal assistants who fail to follow this "feeling rule" for absorbing and internalizing anger were censured. For example, after a very long day in the office preparing for a trial, Michael, the partner, began needling Joe, one of the paralegals I worked with, for not completing a project. Joe pointed out, reasonably enough, that the work would have been virtually impossible to do that day because he had so many other projects to complete. Michael, hardly seeming to listen, relentlessly pushed his point. Joe refused to back down. The exchange went back and forth several times, each person raising his voice more and more. Joe finally blew up and started yelling at Michael: "You've pushed me too far! This is too much. I just can't take this kind of crap from you any more!" He then turned and stalked down the hall. Michael looked furious, glanced at me, and then turned and stalked off in the opposite direction. Several people were standing around watching. The next morning in our team meeting, Michael and Joe resolutely ignored one another. Neither one spoke to the other for over a week. In the meantime, Joe tried to get another female paralegal, Debbie, to intervene on his behalf. Even though she acknowledged that Joe had been treated unfairly, she refused to play intermediary. The stand-off continued. Because Joe wasn't able to successfully "manage his own anger," he was eventually kicked off the case by the attorney and pushed to a peripheral position within the firm.

Law firms explicitly hire people who can deal gracefully with irate attorneys. When I was interviewing for paralegal positions, the question that came up in each of the five job interviews was "How do you feel about working with a difficult attorney?" In fact, in one office I was asked this question by the personnel director, her administrative assistant, and one of the interviewing attorneys. An experienced paralegal told me the question implied that the lawyer with whom I was to work "must be a jerk." Employers, on the other hand, were trying to determine how a paralegal would handle such a personality. In interview number three, when the last interviewer asked me about "getting along with difficult attorneys," I responded: "Look, I have worked with a lot of attorneys who are prima donnas, and I just don't take it personally. That's just the way they are." There was a long silence on the part of my interviewer and then she said huffily, "Well, Elliot is not a prima donna. He just tends to get upset when he works under pressure." I immediately backed down and I said I hadn't meant to imply that Elliot was a prima donna and emphasized that I understood the "tremendous pressures" lawyers worked under and how difficult their job was. The interviewer appeared to be mollified but persisted in questioning me about how I would handle these "difficult situations." In response, I became increasingly submissive and gave examples of situations in which I had deferred to the judgment of the supervising attorney. After the interview, I reproached myself for being careless in my initial response: the employer's reaction served to remind me that I was not to criticize attorneys, just put up with their behavior. Two days later, however, I was offered the job, presumably because I had recovered more gracefully from the faux pas than I had imagined by agreeing with the interviewer, being deferential, and playing up my concern and empathy for the lawyers.

The paralegal's deferential role in the adversarial relationship requires an uncritical stance toward the attorney's written work and professional habits. One way to gauge this particular "feeling rule" is by looking at the mistakes paralegals make when they violate this norm.[9] When I first started working as a legal assistant, I made such mistakes. Whenever an attorney asked me what I thought about a brief or a legal strategy, I assumed that he really wanted to know, and I told him. What I soon discovered was that lawyers didn't want to know what I thought unless I agreed with them or supported their original idea or strategy. Critical feedback was acceptable from other lawyers, but not from non-lawyers. This norm is underscored by the legal assistant's paraprofessional status: she is not simply a subordinate, but also an inferior, a paraprofessional who lacks the requisite training, skills, and credentials to criticize. Sociologists have argued that part of what makes the professions unique is their monopoly of control over the body of knowledge and techniques they apply in their work (Goode 1957; Larson 1977). The current debate over whether "legal technicians" should be licensed or regulated by the California State Bar addresses this issue. Paralegals argue that their occupation should be licensed. Licensing would provide them with more autonomy, allow them to make court appearances, and grant more legitimacy to the occupation (Hall 1988; Goodman-Plater 1988). Attorneys, the main opponents to this measure, contend that paralegals do not possess the requisite knowledge and skills to merit licensing (Meyberg 1989; Alameda County Bar Association Bulletin, February 1990).[10]

The emotional labor involved in being non-critical involves learning to manage one's feelings about being treated as if one were stupid. Perhaps because attorneys, like most professionals, have a monopoly on their "specialized training and knowledge," many in this study had a difficult time believing that a non-lawyer could understand the complexities of the law. As one female paralegal said: "They consider the law the 'inner sanctum of God.' Only the select few are allowed to enter." This attitude created strain for many of the legal assistants I interviewed and observed. Carol, for example, was assigned to work on answering a set of interrogatories with a new, young associate. The associate was busy with another project, so Carol wrote the answers herself. When she gave the completed answers to the partner on the case, he looked them over and said, "Did you do this yourself?" When she said she had, he said with surprise, "Really! They're good! I thought Robert helped you with these." Carol concealed her frustration for the moment but later said angrily to me: "If it's good I didn't do it? What kind of compliment is that supposed to be?" The backhanded compliment simultaneously served to elevate the status of the professional and to demean Carol's efforts.

I discovered this attitude myself not long after beginning my job in the legal department at Bonhomie Corporation. After staying late one night to work on a "mock trial," the supervising attorney asked me what I thought about our presentation of the case. I said I thought it was too technical, and I pointed out several ways to make the legal issues of the case more comprehensible to laypeople on the jury. He paused, stared deliberately at me for emphasis, and then said, "You haven't ever worked on a trial before, have you, Jennifer?" I responded that I had done preparation work on a number of trials that had been continued and had never actually gone out. I also pointed out that I had spent three weeks at the National Institute for Trial Advocacy. He quickly retorted, "Well, trial preparation and a couple of courses in graduate school doesn't qualify you as an expert on juries." He then proceeded to tell me how he thought we should present the case to the jury and why I was wrong. In this case, my credentials were challenged because as a non-lawyer—despite graduate school and paralegal pretrial work—I did not meet his standards for someone qualified to issue a professional opinion. Downplaying my credentials served to enhance his own status and opinion as an attorney.

The frustration and resentment this attitude creates is especially acute for experienced paralegals, who often know much more about the day-to-day practice of the law than the recent law-school graduate. In my interviews, many paralegals had "war stories" to tell about suggestions they made that were ignored until the last minute. But even the experienced legal assistant is supposed to act as if the lawyer, like the husband, is always right. Good paralegals, like good wives, must be uncritical.

Yet another form of deference is "interruptibility." In their study on power dynamics in speech strategies, Zimmerman and West (1975) found that men interrupt women more than the reverse. As subordinates, paralegals are also infinitely interruptible. A paralegal may be racing against the clock to make changes in a brief, but if the attorney comes in and wants to talk, the paralegal is expected to drop everything she is doing and listen. At the private firm, Robert, an attorney, had a reputation for phoning paralegals whose offices were only two or three doors away from his own, yelling into the phone, "Bring me the such-and-such file," and hanging up. Another attorney was known to come out into the hall, yell his paralegal's name, and go back inside his office to wait for her to run down the hall to his office. Some lawyers barged into paralegals' offices without knocking. For example, Mark had the habit of walking in while completely ignoring what the paralegal was doing, loudly shouting out a list of projects in an almost indecipherable rapid-fire manner, and then turning around and walking out again.

Like other deference behaviors, this is not a reciprocal arrangement. Attorneys are not to be "bothered" when they are busy. The paralegal is expected to wait for the appropriate moment to speak to them. One attorney even went so far as to set up "office hours" between nine and ten A.M. Paralegals and secretaries were allowed to discuss things with him only during this limited window of time. If something came up at another time—even an emergency—the paralegal was supposed to wait.

A closely related form of deference is invisibility. On the surface, this appears to be a contradiction in terms. If paralegals are infinitely interruptible, then how can they also be invisible? Actually, though, invisibility is simply the flip side of being interruptible—a subordinate can be interrupted at will and can also be ignored. Most attorneys rarely speak to paralegals unless they need something work-related. Walking down the corridors of the private firm, attorneys greet one another but rarely acknowledge a paralegal or a secretary. At some firms, new associates were actually discouraged from "mingling" with paralegals and other members of the staff because such behavior was considered "unprofessional." Much as in a caste system, in the law firm one's occupational status determined how one would be treated. When I first started working at the private firm, I was temporarily using the office of a lawyer who was away on vacation. Several lawyers approached me in a friendly manner and introduced themselves. When they learned that I wasn't an attorney—and this was usually one of the first questions I was asked—the conversation ended abruptly. Other paralegals reported similar incidents of suddenly "becoming invisible." One new paralegal attended a firm party shortly after she was hired. She told me that one lawyer literally walked away in mid-conversation when he learned that she wasn't an attorney: "He didn't even try to be polite about it. He just walked away and started talking to someone else!" While most experienced paralegals came to see this type of behavior as just another unpleasant feature of the job, most resented such treatment and complained to one another about it. Managing their own resentment about being treated as if they were invisible became yet another facet of emotional labor.

Another way the paralegal's invisibility manifests itself was in what I call attorney's "speaker-phone etiquette." At Lyman, Lyman and Portia and at Bonhomie Corporation, speaker phones enabled lawyers to hold conference calls while other attorneys, paralegals, or secretaries were present to listen, participate, or take notes. Some attorneys, however, left their speaker phones on not only for business calls, but for personal ones as well. With the speaker phone on and the door wide open, the details of a personal call blasted up and down the hall. For example, when Roger and his wife argued about his wild credit-card spending sprees, I knew about it the moment his wife called because the argument blasted across the hall from his office into mine. Similarly, legal assistants at the private firm complained about several attorneys who discussed the details of their dates, recent parties, and other gossip over their speaker phones. Although paralegals sometimes found these conversations amusing—particularly when the details made public an embarrassing moment for an attorney they disliked—they also found them to be annoying, disruptive, and personally offensive. Karen, a legal assistant, describes her reaction to a personal phone conversation:

Yesterday, Rachel was on the speaker phone talking all about her date, where they went, what they did. . . . At first, I thought it was funny because she was so oblivious to the fact that we could all hear this private phone conversation in the hallway, and she did go into detail. . . . But later, it occurred to me, that she just didn't care if we heard. For her, we really aren't there.

Karen's reaction echoes Judith Rollins's (1985) provocative descriptions of her experience of "invisibility" as a domestic worker:

It was this aspect of servitude [invisibility] that I found to be the strongest affront to my dignity as a human being. [To the employers] I became invisible; their conversation was as private with me, the black servant, in the room as it would have been with no one in the room. . . . These gestures of ignoring my presence were. . .expressions of the employers' ability to anni- hilate the humanness and even, at times, the very existence of me. (1985: 209)

Caretaking

Whereas deference is the first major component of emotional labor, playing a caretaking role for the attorneys and, to a certain extent, witnesses and clients is the second. This form of emotional labor also reflects the asymmetry of the attorney-paralegal relationship: the lawyer is the recipient of care, the legal assistant the caregiver. It is also consistent with a particular cultural construction of mother- hood—what some feminist scholars have termed "the fantasy of the perfect mother" (Chodorow and Contratto 1982). Nancy Chodorow and Susan Contratto describe this oppressive cultural representation of the "perfect mother" as one who meets all her children's needs and wishes while suppressing her own. Such a mother is the ultimate caregiver, the object of others' needs, whose own subjectivity is de- nied and devalued. As Johnson (1988) suggests, such a fantasy turns caring into a one-way street—women's caring comes to mean cater- ing to the needs of others but not being cared for in return. In the context of the male-dominated workplace, caretaking, like defer- ence, privileges the needs and desires of male trial lawyers while denying those of female paralegals, and at the same time it repro- duces the gendered hierarchical structure of the law firm.

The first element of the caretaking dimension of emotional labor is being pleasant. As one paralegal described her job: "I was trying to be pleasant, pay attention, and take notes [while the witness was talking]. Not an easy feat, [because] I felt like I was sitting next to a human time bomb [the lawyer]." Legal assistants are expected to ap- pear pleasant and cheerful no matter what else they are trying to ac- complish. As the personnel director for a private firm told me in a job interview, "It's important to maintain a pleasant manner while attending to the not-so-pleasant side of the job, don't you think?" Being pleasant not only involves inducing a feeling—being cheer- ful—but also calls for a specific facial display—a smile. Many women paralegals (but not men) grimly reported the consequences of not smiling: "Why aren't you smiling today?" "What's the matter with you, give me a smile!" "You look like someone just died." Such remarks were typically made by male attorneys, clients, and witnesses to female legal assistants. However, one personnel director, who was a woman, could also be counted on to make comments about one's demeanor. A female paralegal wryly observed, "Sometimes I think she thinks smiling is supposed to be part of my job."

Another element of caretaking is reassurance, alleviating the anxiety of the attorneys for whom one works. Reassurance as caregiving goes beyond the deference expectations of the job, which require that a paralegal be non-critical of an attorney's written work and professional habits to affirm his status and knowledge as a competent professional. By contrast, reassurance focuses on alleviating the anxiety that such professional work entails. For example, Jenna spent most of an afternoon doing what she called "handholding." By this she meant repeatedly reassuring John that he would make his five o'clock filing deadline. Similarly, Debbie spent much of her time acting as Michael's "therapist." She patiently listened to all his work-related anxieties and concerns, gently asked questions, and offered reassurance. Similarly, Sarah, the paralegal who opens this chapter, devoted most of her interview to descriptions of reassuring behavior. And Cindy, another legal assistant, was constantly called upon to "massage the ego" of her boss. "I don't know which is worse, when he wins or when he loses—either way I spend lots of time massaging his ego."

Like other caregiving behavior, this form of emotional labor went only one way. Lawyers rarely reassured paralegals about work-related matters. For example, when Lisa, an experienced legal assistant at Lyman, Lyman and Portia, asked her boss to hire a temporary employee to help her with the review of files for an enormous document production, he told her she would have to complete the project by herself. Lisa persisted, arguing that she was worried about completing the project on time. The partner curtly responded, "I'm not interested in what you worry about—just get the job done." Similarly, when Cindy expressed anxiety about doing a good job answering a set of interrogatories, her boss said, "I don't want to hear it."

Although a small number of women attorneys attempted to create more reciprocal relationships with their legal assistants, such exchanges were not typical. (These exchanges are discussed in Chapter 5).

In addition to taking care of their bosses' feelings, paralegals were also expected to alleviate the anxiety of witnesses and clients before, during and after trials, depositions and court appearances. Every time a particular case was reset for trial, one female legal assistant had to call all thirty-five of the witnesses involved in the case to apprise them of the case's status, the new trial date, and their responsibilities. Inevitably, when called, many of the witnesses expressed reluctance to testify. Their concerns made a short, to-the-point, informational call last much longer, as Sally found herself listening over and over again to their individual fears and then attempting to allay them. When she suggested to her boss that it would be much less time-consuming to send out letters, he objected and said, "This is how you keep the personal hook in your witnesses." In other words, the personal call and the "emotional hospitality" were important psychological means for maintaining contact with the witnesses and encouraging their interest in testifying.

While Sally worked to reassure witnesses about an upcoming trial, other legal assistants sought to reassure the clients. Debbie often worked in her boss's absence to reassure the client about his case's disposition. She sometimes spent as long as forty minutes on the phone talking to him about the details of his case. The client often claimed to prefer talking to Debbie. "He told me that I don't use legalese and I don't bill one hundred-eighty dollars an hour." Similarly, Naomi sometimes spent half an hour or longer on the phone talking to her boss's client. "Mostly, he just wants to know that, you know, everything's okay—and usually Ron's way too busy to talk to him. So, I do it."

In addition to reassuring clients and witnesses, legal assistants also spent time expressing gratitude to other people in the firm on the lawyer's behalf. For instance, after completion of a big project involving a lot of overtime by several paralegals and secretaries for one of the private firm's partners, Carol, the head legal assistant, sent everyone on the team thank-you cards, with notes such as "David [the attorney] and I don't know what we would have done without you!" Because David was lax about thanking people himself, Carol did it for him. In doing so, she made the paralegals and secretaries feel appreciated for the efforts they had made and, at the same time, smoothed over relations between the attorney and these workers.

Another caretaking role that paralegals frequently found themselves in was that of interpreter or arbiter of an attorneys' feelings toward other people. Much like a mother who reads "dad's" moods and explains to the children why he is having a bad day, as a paralegal Debbie apologized to others for Michael when he was "in one of his moods," explaining that he was under "a lot of pressure." Cindy protected Mark's time from other demands by keeping people at arm's length. And Jenna ran interference between John and the client when John didn't want to be bothered because he was too busy. Legal assistants also interpreted the feelings of others for the attorneys for whom they worked. David relied heavily on Carol to read witnesses' reactions to his questions in interviews and depositions and even during breaks. During the break in one deposition, Carol made small talk with the plaintiff to get a "feel" for his frame of mind and his attitude about the case. (David represented the defendant in the lawsuit.) Rather than discussing the information obtained from the plaintiff during the deposition itself, the attorney later quizzed Carol about the plaintiff's attitude, the significance of his recent weight gain, and other psychological clues that might give him greater insight into the weaknesses of opposing counsel's case and their key witness. Carol's ability to obtain such clues provided David with a secret weapon for anticipating sudden changes in tactics and strategy by the other side.

Similarly, in a weekly team meeting before a trial, Michael, the partner on the case, asked each of the female paralegals for her personal reaction to the plaintiff. (He represented the defendant.) Did they instinctively like him? Dislike him? How did they think a jury might respond to him? He specifically asked for the female point of view because, as he said, "I have a complete male reaction to the guy. I hate his guts because he's such a wimp!" Debbie said she thought he would appeal to older women because he was good at playing the "helpless little boy." Mary thought the plaintiff was a phoney but agreed with Debbie's assessment. I said I doubted whether he'd be popular with men, but possibly with older women. Michael took these comments seriously and spent the rest of the meeting discussing strategy and favorable demographics for jury selection.

Paralegals are expected to utilize certain feminized components of emotional labor: deference and caretaking. These emotional requirements reflect the traditional female roles of wife and mother. Much like the traditional wife in relation to her husband, the paralegal defers to the attorney's authority and affirms his status by submitting to and smoothing over his angry outbursts, being non-critical vis-à-vis his written work and professional habits, submitting to constant interruptions, and being treated as if she were invisible. And like the "perfect mother" who tends to the needs of the family while suppressing her own, the legal assistant is expected to be pleasant, cheerful, and reassuring, to express gratitude to others for her boss, and to serve as an arbiter of his feelings to others. While many people of both sexes may harbor a "fantasy of the perfect mother," what is distinctive here is that the fantasy itself is embedded in the culture of working relations within law firms. It is male litigators who can expect to receive nurturing and support from women paralegals and not the reverse. As I will argue in later chapters, such a fantasy is not only impossible to fulfill but totally inappropriate to the workplace.

Chapter Five

Women and Men as Litigators
Gender Differences on the Job

In *The Merchant of Venice,* Portia poses as a male judge in an attempt to bring the plea for mercy into the halls of justice. Rejecting a binary logic of justice in which one party wins and another loses, Portia argues instead for a resolution to a legal dispute in which none of the parties will be harmed. Carol Gilligan refers to Portia's stance as an illustration of morality based on what she calls an "ethic of care" (1982: 105). In her early study of moral reasoning, Gilligan finds that women consistently pose moral questions in a "different voice" than men do.[1] In their attempts to resolve moral dilemmas and issues of responsibility, Gilligan's women, like Portia, are concerned with maintaining relationships so that no one will be hurt, whereas men are concerned with abstract notions of universal rights and justice. More recently, in their study of women and men lawyers, Gilligan's colleagues, Dana Jack and Rand Jack (1988, 1989), find that despite variations in behavior between women, as a group women are more likely than men to express a caring orientation in the practice of law.

In contrast to the empirical findings of Gilligan et al., sociologist Rosabeth Moss Kanter (1977, 1978) finds that women lawyers and managers as tokens or the numerical minority in their occupational group feel strong pressures to conform to existing masculine norms within the workplace and as a consequence minimize, rather than emphasize, whatever differences exist between them and the domi-

nant group. Other studies on token women in male-dominated professions and occupations have confirmed Kanter's thesis (Williams
1989; Spangler, Gordon, and Pipkin 1978). These contradictory sets
of findings raise the central questions for consideration in this chapter: Do women trial lawyers conform to male-defined norms of the
adversarial role or do they speak in a Portia-like dissatisfaction with
the male voice?

I observed that some women litigators practiced an ethic of care
in the resolution of legal disputes, others adopted the adversarial
model for the courtroom and a more care-oriented approach in the
office, and a small minority conformed to the male model. To make
sense of these findings, I reject the "either-personality-or-social-
structure" construction of the Gilligan-Kanter debate and argue instead that gender shapes the experiences of women in the legal profession at the structural level at the same time that women and men
as litigators reproduce gender at the micro-level of interactions and
identity. To make this argument, I examine gender differences on
the job at three levels of analysis: structural, behavioral, and the level
of individual identity. I discuss the gendered structural constraints
women (but not men) face in the law firm, such as their location in
the internal system of stratification and their experiences within the
male culture of the law firm and the corporate world and within the
"male clockwork" of the legal profession. Being a litigator is not the
same job for women as it is for men. Moreover, the gendered "feeling rules," or informal norms for appropriate emotional labor that
women and men face further reinforce these structural constraints.
Women, unlike men, encounter a double bind between the role of
the "good woman" and the emotional requirements of the adversarial role.

In the final section of the chapter, I turn to the micro level of interactions and consider the actual differences in emotional labor that
women and men perform. Compared to men, women as a group are
less likely to embrace the adversarial model in all aspects of their
work, instead expressing a caring orientation toward others, either in
the resolution of legal conflicts and/or in relations with staff in the
office. Here, I introduce West and Zimmerman's (1987) concept of
"doing gender" as the mediating behavioral link between the struc-

tural and individual levels of analysis. In my argument, women litigators, as token members of a male-dominated profession, do not passively conform to the norms of the adversarial model. Instead, they actively construct an emotional style that is consistent with their notion of gender-appropriate behavior. Furthermore, their choice of doing gender is informed in some way by their identity and sense of self as relational or feminine. As I will show, even women who most closely adhere to the male model are preoccupied with relational issues. In my dynamic account, gender shapes the structure of the legal profession, thereby setting gendered limits on lawyers' behavior. At the same time, women attorneys negotiate in and around these constraints, reproducing gender in their interactions with others by constructing a more caring practice of lawyering, creating more humane and caring relations with office staff, or simply by expressing their preoccupation with relational issues.

Structural Differences and Boundary Heightening

The first structural difference can be found within the internal system of stratification within law firms. In 1988, the same year I began my fieldwork, only 8 percent of the partners in the nation's 247 largest law firms were women (Abramson 1988). This contrasts sharply with the percentage of law students nationwide who were women—42 percent that same year (Prokop 1989). While this figure is reflected in the increasing number of women who were hired in law firms across the country at this time (40 percent), it is not reflected in the total percentage of women lawyers (19 percent) or in the percentage of women who achieve partnership (Epstein 1993: 426).[2] Journalists argue that the reason so few women are partners is that women, in significant numbers, have only been on the partnership track in the last fifteen years (Rinzler 1986). In such accounts, parity will be achieved when women have been within the profession for a longer period. The fact that so many women are leaving the legal profession for reasons of discrimination, sexual harassment, the improbability of breaking through the "glass ceiling," and incompatible demands between work and family suggests that such media accounts may be overly optimistic (Jacobs 1989; Loden 1986; Holmes 1988; Kahler 1988; Liefland 1986).

In this study, at the private firm, less than 9 percent of the partners are women; at Bonhomie Corporation, 10 percent. These differences in status are further reflected in income differentials. Although the private firm started associates at $58,500 in 1989, after two years men on the average made $2,000 more per year than the women did. Similarly, at Bonhomie Corporation, after two years men on the average were making $1,600 more per year than women lawyers. These salary differentials reflect those found in a national survey conducted by the National Association for Law Placement.[3] Thus, structurally, women are unlikely to be located in positions of power within the law firm and likely to make less money than men with comparable experience.

Not only do men predominate in numbers and in their positions of power, but private elite law firms represent in Epstein's words, "the quintessential upper-class male culture." "Nowhere is the 'old boy' network so characteristic of the formal and informal structure of an occupation as in the 'establishment bar'" (1983: 178). Recent articles in the legal trade press, such as the *National Law Journal* and *American Bar Association Journal*, suggest that little has changed since Epstein conducted her study in the late seventies (Hazard 1989; Salaman 1989; Bay 1989; Jordan 1989).[4] In a California study conducted by the State Bar Women in Law Committee, 88 percent of the women surveyed believed there is a "subtle pervasive gender bias" in the legal profession, and two-thirds of the respondents said that women are not accepted by their male peers (Bay 1989). Hearings conducted by the American Bar Association Commission of Women in the Profession drew similar conclusions (Salaman 1988). Commenting on these findings, executive vice-president of the American Bar Association, Jill Wine-Banks stated,

> Discrimination is perhaps more dangerous now. It is more invidious because people know enough not to be so blatant in their behavior. They're much more careful about what they say. But what they think remains. (quoted in Salaman 1988)

These studies as well as my own suggest that women still have a hard time gaining admission to the old-boy network. One area in which women lawyers continue to face exclusionary practices is informal socializing with male colleagues. In large law firms, such socializing is an important mechanism for obtaining interesting or important cases and information and for garnering trust and political capital with influential partners. Kanter (1977) argues that token members of an occupational group are less likely to be included in informal socializing. This is frequently the case for women attorneys in this study, such as Kelly, a thirty-five-year-old associate from Bonhomie Corporation:

My supervisor is so disengaged [from me]. But there is an underlying unspoken camaraderie between him and the male associates. There is just no way for me to crack through it. They play golf together, go on long bicycle trips together. . . . I'm never included.

Leslie, a twenty-nine-year old associate, said:

I dislike the "macho" atmosphere [at informal social events]. I went once, and all the associates were trying to see who could drink the most beer. Maybe they did it because I was there. I don't know, but I never went again.

Another woman said that when she first started working at Bonhomie, she "went out for drinks with the boys" but found the talk always turned to baseball. "I thought 'Oh, no. Here they go again.'"

These examples suggest not only that women are often excluded from all-male informal social groups but that even when they were included they still felt they did not belong. The response of their male colleagues exemplifies what Kanter calls "boundary heightening," that is, the exaggeration of differences by the dominant group between themselves and tokens. Male lawyers exaggerate the differences between women lawyers and themselves by talking about stereotypical male topics such as sports when women are present and by turning social events such as after-hours drinks into competitions. Such behavior serves, consciously or not, to underscore the differences between women and men, thereby constantly reminding the women that they are different and do not fit in.

Another way that male attorneys remind women they are not part of the "male culture" is by deflating women's occupational status. When Sandra Day O'Connor graduated from Stanford Law School

in the early 1960s with a distinguished academic record, no employer was willing to hire her at a law firm except as a legal secretary
(Morello 1986). Rhode (1988) notes that O'Connor's experience was
not uncommon at that time. Today, such discriminatory hiring practices are illegal.[5] Women are no longer denied jobs as attorneys;
however, they are frequently mistaken for secretaries. Many of the
women I interviewed expressed anger and annoyance at such incidences. Jeanette, a thirty-two-year old associate said:

I'd been with the firm for about eight months working with James [a part-
ner] when Jerry [another partner] came up to me and asked me to type
something. I looked surprised and said, "I'm an attorney, not a secretary." I
actually sat next to this man at a litigation department luncheon [for attor-
neys] the week before, so I knew he knew me. He laughed and said with a
conspiratorial wink, "Oh yeah, but don't all women know how to type." He
sauntered down the hall. I was furious.

Several other women attorneys recalled similar experiences. As one
commented sardonically, "Men seem to think women are born to
type." Such derogatory remarks serve to deflate the status of women
as attorneys. Deflating the occupational status of female attorneys
also serves to heighten boundaries between men and women. It reminds women that male lawyers think of them in stereotypical, sub-
servient female roles, and not as competent professionals, suggesting
a reluctance to accept women as colleagues or as equals.

Another means of heightening boundaries between male and female attorneys is through sexual harassment. The sexualization of
women is perhaps the most blatant way to exaggerate differences between the sexes. Recent studies of the legal profession suggest that
sexual harassment is much more common than was once supposed.[6]
Many of the women lawyers I interviewed reported incidences of
unwanted sexual invitations, attention, and behavior. For example,
Gabriella, a twenty-six-year-old associate, was harassed by a male
partner at a firm cocktail party who was notorious for such behavior;
she slapped him in response.

Everyone else knew about George, but I was new, I didn't know to avoid
him. So, when he tried to grab my breasts, I didn't even think, I just came
out swinging. . . . It was so humiliating. Then, afterwards . . . the snide re-

marks, the knowing glances, the comments, "How's your left hook?" It was the second public humiliation.

Another young women lawyer, Nancy, described the sexual harassment she experienced with a judge for whom she had clerked her first year out of law school:

He used to flirt and talk to me all day long. Most of the time I just tried to ignore it. . . . Finally, one day he said to me, "Nancy, do you work out?" I said, "Why do you ask?" He said, "I'm wondering what you look like in a sweatsuit." I replied, "Keep your sexual fantasies to yourself!" Later, I reported him to the court. They had gotten tons of complaints and told me [the judge] specifically requested female law clerks. . . . They never did anything about it.

Denise, another woman attorney, described a pass that a male attorney had made at her while they were away together on a business trip to the East Coast. "He put his hand where it didn't belong," she told me. When I asked how she reacted, she said, "I put it back where it belonged." John, a male attorney who was sitting nearby as we conversed, interjected, "That's all you did?" in a tone that suggested he believed Denise had enjoyed the other lawyer's advances. His sarcastic remark captures the attitude that many male attorneys held about sexual harassment. Although none experienced sexual harassment personally, they knew it went on at the firm and many, but not all, found it humorous.[7] Similarly, the comments male attorneys made about Gabriella after the incident with George suggest that not George's behavior but rather Gabriella's reaction—slapping George—was what they considered inappropriate and worthy of derision. Reminding Gabriella of the incident in this way also drew attention to her status as a woman. By treating women lawyers as sex objects, male lawyers simultaneously heighten the boundaries between themselves and women and assert their authority as men in the workplace.

Not only were women reluctantly accepted by the male culture within the firm, but they also faced serious obstacles in dealing with their predominantly male clients in the corporate world. A recent trade press article titled "New Trouble for Women Lawyers," found that women have more difficulty than men in bringing clients into the firm because clients are still more likely to turn to a man. As one woman lawyer said, "It wouldn't occur to them to call up a woman. They'll call up a law-school buddy" (quoted in Chiang 1990: 1). Another female attorney recalled chatting with a prospective male client at a business dinner about her work, her husband, and her children. She felt confident that she was on the way to making a good business contact until the client tried to kiss her goodbye. And a partner from a prominent San Francisco firm recalled meeting with a client who refused to make eye contact with her, even when she asked him direct questions. Rather than responding to her, the client turned to the junior associate, a man, who had been sitting silently next to her (Chiang 1990).

Women at the private firm encountered similar problems. Judith, a young woman associate, said that the client on one case wouldn't talk to her because she was a woman—the client was the executive officer of a conservative corporation. When she complained to her supervisor he told her that she just had to understand that this was nothing personal. Since a good portion of the firm's business drew from this corporation, Judith and other women faced unusual difficulty in "wooing" and working closely with clients. As Leslie said, "They keep saying all the women leave. Do they ever wonder why? Most of the clients don't want to work with us." The two women partners in the litigation department avoided this dilemma by bringing in business in other areas, such as insurance and the electronics industry. Candace, one of the women partners, explains how she had acquired her first "big client":

It wasn't easy. At first, I thought I should try to work with the firm's major client. When I realized that wouldn't work, I went elsewhere. Before I had any reputation as a litigator, I heard "No" a lot. No explanations, just "No." One of those young computer whiz kids in the Silicon Valley gave me a break. The first day he came to the office in jeans, a t-shirt and cowboy boots. You should have seen the other attorneys look. [Smiles.] Today, his company is my biggest client. He gives me all his business and referrals. I have more work than I know what to do with. But I was lucky. Other women haven't been so lucky.

At Bonhomie Corporation, because the company itself was the client, attorneys did not have to woo clients or "make rain." Nevertheless, relationships with the "client" were of tantamount importance, and women faced problems that most men did not. As Gail, a thirty-five-year-old junior associate, said:

There is this rule with clients [where] senior counsel men and junior counsel women go to meetings with the client. Lots of times, in that situation, I'm expected to take the silent-assistant role. It's not the same for men.

Despite Gail's claim, male associates did not always find it easy to "make rain" either, though for different reasons. Men from upper-class backgrounds with family money, connections, and "cultural capital" (Bourdieu 1977b) found it easy to exploit pre-existing family business connections and to make new ones. Their broad cultural knowledge and familiarity with upper-middle-class social etiquette made socializing with elite CEOs and company presidents easy for them. The few men from lower-middle-class and working-class backgrounds simply did not feel at ease in these situations. Rafe, a twenty-nine-year-old Boalt Law School graduate, posed the problem in this way:

Stanley [an upper-class Ivy League law school graduate] already knows these people [the clients]. His father is the CEO for Blinky, Inc. [a large multinational corporation]. He grew up talking to these kind of people. He knows their language—how to say the right things, which clubs to belong to, which stocks to invest in. . . . I'm lucky if I figure out the right color suit and tie to wear to these meetings.

In the legal department at Bonhomie Corporation, men made their way to senior counsel positions not by making rain but by making influential contacts with superiors in the corporate hierarchy. Successful senior counsel were on familiar terms with the CEO and vice-presidents. Randy, a thirty-year-old African American man, complained about feeling excluded from this process:

They have an affirmative-action program here . . . so there are more Blacks, and women too. But look at who makes senior counsel. I have been here six years and I see the writing on the wall. I don't socialize with CEOs—they probably wouldn't want to socialize with me. I've never even met one of them. I'm just not a company man. The only Black man who made senior counsel did so after eight years of service with the threat of a discrimination suit. Now, he's their token. I don't want that.

The comments of women lawyers and these two men suggest that wooing clients requires a degree of acceptance on the part of the client and a social ease on the part of the lawyer. Lawyers from minority or working-class backgrounds as well as women often do not feel completely at ease socializing with corporate executives. As one women said, "These people belong to the Bohemian Club.[8] How is that supposed to make me feel?" On the other hand, clients who work in homogeneous corporate environments are unused to working with people of color and white women as equals. The fact that the corporate world is still unable to accept women and men who do not fit into this white, upper-middle-class male culture has serious negative repercussions for lawyers whose intrafirm mobility is based on recruiting new clients.

Not only is the culture of law firms strongly male, but the model of the professional career itself is distinctly male. In her classic article, "Inside the Clockwork of Male Careers," Hochschild (1975) argues that academic institutions support careers that are implicitly based on the male life cycle. If the male professor has a family, the underlying assumption is that his wife will devote her time and energy to managing the potential disruption this could create in his career. Hochschild writes: "Other things being equal, the university rewards the married, family-free man" (1975: 67). Law professor Geoffrey Hazard makes a similar argument about the legal profession:

This model of a professional career is distinctly male, and does not work for most women. Apart from everything else in life, a woman's biological clock has a different setting. Most women who become lawyers follow the same pathway as men until they complete college at about age 21. . . . Only a few women these days are firmly committed to having no children . . . a decision male lawyers need not impose on themselves. If women wish to keep open the option of having children, they face strategic choices in relating professional career to personal life. (Hazard 1988: 24)

The clockwork of male careers played itself out in the legal department at Bonhomie Corporation and at Lyman, Lyman and Portia. Although Bonhomie had an eight-week maternity-leave policy, many women lawyers complained that while men were able to obtain part-time work assignments for "health reasons," they were unable to work part-time after having a baby. Mary, a woman lawyer and a single mother, confronted the managing partner with this double standard.

He told her that "the men had families to support." On the other hand, the private firm had no official maternity-leave policy. "They do it on a case-by-case basis," explained Jessie, a young women in her sixth month of pregnancy. She added, "I have no idea what's going to happen after I have the baby. The management committee hasn't decided my case yet. I am facing this big transition in my life, and I don't even know if I will have a job after I have the baby." Deborah Rhode sarcastically describes management's viewpoint about this issue: "The prevailing view at some firms is that 'having a baby is a personal decision, rather like vacationing in Tahiti' and unworthy of significant organizational support" (1988: 1185).

Gendered Feeling Rules

The double standard posed for women by the "quintessential male culture" of the law can also be seen by looking at the divergent "feeling rules" men and women face about appropriate display of emotional labor. In Chapter 3, I described the two main components of the gamesmanship required of litigators—intimidation and strategic friendliness. Unlike male attorneys, women encounter a double bind in the aggressive component of emotional labor. At NITA and both law firms, women attorneys were criticized for being "too nice to the witnesses," "not forceful enough," "too bashful," and "unaggressive," at the same time that they were admonished for being "too aggressive." Men, on the other hand, were sometimes criticized for being "too aggressive" and not listening carefully to the witness but were more likely to be praised for their ruthlessness. This double bind emerged not only in the aggressive component of gamesmanship, but in its less confrontational—though equally manipulative—form, strategic friendliness. For example, when male attorneys used cajoling and placating strategies to achieve an instrumental end, they received support and encouragement from their colleagues. Women who adopted similar tactics, were accused of using their "feminine wiles" to get their way with the witness or opposing counsel.

Underlying such attitudes is a gendered division of emotional labor, in which men are expected to be aggressive, manipulative, and instrumental, and women are not. Women who display these qualities are regarded as "unladylike," "domineering," "strident," and "shrill." In her classic study on women lawyers, Epstein (1983) suggests such women violate the cultural myth of the "good woman."

A pervading myth about women is that they possess or should possess higher moral standards than men. . . . In the view that women are good or ought to be so, "good" usually translates as "too good"—too good for politicking and therefore governing, too good to make deals and therefore to enter business, too good to be tough-minded and therefore to make good scientists, physicians, or lawyers. (1983: 268–69)

The myth of the good woman suggests that women lawyers, like women in other occupations, are expected to express care and concern for others. However, because gamesmanship requires intimidation, manipulation, and artifice, women lawyers are placed in a constant double bind between the requirements of the role of the "good woman" and the role of the adversary.

The double bind posed by the aggressive component of gamesmanship is evident in a presentation made by a young woman lawyer at the National Institute for Trial Advocacy. Amanda performed a confrontational cross-examination of the witness, badgering him until he began to admit that he wasn't absolutely sure about the date of the incident in question. Amanda, however, had one mannerism that the teacher did not like—her smile. At the end of one of the leading questions, "You don't remember what you did on August 28th, do you, Mr. Jones?" she smiled. In his comments at the end of her presentation, the teacher said that her smile detracted from the seriousness and aggressiveness of the cross-examination. He told her half-seriously and half-jokingly that if she smiled again, he would hold her in "contempt of court." His advice to Amanda was to "lose the smile and be more forceful."

At the break, Amanda talked at length with me about the teacher's comment. She knew that she smiled a lot, but she didn't know she smiled so much until she saw the video of her presentation. She added that she smiled at the end of one of her particularly aggressive questions because she didn't want to be perceived as a "bitch." Her comment suggests that although she was capable of playing the part—being aggressive—she was still concerned about, or preoccupied with, how other people thought of her.

In the afternoon session, when Amanda went back to class, she did another cross-examination. This time she didn't smile at all, and instead hammered away at the witness with question after question, looking serious and stern. This time, the teacher told her that her cross-examination was "dull, lacking animation and interest." As Amanda herself said afterwards, "I feel like I can't win. If I smile, I'm not aggressive enough. If I'm aggressive and don't smile, I'm boring. What am I supposed to do to be a good trial lawyer?"

This question plagued many of the women lawyers in this study. They found that if they were polite to the witnesses they cross-examined, they were criticized for not being forceful enough. When they became more aggressive, they were admonished for "overplaying it" or "being phoney." Lyn, a pleasant young woman associate, was censured in her performance evaluation for not being "tough enough" because she "got along too well with opposing counsel." Similarly, the male attorneys in Leslie's office thought she "wasn't tough enough to go to court," despite the fact that she had won the moot court competition in law school and been a debate champion in college. Both women found that when they tried to be more assertive, they were described as "too hyper" or "too shrill." As one of the NITA's female teachers astutely observed, "Unlike men, women lawyers have to find a balance in the courtroom between being forceful, but not being too shrill."

These findings confirm other studies that show that young women lawyers often experience a double bind between their personal identity as female and their membership in a profession that is strongly masculine (Rhode 1988; Spencer and Podomore 1987; Epstein 1983). Rhode writes: "Those conforming to traditional characteristics of femininity are often thought to lack the requisite assertiveness and initiative, yet those conforming to a masculine model of success may be ostracized at work settings as bitchy, aggressive and uncooperative" (1988: 1183).

This lesson was rigorously reinforced by the sessions I attended at the National Institute for Trial Advocacy. The demonstrations of destructive cross-examination were very aggressive. However, when women performed, they were much more likely than men to be criticized for being "too nice." As discussed in Chapter 3, both Laura and Patricia were admonished for "losing control" and "being too nice" to the witness. Yet when these same two women performed a more confrontational cross-examination in the afternoon session, Laura was described by one teacher as "shrill" and "affectless" and Patricia by another as "impassive" and "nervous." The fact that each woman's presentation could be simultaneously described as overly emotional and not emotional enough highlights the impossibility of performing satisfactorily. Teachers perceive aggressive women, consciously or not, as inappropriate.

Just as NITA teaches and reinforces an aggressive stance for male litigators, in the weekly litigation meeting at the private firm, attorneys regularly demonstrated support for male lawyers' "hard-ball tactics." For instance, one of the partners, who was well known in the city as a highly successful litigator, described how he had been hired as "a big hired gun" by an insurance company for the "intimidation factor." He told the group: "When opposing counsel saw me come through the door with the client, they dropped their jaw. That was before I made my argument." He went on to describe a confrontational settlement conference. His description was met with appreciative laughter and supportive comments such as "Good going," "That'll get the other side," and "You showed them." His colleagues' comments served as a collective reinforcement for his intimidation tactics.

At the same meeting, another lawyer commented that "If you want to make a tough case, ask James. Ever since he's worked on the Waverly case, he's gotten tough." Following this comment, attorneys laughed and teased about how tough James had gotten—"He's so tough, he could take on Arthur Liman," and "He'd prosecute the dress off his grandmother." Far from censuring James's behavior, these remarks suggest a macho admiration for this quality. In addition, the remark about his grandmother underscores James's ability to depersonalize the attack and compete against friends or even family members to achieve the desired result.

This kind of behavior was also reinforced in the legal department at Bonhomie Corporation. A young male associate spoke admiringly to me and another paralegal of his supervising partner's manic, aggressive style:

When we were in Washington, D.C., we started depositions every morning at 8 A.M. That's five A.M. West Coast time. Mack and I just kept speeding through depositions. Mack never got tired at all. And opposing counsel didn't know what to do, they just couldn't keep up with us or fight off the attack. And if anyone should have been tired, it should have been us. We were three hours behind them.

When the other female paralegal suggested that Mack's behavior was somewhat extreme, Doug quickly responded, "Mack's the greatest!"

At the private firm, some associates demonstrated admiration for the combative style of Michael, one of the senior partners. In interviews as well as in my fieldwork, several young male lawyers described with respect how Michael had "reduced a witness to submission with a stern glance," "cut the other side down to size," and "torn the witness's testimony into bits." Michael treated secretaries, paralegals, and young associates who worked for him with the same adversarial vigor. He yelled, rather than requested; he picked and criticized instead of expressing gratitude for tasks completed. One paralegal described him as a "shark who ate the people who worked for him alive." By contrast, young associates greatly admired his force of personality and cunning in the courtroom. In their interviews, these young male attorneys viewed Michael as a role model. Several expressed the desire "to be a litigator like Michael." Dan, a twenty-nine-year-old associate who did not work with Michael, said enviously, "When I see these other associates working with Michael, I have felt like the 'orphan child.' Although I realize working with him can be problematic, I wish I could work with him. He's the best."

The reception of Michael's behavior contrasts sharply with the experience of Chris, a young woman associate at the private firm. Other lawyers regarded Chris as brash and obnoxious. In her communications with opposing counsel, she was brusque and confrontational. Once, while I was sitting in her office, she yelled on the phone to opposing counsel, "I'm not accusing you of lying, I know you're lying!" In her interactions within the office, her abusive behavior toward the staff had caused two secretaries to leave within two months. Far from receiving praise for this behavior, Chris garnered a shower of criticism. The personnel director gave her an ultimatum about learning how to "get along with support staff." The managing partner told her point-blank that she was "the most obnoxious person" he had ever met. But the most extreme sanction for her behavior came in the form of a "surprise" she received in interoffice mail. Someone from within the firm anonymously sent her a pig's foot in an elaborately wrapped gift box.[9]

Chris was not disliked simply because she was obnoxious, however. Comments by her colleagues and subordinates suggest she was also disliked for being a woman who emulated the behavior of successful men. One of her male colleagues said about the incident, "Women who act like Chris deserve what they get." Some paralegals and secretaries were inclined to agree with this view. As one female secretary said, "Women who act like Chris don't have any class." The same secretary said of Michael, " Yeah, he's a pain to work for. I don't like him, but who expects men to be nice?" Her response underscores the double standard women lawyers face—women who aren't nice deserve to be treated disrespectfully, whereas the same behavior in men is grudgingly accepted. In light of these responses, the gift can be seen as a symbolic sanction not only for unpleasant behavior but for gender-inappropriate behavior.

Other women lawyers were censured for their aggressive behavior, though none as severely as Chris. For example, in a litigation department meeting, Anne described the tactics she had used in a recent deposition. In her cross-examination, the plaintiff claimed that he knew the defendant had lied to him on the phone. Anne successfully showed that the plaintiff couldn't know this.

Q: How did you know she was lying?

A: She, her voice volume changed.

Q: How did her voice change?

A: Well, if you're trained into the art of recognizing people's responses, I felt that I recognized that she got upset, that they went, came into light.

Q: Mr. Diamond, what training have you received in interpreting changes in people's voice patterns?

A: I have studied psychology books myself, and I have daily contact with tons of people in the performance of my job.

Q: What psychology books have you read which have discussed the interpretation of voice patterns?

A: Several.

Q: Could you identify these?

A: Not specifically, specific to the subject, but specific to the methods of lie detectors, and I know that one of the forms of recognition is when someone's lying or he's been confronted with an unpleasant situation, there is sweatiness. There's change in the resistance of the skin, sweatiness, redness.

Q: Were you speaking to the defendant face-to-face during this conversation?

A: No, over the telephone.

Q: Didn't you say that you thought the defendant was lying?

A: Yes.

Q: And, didn't you say that sweatiness is a sign that someone may be lying?

A: Yes.

Q: Tell me, Mr. Diamond, how did you detect sweatiness over the telephone?

A: Uh.

Q: That's all for today.

At the conclusion of her story, Anne repeated the phrase, "Tell me, Mr. Diamond, how did you detect sweatiness over the telephone?" in a stern, serious voice. Several attorneys laughed. One man curtly responded, "Well, we'd better not call Anne up for a date." More laughter followed his comment. Rather than supporting Anne's strategy, his remark undermined her presentation by sexualizing her as a potential "date" rather than congratulating her as a professional colleague, and thereby rendering problematic her behavior in the deposition. The "joke" also reflects a hierarchical pattern. In her article, "Laughter among Colleagues," Rose Laub Coser (1960) argues that in interactions between superiors and subordinates, superordinates such as male residents initiate jokes, while female nurses "receive" them. In this case, the joke is initiated by a male at his female colleague's expense, thus, serving to put Anne in her place as a woman.

Aggressive women lawyers were put in their place in other ways as well. Yolanda, a Black woman, had been dubbed the "queen of sanctions" by the head of the litigation department for her persistence in castigating opposing counsel for failure to comply with discovery requests, pleading with the judge for sanctions and successfully obtaining them.[10] During a meeting at Bonhomie Corporation, the managing partner designated Allen, a young male associate, to become the new insurance expert for the department. A discussion followed about the need for a coffee machine for the group and the company policies that precluded this. To resolve the problem, the partner selected Yolanda to look into it. "You'll be our litigation hostess," he said jokingly. One of the male associates corrected him, "You mean she'll be our hostess czarina." Everyone laughed and the managing partner added, "Let's see, we have Yolanda the hostess czarina, Yolanda the queen of sanctions, what's next?"

The banter about Yolanda's reputation appeared to be quite friendly. Beneath the teasing and joking, however, lie assumptions about a gendered and racial division of labor. Allen, a white male and one of the least experienced associates, is assigned the role of insurance expert. Yolanda, the only African American female, the most experienced associate, and one of the department's more successful litigators, is assigned the task of looking into company policies about obtaining a coffee machine. The man has been assigned the role of expert, the woman the task of housekeeper. Thus, Yolanda, the "queen of sanctions," is not only put in her place as a woman, the litigation hostess, but is relegated to a domestic assignment, the historic lot of a Black woman (Rollins 1985).

Doing Gender: Variation and Continuity

The male-dominated structure of the legal profession, as well as the gendered nature of "feeling rules," sets the limits for gender-appropriate emotional labor for male and female litigators. Men as a group were more likely to follow the dictates of the adversarial model and to refrain from developing social relationships with support staff. On the other hand, women were less likely to embrace the adversarial model wholeheartedly, instead performing a relational form of emotional labor emphasizing a caring orientation toward others, either in the adjudication of legal disputes or in office working relations. Women and men did not conform precisely to these limits but rather varied in the degree to which they performed gender appropriate emotional labor. Much like the women lawyers in Jack and Jack's (1988) study, women's behavior in this study also varied. At Lyman, Lyman and Portia and in the legal department at Bonhomie Corporation, women's emotional labor fell along a continuum ranging from those who sought to reshape the adversarial role to fit their caring orientation (26 percent), those who "split the role" (58 percent), and those who minimized the feminine self by adopting the male model (16 percent).[11] Men also varied in how closely they adopted the strategies of gamesmanship. Some wholeheartedly embraced the adversarial role (40 percent), others did it but expressed a more distanced relation to it (50 percent), and a small minority rejected the model altogether (10 percent).

Resisting and Reshaping the Adversarial Role

Women lawyers who attempted to reshape the adversarial role to fit their caring orientation expressed a strong dissatisfaction with the traditional adversarial role. Twenty-six percent of women fell into this category. They paid more than "lip service" to their expressed values by actively seeking to incorporate alternatives to gamesmanship in their daily practice. Like the feminist lawyers Epstein interviewed, these women were dedicated to social goals rather than making money and valued egalitarian working relationships with colleagues and with support staff (Epstein 1983: 139–40).[12] Men in this category were also critical of the adversarial role and its emotional requirements. Although they attempted to reshape the adversarial role, they did little to challenge hierarchical working relations with support staff in the office.

The following conversation between two lawyers illustrates the feelings expressed by women in the first group:

Tom: Dealing with the aggressive role is purely personal. If people aren't aggressive by nature, they won't be good litigators. If I had to I could persuade any client to do whatever I wanted. . . .

Linda: But isn't that unethical? You have to inform clients of the downside as well. . . . [*Later, in a private conversation*] Tom's partially correct, you sometimes do have to be aggressive to survive. But the majority of lawyers aren't cutthroat. There are other possible ways to resolve problems.

Linda's suggestion that there are ways to resolve legal disputes other than being aggressive is not a reference to strategic friendliness. She doesn't believe one has to be manipulative to be a good lawyer. In her view: "I often see my relationship to clients as the creation of a personal relationship. Some would say that's unprofessional. But I really think that relationships based on trust don't emerge from manipulation. I treat clients with respect. I provide them with alternatives and urge them to think for themselves." Thus, Linda is concerned about the quality of her relationship with the client as well as the procedure for obtaining a decision. By contrast, Tom is unconcerned with the relationship and is solely interested in pursuing whatever it takes to win.

The difference in these approaches is reminiscent of Carol Gilligan's (1982) early findings on gender differences in moral development. In her study, Gilligan finds that men tend to resolve moral dilemmas using a language of rights and responsibilities and an abstract notion of justice. Men identify the legal issue, balance the rights of each party, and declare one the winner. By contrast, women utilize an "ethic of care," considering the needs of all the parties involved as well as their relationships, and attempt to find a solution that will satisfy everyone, rather than selecting a winner and a loser. Thus, Gilligan finds that women are more concerned with how moral dilemmas are resolved.

Many of the women I interviewed expressed concern for how legal disputes were resolved. Margaret, a young associate at the private firm, expressed a Gilliganesque concern about her working relationship with opposing counsel:

I don't give into being aggressive, rude, and snotty to get the best results. You don't have to stand up to opposing counsel by screaming on the phone, for example. You can always hang up. . . . They can't win by playing hardball all the time. Being a feminine woman and being reasonable, that's how I see myself. Howard, the partner I work for, adopts the adversarial relationship. That's not me. I don't know what happened before in this case I'm working on or why it had accelerated to such an ugly state. I decided to be reasonable. Now opposing counsel calls me and says, "Look Margaret, I don't trust Howard, but I trust you, I think we can work this out."

In this way, Margaret found an alternative to the aggressive and manipulative aspects of gamesmanship. Her particular style emphasizes mutual trust and respect rather than suspicion and combativeness. This style carried over into her working relations with secretaries and paralegals as well.

I think it's really important to develop working relationships out of mutual respect. I've seen too many attorneys treat their secretaries badly—like they're not people, like they don't matter. But they do matter, it does matter. Every time you treat someone like that, you hurt them, and you hurt yourself. It's a process of dehumanization, and it works both ways.

Gail, another young woman lawyer, found yet another way to deal with her dissatisfaction with the adversarial model:

When I first came to the legal department, [senior counsel] made it clear I was on the "fast track." After a couple of years under a supervisor who gave me complete autonomy without any kind of psychic reward, I felt burned out. I wasn't contributing to society, plus all the stress and long hours. I decided at that point to find personal satisfaction. I got off the sixty-hour-week fast track. I took a three-month leave of absence. I came back to work part-time. I work [here] four days a week and do pro bono work on Fridays—I work for legal services for kids. I need to do it!

In her pro bono work, Gail found a way to satisfy her interests in the human side of the job: "I can't relate to the psychic manipulation and gamesmanship. When I go to work on Fridays, I feel like I'm doing real work for real people with real problems. I don't have to puff myself up or put other people down. It's about real life."

Other women attorneys also expressed concern with the quality of the procedure for resolving legal disputes and the quality of legal relationships and actively sought alternative means to adjudicate legal conflicts. For instance, Jessie, a young associate, described a situation she tried to resolve in a novel fashion. The case involved a plaintiff and defendant who had formerly been friends. One had sued the other for breach of contract in a business arrangement. The plaintiff refused to agree to any of the settlement negotiations. The case had dragged on for several years with repeated depositions, discovery motions, and settlement conferences. Initially, the plaintiff always seemed eager to settle, but in the end, he refused every offer. After days of reviewing the files and reading deposition transcripts, Jessie developed a theory about the bitter antagonism between the two parties and decided to try it out.

She called a preliminary settlement conference between the plaintiff and the defendant. She sat them both down in the conference room and said,

I've read through the files thoroughly and I see this case as a simple breach of contract. What I don't understand completely is the animosity between the two of you. Mr. Smith has agreed to pay you a considerable sum of money for your loss, Mr. Henry. And you refuse the offer time and time again. It strikes me that you're angry with Mr. Smith about something unrelated to the lawsuit. I wonder if you could tell me what it's about?

This question was followed by a long silence. Jessie added,

I realize that this is unorthodox Mr. Henry, but I have a feeling that the only way you two can ever resolve this dispute is if we get to the bottom of this antagonism between the two of you. If you prefer not to discuss it, I'll respect your wishes.

Mr. Henry finally said, "You really want to know?" Jessie nodded. He went on, "He married my ex-wife!" Mr. Smith said, "What! You left her for someone else. You left her! I didn't know you cared about what she did." The interchange continued for some time, with exclamations, accusations, and laughter on both sides. Finally, Jessie brought the discussion back to business. "Would you be willing to accept Mr. Smith's offer?" Mr. Henry agreed.

Jessie's approach contrasts sharply to the adversarial model. Rather than focusing only on her client's interests, she attempted to create a resolution by considering the interests of all the parties involved. Furthermore, her relationship to the plaintiff was not purely instrumental and manipulative, but one of genuine interest and concern. She wanted to get to the bottom of things, and she believed that a more personal approach would work: "People think I am a pushover because I'm nice and pleasant. But sometimes I think practicing law can be different if you're pleasant and treat people with respect."

Jessie sought not only to transform the practice of law, but to break down hierarchical relations in the office:

A lot of lawyers think because they have a law degree, they're smarter than everyone else. I've never suffered from that delusion. I value what everyone on my team has to offer. . . . If Joan [a secretary] tells me I did something wrong, I listen. She's been in the office longer than I have and she knows a lot of things I don't. . . . The practice of law encourages hierarchical thinking. If we break that down, we can be better lawyers, better people.

By reshaping the adversarial role to fit their more relational orientation, these women contradict Kanter's findings on female tokens. Rather than conforming to the male model, these women self-consciously reject the binary win-lose structure of adversarial practice and construct alternative forms of practice that value mutual trust and respect in relationships. Their active participation in creating a more caring orientation within the legal profession serves as both a critique of and a challenge to the male-defined adversarial role. Furthermore, their emphasis on "real" relationships undermines one of the major assumptions of gamesmanship, that is, that relations with others are a game in which people are treated as objects. Rather than deny the subjectivity of the other, these women recognize the other as an authentic subject.[13]

Some men in this category also expressed serious misgivings about the adversarial role. Patrick, for example, criticized many lawyers for their tendency to behave like "assholes." By contrast, he wanted to practice law in a less adversarial way—one influenced by Eastern philosophy.

I do martial art, aikido. I like to live that as my personal lifestyle. In aikido, you overcome your opponents without being an asshole, but understanding their interests. Let's try to resolve both interests, rather than winning is everything. I think that I am new enough as an attorney that I don't know how well it works in practice. I think that you can apply it to other parts of your life, you know making compromises and not being adversarial.
Do you think you will be successful with that attitude?
Successful? I don't know. I would like to think that I could be successful with this attitude. I can't see it some other way. If this profession demands that I become an asshole and I realize that I become an asshole, I would make a change, because this is just a job. I don't think enough people are concerned with resolving conflict this way. For them, it is zero-sum, win-

lose. And it's a real ego investment, too. I think a lot of people want to win for the sake of winning.

Have you ever put this into practice at the office?

Maybe, I am naive, but I was in a dispute in a banking case. There was a situation where I could have said "fuck you" to opposing counsel, but I didn't. When it was clear that I was not going to do this through reason, I just said, "I can't do it, I'm sorry."

Unlike lawyers who adopt a guerrilla-warfare mentality, Patrick endorses the Eastern philosophy of aikido to describe his position. Rather than trying to overcome opponents by force, he wants to "understand their interests" and "resolve the interests from both sides." Such a concern appears quite Gilliganesque. However, though highly critical of the combative aspects of the adversarial role, his seemingly relational stance did not extend to his working relationships in the office. He was friendly with secretaries and paralegals, but he made no effort to create friendships with them, insisting instead on "professional relationships." Furthermore, paralegals reported that Patrick frequently "pulled rank"—that is, he was quick to remind them that he was the lawyer. While Patrick's critique of the adversarial model is quite similar to that of the women in this category, it did not extend to his behavior in other working relationships in the office.

Several other male attorneys expressed dissatisfaction with the adversarial role. Ben, for example, who complained in Chapter 3 that "litigation turned people into bastards," refused to adopt intimidation tactics, instead utilizing a more "friendly, down-to-earth approach." He was nice to opposing counsel "because it's amazing what you can find out if you are nice." Similarly, he was pleasant to his secretary because it "pays to have good relations with support staff." Compared to many other male lawyers, Ben was much more friendly and upbeat in his interactions with secretaries and paralegals. However, his stance differs from the more relational concern for others that women attorneys express. Rather than concern, Ben's friendliness exemplifies a form of manipulation. He is friendly with his secretary not because he values her friendship, but because she is useful to him. His cost-benefit calculation—"It pays to have good relations with support staff"—underscores his instrumental understanding of the relationship. Even though Ben eschews the intimidation strategy, he continues to utilize its no-less-manipulative counterpart—strategic friendliness.

Splitting the Roles versus Distancing

In their study on women lawyers, Jack and Jack (1988) found that some women lawyers "split" the lawyering role by living up to the demands of the professional role and, at the same time, maintaining their personal caring morality. They accomplished this by splitting their roles at home and at work, adopting an adversarial role at work but embracing a caring ethic at home. In my research, women also split roles, but in a different way. The second group of female lawyers (58 percent of women) assimilated to the masculine norms of gamesmanship in their dealings with opposing counsel and with clients, but their actions and feelings in the office often belied this stance. Some adopted a combative style with opposing counsel but treated staff and colleagues with concern and/or respect. Others utilized gamesmanship but often expressed strong feelings of guilt and dissatisfaction. On the other hand, men in the second group distanced themselves from the adversarial role. Unlike men in the first group, who criticized the combative aspect of the adversarial role, these men were not critical but instead expressed a curiously detached relationship to the emotional requirements of the job.

Mary exemplifies women who split the roles. She appeared to adhere to the model of the combative litigator, as in an incident typifying her response to communications with opposing counsel: during a heated argument with opposing counsel on the phone, she told him he was "the most patronizing man" she'd ever met in her life. "Who do you think you are to presume that Sam [the other attorney on the case] and I don't know what we're doing?" Mary, who is five-foot-eleven, explained her future strategy for dealing with this lawyer, who was only five feet tall: "From now on, in every meeting with him, I am going to wear three-inch heels, so that I tower over him. And, if he gets in my way, I'll squash him like a bug with the end of my stiletto heel!"

In another context, Mary appeared ambivalent about being so aggressive. She had a reputation among secretaries and paralegals for being difficult to work with. However, what made her behavior different from that of her male counterparts lay in her interactions with subordinates. She usually gave flowers or candy to subordinates before she went into her work frenzy. In fact, one of her paralegals said that she could always tell when Mary was going to be difficult to work with, because she gave her flowers, as if she were apologizing in advance for what she knew would be inappropriate behavior. Furthermore, the day after she had given paralegals and secretaries a difficult time, she thanked them excessively for the work they had done. Mary's attitude about gamesmanship clarifies this seemingly contradictory behavior:

> Winning is great, it's important to me. But winning isn't everything.
> *Meaning?*
> Some lawyers turn every encounter into a win-lose situation. In the courtroom, there's one kind of winning. In the office, it means putting someone else down. I think that's lousy. When I'm in the office I try really hard not to be like that—people matter to me. I don't always succeed, but at least I try.

Mary effectively performed the combative aspects of the adversarial role, and enjoyed winning her cases, but she also placed a high value on relationships in the office.

Jeanette was another litigator who had a reputation for being "tough." Watching her practice her "mock trial," I was struck by the contrast between her angry demeanor in the courtroom and her typically pleasant presentation of self in the office. While opposing counsel was presenting his side of the case, she rolled her eyes dramatically, scowled, and made faces suggesting to the jury that she thought the other lawyer was an idiot. When it was her turn to cross-examine the witness, she utilized a confrontational approach, simultaneously questioning and berating the witness.

In the office Jeanette's behavior took on a more relational tone. She planned surprise birthday parties for all the secretaries, paralegals, and lawyers on her team, and often baked the cake herself. During the holiday season, she personally delivered Christmas cards and candy canes to all the people who worked for her. Moreover, when I left the legal department she made a special effort to take me out to lunch to thank me for all the work I had done for her. Jeanette defended her behavior in this way:

I really like my secretary. She's great. Our friendship is important to me. . . . [But] some lawyers have lectured me on my lack of professionalism. You know, [she adopts a deep voice] "It's not professional to be friends with your secretary." To me, that's a male attitude. If I were professional all the time, I wouldn't have any friends at all.

Again, we can see that Jeanette self-consciously rejects what she considers to be the male-defined professional stance for office etiquette, opting instead for more personal relationships.

Yolanda, the "queen of sanctions," also fell into this category. Despite her no-nonsense attitude in the courtroom and her reputation at the courthouse, in the office Yolanda was attentive and friendly in personal interactions. During department meetings, she was usually one of the few attorneys who chatted and joked with paralegals. She made an effort to include people in conversations, doing what Pamela Fishman (1978) calls "interaction work." Moreover, unlike the other women attorneys, Yolanda freely discussed make-up, clothes, jewelry, and dieting in public situations. During one meeting, she described at great length a new leather mini-skirt she had bought and where she planned to wear it. When senior counsel cast a disapproving glance in her direction, she shot back, "I'm just trying to liven things up, Sam. These meetings are so dull!" Everyone laughed. Again, her attention to personal interactions belies the more aggressive style she develops in the courtroom.

Yolanda describes these different presentations of self:

What I do in court, I do because I have to. I'm a damn good litigator and I'm not afraid to be tough. In the office, I can be Yolanda and joke around and talk to people. That's when I get to be myself.

Other women who "split the roles" discussed the guilt they experienced in performing the combative role. As one woman said, "Unless I really hate the other side, I always have this lingering feeling of guilt, like I'm not doing the right thing. It doesn't stop me from doing it, but it's there." Rachel, a partner, also expressed these feel-

ings after watching a re-enactment of her behavior in a skit presented by support staff at the annual Christmas party. In the skit,
one secretary dressed up as Rachel and another dressed up as
Michael, one of the senior partners. The secretary portraying
Michael imitated his walk and his mannerisms and ran around the
stage barking orders and singing, "I'm Michael Bond, I'm such a
busy man. I'm such a busy man." The other secretary followed suit
by barking orders and singing, "I'm Rachel Rosen, I'm such a busy
man, I mean woman. I'm such a busy man, I mean woman."

The skit pokes fun at both Michael and Rachel. However, for
Rachel, the humor has a double edge, depicting her not only as a
tyrant barking orders to her subordinates but as a woman who is
confused about her gender identity—is she a man or is she a
woman? Or, more accurately, is she an attorney, or is she a woman?
Michael responded to this spoof in stride, teasing the secretary for
imitating him. Rachel, on the other hand, was very upset:

> It gave me sudden insight into how people see my personality. I guess I
> didn't know that's how people saw me—as this abusive tyrant. I didn't say
> anything at the time, but I felt terrible. And I feel guilty. I have high stan-
> dards, and I believe in doing the best job possible, but I don't like the idea
> that I'm hurting people in the process.

Although Rachel embraced the aggressive component of gamesmanship, she felt guilty about doing so when she realized it would hurt
other people's feelings.

Many of the women I interviewed who fell into the second category were aware of the conflict between their personal morality and
the adversarial role. Yolanda described it in this way:

> Personal relationships are important to me. I like my colleagues, I like
> my secretary. And then there's court, I love going to court. I like drama,
> getting dressed up, playing the role. But sometimes it's hard. When I
> worked for the district attorney's office, I prosecuted a lot of poor people,
> Black people. As an African-American woman, I had problems with that.
> People were always telling me, "Yolanda, you're not down for the commu-
> nity." I didn't like thinking about that, that's why I got out. Now, I defend
> the company, it's different.
> *How is it different?*
> I don't prosecute poor people any more. But the conflict is still there, it's

just not as great. Now I defend Bonhomie and we all know what a pristine, innocent, and pure-as-snow company it is. [*Laughs.*] I don't like knowing what I do hurts people.

Similarly, Mary said:

Sometimes I feel the conflict, sometimes I don't. I'm from the Midwest. People are more down to earth in the midwest, more concerned about other people. I know it's a stereotype. . . . Anyway, I try to be a Midwesterner. But it doesn't always work. You know, if you really don't like the other side—no problem. But when it's less black and white, I don't know. Once I did a [personal injury case]. The woman [the plaintiff] really got hurt, and it was definitely the company's fault. But she didn't have a good lawyer. I got the company off on a technicality. I didn't sleep nights after that one. [*Sighs.*] And I'd be lying if I said I still didn't feel guilty about it.

By splitting roles between conforming to masculine norms of gamesmanship in relations with opposing counsel and clients and adopting a caring orientation in the office, the behavior of the women in the second category contradicts Kanter's thesis about the behavior of token women. While these women seemingly conform to the masculine norms, thereby making themselves less visible in Kanter's formulation, their behavior toward support staff and colleagues in the office and the expression of their Gilliganesque concern for relationships suggests that they have not fully assimilated the masculine demands of the profession. Their behavior and expressed feelings underscore instead a fundamental conflict between the adversarial role and their personal feelings about the importance of relationships, civility, and fair play.

Like these women, the male lawyers in the second group accepted adversarial tactics in the courtroom. However, they did not split roles—their behavior did not take a more relational tone in the office. They did not pursue friendships with secretaries, remember birthdays of colleagues or support staff, bake cakes, or buy flowers. Nor did they embrace the adversarial model enthusiastically. Instead, they expressed a distanced attitude toward their courtroom behavior. One lawyer commented dryly on his use of adversarial tactics: "I put on my mask for battle. I parry, I thrust. I score. It's like fencing." His lack of affect contrasts sharply with lawyers who describe their victories and strategies with vigor and enthusiasm. Similarly, Nathan, another lawyer, said, "I've done it so many times, it's like going through the motions. I turn on when I go to court. When I come back to the office, I shut down. It's a male thing." Another lawyer described the emotional dimension of the job as "the lubricant. It's like oiling a bicycle wheel to keep it from squeaking." These men perform the requisite emotional labor in the courtroom, but they appeared to remove themselves from it. By distancing themselves, they have created an additional component to emotional labor. Not only do they treat other people as objects to manipulate, but they seem to regard their own feelings and behavior in the same way.

Robert Connell (1990) made a similar observation about men in the Australian environmental movement. In his study, Connell found that despite these men's encounter with feminism and their personal attempts to "remake masculinity," they continued to encounter personal dilemmas. For example, although a man might have learned from feminists to listen to his body and treat his body better, he still tended to treat his body as a "naturally constituted object" (1990: 469). For example, one of his interviewees went so far as to talk about his body and "me" as if they were two separate people. Similarly, male lawyers tended to talk about themselves and their feelings as if they were separate entities. Moreover, unlike women who expressed a conflict between their personal morality and the adversarial role, these men remained uncritical of the legal profession. As one remarked dryly, "That's just the way it is." And another said, "It's a job." Finally, in contrast to women litigators, they objectified not only other people but their own personal feelings and behavior.

Talk Like a Lawyer, Think Like a Lawyer, Act Like a Lawyer

The third and smallest group of women lawyers (16 percent) emulated the behavior of aggressive male litigators in the courtroom and in the office. Jack and Jack describe this type of woman lawyer as one who "accepted the male model and tried to mold herself to fit its dictates" (1988: 269). In their study, women who fell in this category "minimize the caring self . . . [and made themselves] talk like a lawyer, think like a lawyer, act like a lawyer" (1988: 270). This particular model of behavior has been encouraged in popular advice books and articles written for career women (Harrigan 1977; Strachan 1984). For example, in an article in the American Bar Association Journal, a female attorney advises women who want to succeed in a "man's world" to establish themselves as committed and competent professionals by doing top quality work, working long hours, and never shirking late hours or weekend projects. In addition, she suggests rejecting any association with the traditional female role:

Don't go home to cook dinner—or if you do, don't tell anyone. Keep your personal life in the background. . . . Never make excuses based on the needs of a spouse or children. Dress and talk in a conservative and professional manner. . . . Dress like a lawyer. Don't chew gum. When called "dear" or flirted with in business meetings or professional situations, respond only with entirely professional business-like statements, so that all communications are placed on and remain on a highly professional plane. [And finally] Don't think of yourself, or allow anyone to think of you, as anything but a hard driving, capable lawyer. (Strachan 1984: 94–95; passage reordered from original)

The women who fell into the third category closely adhered to the male standard for success. Not only did they adopt hardball tactics in the courtroom, but unlike women lawyers who reshaped or split the adversarial role, they maintained "professional working relationships" with their secretaries and paralegals. Kathryn, for example, said, "I'm not friends with my secretary and I don't intend to be. It's simply a working relationship." And another asked rhetorically, "Why should I be friends with her? She's my secretary." In addition, these women strongly rejected seeing themselves as women lawyers. Kathryn believed, "Being a woman is just not an issue. I never think that because I happen to be a woman, blah, blah, blah will happen." Such a gender-neutral view carried over to her experience of discrimination:

Discrimination? Sometimes clients will say that it's odd to have a woman on the case. But I don't pay attention to that. You just get in there, roll up your sleeves, and you do the work. I worked hard, I put in the hours and I made partner. In fact, I was the first woman partner in this department. But being a woman had nothing to do with it.

Candace, another partner from the private firm, echoed Kathryn's
sentiment about discrimination:

Of course, it bothers me. So does nuclear war. But the bottom line is that I
can't do anything about it. All day long, this client avoids my phone calls because he thinks women are incompetents. Hell, it bothers me, but I can't
let myself dwell on it, because dwelling on it just depresses me. So I focus
on my work. That's what women have to do, work and work hard!

*It sounds like you use a lot of energy to keep these feelings beneath the
surface.*

To survive I have to *not* think about all these things. If I did I would go
crazy.

Both these women deny discrimination is a significant factor, though
in slightly different ways. Candace acknowledges its existence but
doesn't let herself dwell on it and focuses instead upon her work.
Kathryn simply refuses to pay attention to it. For both women, "hard
work" is viewed as the key to their success—being a woman has
nothing to do with it.

Candace's gender-neutral stance appears less firm than Kathryn's,
however. Earlier in the chapter, she mentioned she was lucky to get
clients—"Other women weren't so lucky." In addition to recognizing
the differences women face in getting clients, Candace also appears
to falter when discussing discrimination. The intensity of feeling behind her statements, such as "Hell, it bothers me, but I can't let myself dwell on it," suggests anger, not denial. Over coffee several days
after the interview, Candace told me she had been thinking about
the psychological costs being a lawyer posed:

You asked some really difficult questions. I really had forgotten how much
anger I've buried over the years about what happened to the woman who
became a lawyer. I've fought so hard to be recognized as a lawyer—not a
woman lawyer. I actually used to be flattered when people told me I think
like a man. But a couple of years ago my ten-year-old daughter told me that
I acted just like a lawyer when I was helping her with her homework. She
was not paying me a compliment. I felt it meant I'd become some awful
caricature of a man totally unconcerned with the feelings of other
people. . . . To be a lawyer, somewhere along the way, I made a decision
that it meant acting like a man. To do that I squeezed the female part of me
into a box, put on the lid, and tucked it away. I see these young women like
Jessie, talking about being a woman and doing law in a different way.

Sometimes I admire her spirit and self-confidence, and sometimes I think she's very naive. I couldn't do the things that she does. Twenty years of socialization doesn't disappear over night.
Socialization as a lawyer?
[*Laughs.*] I was going to say as a man, but I guess it's the same thing.

Candace's metaphor for her femininity—squeezing it into a box, putting on the lid, and tucking it away—is similar to those used by the women lawyers in Jack and Jack's (1988) study who denied their relational needs. For example, Jane, one of the women who described herself as a workaholic, observed:

Because of the age I was in, my confusion was that I thought it [a relationship] was feminine and I thought that's what I was denying, and then I would achieve success and pursue things just as a male. All I had to do was deny the feminine, okay? Well, as I come along, I've decided that what I'm denying is not necessarily male or female but is human, and to be a whole person you don't go around denying need and love and nurturing and those kinds of relationship things. I just denied it all because I was intent on succeeding. That's what I did and it took a couple of major traumas for me to step back and look at it. (1988: 275)

Initially, Jane associates relationships with femininity and regards them as an obstacle to success. If she could deny that aspect of herself, then she could "pursue things just as a male." Both Jane and Candace appear to reexamine what it means to deny that part of themselves. Jane attempts to reclaim the formerly denied self, renaming it as human. Candace appears more ambivalent. She doesn't like the implication of her daughter's statement that she "acts just like a lawyer." Further, she admires women lawyers like Jessie who attempt to reshape the adversarial role. However, she also thinks Jessie is sometimes naive and doubts whether she could ever practice law the way Jessie does.

The women in the third category most closely approximate Kanter's predictions about the behavior of tokens. However, these women also represented the smallest group of women lawyers numerically—only 16 percent fell into this category. Moreover, while these women have conformed outwardly to the male model, they have strong feelings about the personal costs such conformity has entailed, feelings that are related to gender. It is femininity that is put in a box and tucked away or denied.

These styles are similar to the behavior of men in the third group who emphatically embraced the adversarial model. They considered aggression and strategic friendliness to be central and acceptable parts of the job. Bill, a young associate explained, "I do my best work when I hate the other side. The more obnoxious they are, the harder I work against them." Bill has no interest in changing the nature of the relationship with opposing counsel. He doesn't believe that you can trust the other side and has no interest in trying. "They lie all the time—that's the way it is."

In addition, the men in this category strongly reject alternatives to the adversarial model. When I asked one man whether he had ever utilized any means to resolve disputes other than adversarial tactics, he responded, "That's pie in the sky. Everyone can't win. There are winners and losers in litigation. It's zero-sum. And I want my client to win." Similarly, when I asked a partner what he liked best about his job, he said:

Winning for sure. Of course, you usually only win part of the case, not the whole thing. But winning is definitely emotionally satisfying—it's emotionally satisfying to know you did it.

For these men, the adversarial model and its emotional requirements were viewed unproblematically as part of the job. John, a middle-aged junior partner summed up the situation in this way:

Sometimes I hear these young lawyers complaining about how aggressive and sleazy other attorneys are. But you have to be aggressive and sneaky in this business. It's part of the job. People who don't like it should stop whining or get the hell out.

For these men, conforming to the adversarial model does not pose any personal costs. Whereas women in this category felt that adopting the adversarial role involved suppressing their gender identity, men saw the role as a natural extension of their masculinity. For example, John asserts later in the same interview, "No offense, but [women] just don't have the balls to be tough litigators. It's just one of those things that men do better. Women are good at writing briefs." Similarly, Bill not only embraces the adversarial role but describes it as "something men get into." "You've got to be tough and ruthless. Most women can't do that."

In this section, I have shown that female attorneys perform a more varied range of emotional labor. Existing theoretical accounts do not adequately explain the variation in the behavior of these women lawyers. While Kanter's proposition that women conform to male norms of the legal profession describes the behavior of women in the third group, it does not account for those who split roles or those who reshaped the adversarial model. Similarly, Gilligan's social psychological theory explains why some women created alternative, caring practices of lawyering, but it does not explain why others did not. How then can we explain the variation in behavior?

To answer this question, the experiences of women attorneys must be theorized as a dynamic relationship between occupational structure, behavior, and identity. Gender is an integral part of this analysis. In my explanation, gender shapes the experiences of women lawyers at the level of occupational structure while legal workers reproduce gender in their interactions with one another. At the structural level, female litigators find themselves a token minority in a male-dominated occupation, encountering a professional socialization and a career track based on a male model of success. They must contend with boundary heightening, and they face contradictory messages about the appropriate display of emotional labor: when they adopt gamesmanship strategies they are criticized for "unladylike" and "shrill" behavior, but when they are "nice" or "pleasant," they are judged "not tough enough" to be good lawyers.

The double bind women attorneys invariably experience explains, in part, the variation in their behavior. There are simply no clear-cut "feeling rules" for women lawyers. Nor is there any one form of acceptable emotional labor for them. Whether they closely adhere to the adversarial model or not, they garner criticism, disapproval, and even ostracism. However, assuming that structure determines behavior in a simple one-to-one relationship denies agency to social actors and neglects the continuous and reciprocal relationship between the two levels of analysis. To improve upon this theoretical weakness, I view the masculinized structure of the legal profession as setting limits on female litigators' behavior. Some women attorneys cross over these boundaries, others move within and around them, and still others remain safely inside the lines.

Regardless of which strategy women select, their negotiation within these limits poses a nagging question: How can I be a lawyer and at the same time be a woman? Answering this question entails choosing behavior congruent with their notions of gender-appropriate behavior—which is not necessarily the same thing as behaving in traditionally female ways. Socialization in a masculinized profession has provided these women with life experiences as well as an education that provides them an array of choices for "doing gender" (West and Zimmerman 1987). Women lawyers who split roles do gender in accordance with professional norms in the courtroom and with their conceptions of feminine behavior in the office. Those who adopt a more relational orientation reshape the adversarial role to be consistent with their notions of how law ought to be practiced and their sense of how women as traditional caregivers should do law. Finally, even the women who adopt the role of the professional combatant do gender by accepting the advice for women lawyers that encourages them to establish themselves as competent professionals and to downplay their association with the traditional female role. Ironically, this group of women sought to be lawyers and women by minimizing the feminine side of themselves.

Despite the variation among women lawyers in doing gender, there is also some continuity, notably their recurring concern with relationships. Those who sought to reshape the adversarial role as well as those who split the role expressed a relational orientation. Although it is most strongly expressed by women who actively sought to create alternatives to the adversarial model, it is also expressed by women who emphasize the importance of relationships in the office. Even the women who most closely adhered to the male model of success expressed misgivings and ambivalence about denying the relational part of themselves.

This recurring concern with relationships supports Chodorow's theory of feminine gender-identity. In her formulation, women develop a sense of self as empathic and nurturant through the early mother-daughter relationship. As a consequence, feminine identity comes to be defined through attachment and relations to others. For some women litigators, this sense of self is expressed in their alternative practice of law, for others in their relationships in the office, and for still others in their continuing preoccupation with relational issues despite their adherence to the male model.

While Chodorow's theory sheds light on this common theme, it does not explain why some women lawyers are more relational than others because it does not theorize the influence of the workplace on personality. However, by integrating her concept of gender-identity within this historically specific occupational context, the continuity and variation in women's behavior can be explained by theorizing a dynamic relationship between occupational structure, behavior, and gender identity. In a dynamic understanding, the male-dominated legal profession poses a double bind for women in the performance of emotional labor, thereby setting gendered limits on their behavior. In response, women lawyers actively construct an emotional style that is consistent with their notion of gender-appropriate behavior and is informed in some way by their sense of self as relational or feminine. Women attorneys negotiate in and around the gendered constraints of the legal profession, reproducing gender in their interactions with others by constructing a more caring practice of lawyering, creating more humane and caring relations with office staff, or simply becoming preoccupied with relational issues.

This alternative explanation also applies to the behavior of male litigators. Structurally, the gendering of the legal profession is advantageous for men, who are more likely than women to be located in positions of power within the firm and to find a homogeneous working environment. Moreover, the culture of the firm (i.e., the old-boy network) and the pacing of career development are congruent with their interests and lifestyles as men. In addition, they have access to informal social networks that women do not, which can lead to important case assignments and potential contacts for new clients. Furthermore, male attorneys do not encounter sex discrimination or sexual harassment, and they do not face a double bind in the performance of emotional labor; there is no conflict between their gender-identity as men and the emotional requirements of the adversarial role.

The gendered structure of the legal profession benefits men politically and economically, suggesting that men have greater incentives than women do to embrace the adversarial role and its emotional requirements. As this chapter shows, most male litigators adhered to the adversarial model in practice. Men do not automatically fall in line with the practices of the profession but instead make active choices within this socially and historically specific occupational structure; some embrace the adversarial role, some adopt a more distanced relation to it, and a small minority criticize or reject it. Moreover, their choice is influenced not only by the demands of the legal profession and the benefits it holds for them as men but also by their thinking about masculinity.

Incorporating Chodorow's theory of masculine gender-identity further enhances our understanding of the way men do gender in this specific occupational context. In her formulation, a masculine gender-identity emerges as a sense of self as separate and autonomous from mother, as "not female." As I argued in Chapter 3, intimidation and strategic friendliness are utilized for the purpose of winning a case. Male litigators' constant focus on winning cases, the size and amounts of wins, and bragging about other types of accomplishments and achievements all serve as ways for men to distinguish themselves as autonomous and separate from others and as "manly" men. Moreover, their lack of interest in creating friendships with support staff can be read as another assertion of autonomy and denial of relatedness. And finally, their use of boundary heightening emphasizes the differences between themselves and women lawyers and also serves as a means to repeatedly distinguish themselves as men. Thus, gender shapes the experiences of male litigators at the level of occupational structure at the same time that men reproduce gender through the performance of emotional labor and through boundary heightening with women.

In this theoretical account, gender shapes the experiences of women and men attorneys at the level of occupational structure, behavior, and identity. In other words, gender at once organizes and is organized by social processes in the occupation.

Conclusion

The findings in this chapter demonstrate that women face different structural constraints in the legal profession than men do. Women are the numerical minority in this profession. They are less likely than men to hold positions of power within the firm and more likely to make less money. In addition, they experience having their status deflated, have more difficulty in creating new business contacts, experience sexual harassment, and face obstacles to balancing work and family.

These differences also operate on a more subtle level. Women face a double standard that men do not in displaying occupationally appropriate emotional labor. Whereas men are praised for using intimidation and strategic friendliness, women are not. Women who are aggressive are censured for being difficult to get along with and women who are nice are "not tough enough" to be good litigators. Similarly, women who utilize strategic friendliness are accused of using their feminine wiles to get their way.

Finally, women and men perform different kinds of emotional labor. As a group, women did not embrace the adversarial role as emphatically as men did. Some sought to reshape the adversarial role (26 percent), some "split" roles (58 percent), and a minority (16 percent) adhered to the male model. Neither Gilligan's (1982) social psychological account nor Kanter's (1977) structural thesis alone can explain this variation. To make sense of these findings, I have proposed a dynamic theory which examines the interplay of gender between the structural and individual levels of analysis. Doing gender is the mediating link between these two levels of social relations. These levels are distinct only analytically, however. In day-to-day experiences in the law firm, they are continuous and reciprocal. Sex discrimination as a structural practice has obvious consequences for individual women. And masculine gender-identity, as a complex of practices and consciousness, shapes the universe of collective action, including boundary heightening and other practices which exclude women. Furthermore, the reproduction of gender among litigators is not a smooth or uncontested process. Although women face strong pressures to conform to professional norms, they do not passively acquiesce to them. Their alternative practice of law, which values an ethic of caring and mutual respect, and their efforts to create a more humane office environment at once challenge and disrupt the male defined adversarial role and norms for professionalism.

Chapter Six

Gendering Consent and Resistance in Paralegal Work

According to Kanter (1977), tokenism emerges in groups that are highly skewed, with a preponderance of one group of workers, the dominants, over another, the tokens.[1] Male paralegals, like women lawyers, are tokens—they represent the numerical minority in this feminized occupation. As I discussed in the previous chapter, Kanter's thesis suggests that tokens face greater performance pressures on the job because they encounter more scrutiny than their counterparts in the numerical majority. For example, in response to their greater conspicuousness, women managers in her study attempted to limit their visibility by being more secretive, less independent, and less oppositional. In both the private firm and in the legal department at Bonhomie Corporation, male legal assistants as token members of the occupation are treated in dissimilar ways from women, face divergent expectations, and do different kinds of emotional labor. However, unlike the female managers in Kanter's study, male paralegals do not attempt to limit their visibility within the occupation or conform to the behavior of the numerically dominant group. Nor do they encounter the exclusionary practices Kanter's women executives faced.

These findings corroborate recent feminist scholarship suggesting that the experiences of male and female tokens are not equivalent (Zimmer 1988; Williams 1989, 1993). Williams (1989), for example, finds that compared to female marines, male nurses strive to be visible in their field by emphasizing their masculinity and by occupying the few high-status positions within the occupation. This chapter also considers how male tokens reproduce gender in a feminized occupation, and it shares Williams's psychoanalytic interpretation of gender identity. However, my argument departs from hers in theorizing a dynamic relationship between occupational structure, behavior and gender identity.

This chapter begins by examining how gender influences the positioning of paralegals in the occupational structure, their treatment by their employers, and the expectations they face about the emotional division of labor. Next, it focuses on legal assistants themselves, who do gender through their interactions with others in the firm and by performing emotional labor. In the final section, the strategies paralegals utilize to resist emotional degradation on the job are explored. As I will argue, even when paralegals resist the "feeling rules" implicit in their occupational life, the individualized coping strategies they choose serve to reproduce the gendering of the labor process within law firms.

Gendering Constraint and Consent

Among paralegals, gender shapes the internal stratification of the occupation: men are more likely than women to hold positions of influence and authority. This suggests that among legal assistants, much as in other occupations and professions, an internal hierarchy exists wherein men occupy the "good" jobs, and women, the "bad" ones (Bielby and Baron 1984; Reskin and Roos 1987). For example, in research on lawyers, sociologists have found that men and women are located within different specialties: men were found in the highly paid, prestigious specialties, such as litigation, whereas women were more likely to found in less prestigious, lower-paying areas, such as family law (Podomore and Spencer 1986; Epstein 1983). Among paralegals this finding is especially striking, given that the occupation is female-dominated and that only a few such positions existed in any one firm. For example, in the legal department at Bonhomie Corporation, Brian, a paralegal, was the managing partner's "right-hand man," privy to information such as how and why various department political decisions were made, who would make partner, and who was going to be hired. Bonhomie employees without access to the managing partner relied heavily on Brian for information about internal political struggles. Similarly, at the private firm, Kenny worked for one of San Francisco's most successful and influential litigators. His boss's influence in the legal community as well as within the firm gave Kenny a certain amount of informal influence. He knew when new business came into the firm, what was going on in other firms across the city, and so on. Only one woman at both field sites held a managerial position—she was the paralegal coordinator. She was highly regarded by attorneys for her slavish devotion to cases and her ability to smooth over conflict between attorneys and paralegals, but not for her political savvy or influence. In fact, she had very little autonomous decision making power either formally or informally and was rarely consulted about department politics.

Men not only found themselves in different positions within the occupational hierarchy, but they were also treated differently by virtue of their gender. Because they were men, male paralegals were often mistaken for attorneys; because most secretaries are women, female paralegals were often mistaken for secretaries. Female paralegals, like some women lawyers, reported that they were asked to type things for attorneys. When they said that they weren't secretaries, lawyers expressed surprise—but rarely apologized for the misunderstanding. Some attorneys, in typical adversarial style, even persisted—"Can't you just do it anyway? My secretary is leaving in five minutes." Here, the experiences of token male paralegals contrast sharply with those of women lawyers and legal assistants. Male lawyers often assumed that male paralegals were attorneys or, at least, law-school bound. For men who worked as paralegals, their gender inflated the perception of their occupational role. For women paralegals and for women lawyers, as Chapter 5 showed, gender deflated such perceptions.

These status differences were also played out more informally. Male legal assistants, unlike women lawyers or women paralegals, were often invited to go out for drinks with male partners and associates after work, to play on the firm softball team, or to go to sporting events together, such as baseball and basketball games. These informal get-togethers were a means of getting to know the attorney better who might write a letter of recommendation for professional school, provide one with more interesting work assignments, or affirm work performance. One male paralegal, for example, managed to finagle his way out of a deadly boring case into a more interesting assignment. Women were rarely included in these events. These differences in informal patterns of socializing also contradict Kanter's analysis. In her account, secretaries and other workers in positions of blocked mobility tend to socialize among themselves, whereas managers moving up the corporate ladder tend to socialize upward in an effort to advance their careers. Female paralegals socialized together and sometimes with secretaries; however, male legal assistants often chose not to do so.

Men's choice not to socialize within their own occupational group challenges Kanter on a related point. She describes how members of a dominant group heighten boundaries between themselves and the token to exaggerate differences. This is not the case with female and male paralegals. Women actively sought to include the men in lunches, breaks, and other social activities. Although there was some socializing, men often opted out because they were bored with women's conversations: "They talk about boring things—their children, buying new clothes—you know, girl stuff." Others said they preferred to see friends outside the office. When I asked a twenty-six-year-old gay man whether he socialized with the women, he said:

Sometimes it's fun sitting around with the girls. We compare notes on who is the best-looking [male] attorney . . . and laugh and have a good time. But other times I feel contemptuous.
    Why?
    Well, they're straight. They live in Marin County and I live in the Castro. My identity is there, and my friends are dying there. I think about it a lot. . . . Some of the women are sympathetic [about AIDS], but it's not their friends who are dying. . . . I think some straight women like to think that gay men are "special" men.
    Meaning?
    That we are not like other men because we're oppressed. Like we share some similar identity, but we don't.

In this case, he was included but chose to emphasize his difference—his identity as a gay man—and downplay the presumption of similarity.

This contrasted sharply with my own experience. When I managed to include myself in one of the all-male get togethers, the boundaries between me and the men in the group were immediately erected through the initial joking remark made by Daniel, one of the attorneys: "Jennifer's here. I guess we'll have to swap recipes or something." When I made an effort to talk about another topic—movies—Daniel quickly retorted: "Oh, I bet you only like love stories." When I pointed out that I preferred "thrillers," I was ignored. As the lone female in an all-male group, the men foisted difference upon me, thereby excluding me. Male paralegals were included by the women but chose to exclude themselves. Thus, it is not simply the significance of being a numerical minority that determines treatment and behavior but the gender of the "minority group" that must be considered. In law firms, male tokens such as paralegals are treated more favorably than are female tokens.

These differences in status also resulted in a gendered division of labor. Women were expected to be more nurturing than men. Lawyers were more likely to confide their personal problems in women paralegals. Several women, in fact, were referred to as this or that attorney's "therapist." Men were relied upon not to care for lawyers' bruised feelings but to serve as political advisers and yes-men. They were expected to provide political information and gossip to protect their boss's interests. Theirs was a less personal, more rational mode of conduct. This does not mean emotional labor was not required of them, however. As Peter Lyman reminds us, "Rationality is not a dispassionate emotional state, but takes its latent structure in the repression of anger" (1984: 1).

The basis for gender-appropriate emotional labor among legal assistants lies in the degree of affective engagement. Being affectively neutral or polite is acceptable for men but not for women. As a consequence, men must put a lid on expressing deep emotion. For example, attorneys repeatedly criticized one male paralegal for his "giddy" and "flamboyant" behavior. While other paralegals and secretaries were amused by his imitations of the "church lady" from the television show *Saturday Night Live*, the attorneys were not. As he said to me in his interview, "They're always telling me to tone it down. Attorneys are so serious. . . . You'd think this place was a funeral parlor or something." This "feeling rule" for male inexpressivity reflects larger cultural conceptions of masculinity (Sattel 1982).

By contrast, women are expected to be affectively engaged. This can be demonstrated through behavior such as "being nice" or through facial displays such as smiling. As I discussed in Chapter 4, women were repeatedly admonished to express their engagement by smiling. Similarly, women were also subtly prodded to humor attorneys, flirt with them, or pay "special" attention to them. One twenty-seven-year-old woman paralegal said that David, an attorney, was "always trying to get me to pay attention to him." She said he was always asking her, " 'Did you notice my new tie?' Or, 'My new office furniture?' Or, 'My new car?'"

An older woman commented,

After Mark [a twenty-six-year-old associate] gives me an assignment, he just stands around in my office like this little boy waiting for something. . . . When I ask "What's up?" he'll say, "Oh, nothing." But he keeps standing there looking hopeful.

Another woman complained about the partner she works for:

Jerry drives me absolutely crazy—he's such a blabbermouth, he never shuts up. He hates it when I ignore him and try and do my own work. He just can't stand not to be noticed.

These descriptions are reminiscent of the early mother-child relationship. Mothers coo and smile at their babies, and babies coo and smile in response. As the infant gets older and begins to take its first steps away from mother, she continues looking back to mother for recognition and support (Mahler, Pine and Bergman 1975). Similarly, male attorneys look to female paralegals for recognition—Notice me, smile at me—as if they were actually their mothers. As Hochschild writes: "The world turns to women for mothering, and this fact silently attaches itself to many a job description" (1983: 170).

Unlike smiling and being nice, anger is not acceptable for a woman. The job requires that paralegals manage anger—their own and that of attorneys. However, as Hochschild observes there is a double standard in the perception of anger: "When a man expresses anger, it is deemed rational. . . . When women express an equivalent degree of anger, it is more likely to be interpreted as a sign of emotional instability" (1983: 173). In my findings, this double standard appeared in the form of an invisible threshold. Men were given more leeway than women to express anger. Both men and women paralegals were expected to manage their anger. However, in the case of Joe discussed in Chapter 4, it was not until he blew up in response to the attorney's needling that he was sanctioned for his behavior. For women, this threshold occurs sooner. Anna, for example, spent three weeks working on a trial with her boss in Las Vegas. On the return trip, while they were both completely exhausted and were standing in line at the ticket counter with more than twenty-five pieces of luggage, the attorney turned to Anna and said, "Is all my luggage there?" Anna said, "I don't know." He replied, "You mean you didn't count all my bags! Go count it. Make sure it's all there!" Anna who was typically quite pleasant, responded coldly, "I'm not your porter." The lawyer began yelling while they were standing in line, "No one talks to Edgar Markus that way, no one." Anna ignored his tirade and his request. After returning to the office, she was told by the paralegal coordinator that she was being assigned to work for another attorney. Similarly, Karen, another legal assistant, received a stern lecture on her lack of professionalism because she typically answered her phone with a curt "Yes." When she attempted to defend her behavior—she said she was too busy to answer the phone each time with a pleasant "Hello, Karen Anderson speaking," the lawyer screamed, "You do not talk to attorneys with that tone of voice!" and stomped out of her office.

Status differences also translated into differential expectations regarding other deference behaviors, such as invisibility and being treated as if one were stupid. Because male paralegals were more likely to be mistaken for attorneys, they were simply more visible than women paralegals. They had to do less emotional work about being treated as if they were invisible and were shielded from this emotionally degrading aspect of the job. Men were also taken more seriously. Although both women and men had to contend with being treated as if they couldn't understand the finer points of the law, women tended to be denigrated more frequently. Male attorneys referred to various women paralegals as "bimbos," "ditzy," and "Barbie dolls," implying they were sexually attractive but dumb. Male paralegals were sometimes criticized for being "weird" or lacking social skills, but no one called them stupid. This corroborates Schultz (1975) and Lakoff (1975), who found that terms applied to women contain sexual connotations. Schultz (1975) argues that this process of "derogation" has the same characteristics as racial or ethnic slurs, implying that women are viewed as proper subjects for ridicule.

Although men are not ridiculed in this way, some felt embarrassed or defensive about being legal assistants. Being a member of a female-dominated profession does not approximate the masculine ideal of success. When I asked a twenty-six-year-old what he told people he did for a living, he laughed nervously and said, "I just tell them I work for Lyman, Lyman and Portia, and they're impressed. You know, it's a big San Francisco financial-district law firm. If I told them I was just a paralegal, they wouldn't be." Another man, who left the field, told me that he believed male paralegals were treated quite favorably compared to women: "The attorneys always asked me when I planned to go to law school." He interpreted their assumption as a sign of their confidence in his abilities.[2] Other men resented the assumption: "It implies that I haven't accomplished enough, that I should be doing something else." On the other hand, a thirty-year-old who described himself as an artist, not a paralegal, said, "Lawyers always think you should be a lawyer. I used to be offended. Now, I think they lack imagination—they can't imagine anybody would want to be anything else!" Thus, visibility as the male minority meant lawyers made assumptions about their career goals that were not made about female paralegals.

The differences legal assistants faced in expectations correspond roughly to actual gender differences in emotional labor. Women performed what I term a more relational or feminine style of emotional labor that emphasized their concern for others. Men, on the other hand, had a masculine style of emotional labor, which underscored their difference from others as well as their own achievements. These patterns emerged along both the deferential and care-taking dimensions of emotional labor.

Deference involves maintaining a non-critical stance vis-à-vis the attorneys. Along these lines, women tended to do what Pamela Fishman (1978) calls "interaction work." For example, during team meetings, women paralegals listened attentively by nodding their heads and frequently saying "uh huh" and "um hmm." Men listened, but not as actively. They did not attempt to support discussions through verbal assurances but were more likely to be silent and occasionally ask questions about the case in a polite, reserved manner. Women were also more likely to support the attorneys they worked for by saying enthusiastically—"You're doing great," or "You're doing fine." Men said authoritatively: "I think you're doing great." This subtle difference has interesting implications. To say, "I think you're doing great," is an egocentric form of support. It underscores what I think about your behavior. On the other hand, the phrase "You're doing great," reflects a concern with the other person—it's "other-centric." Although both men and women attempted to show their support, they did so in different ways.

This difference is consonant with Carol Gilligan's (1982) work on women's moral decision-making, which finds that women's language is suffused with references to relationships and a concern for others. On the other hand, linguist Robin Lakoff (1975) argues that women's language is often signified by "tag questions" and intensifiers—such as "Don't you think?"—which suggest uncertainty or hesitancy. In my reading, the Gilliganesque interpretation is further supported by the manner in which the statements were made. Male paralegals said "I think" with force and authority, whereas women were more likely to make their statement with warmth and enthusiasm, as is illustrated in the following interchange between an attorney and two paralegals during a meeting: David, a forty-year-old partner, says to two legal assistants,

I've rewritten my opening statement five times and I still don't like it. It's too dry. . . . I need to liven it up for the jury . . . maybe a personal vignette about Max [the defendant] . . . how his hard work transformed his small family business into a successful corporation. . . . How am I doing? Is that any better?

Leslie, a paralegal, responds enthusiastically: "You're doing fine! That will make Max much more sympathetic." Karl, another paralegal, interrupts and says authoritatively, "I think it's a terrific idea!" David nods and says,

> Good, good. I'm also thinking about adding something about the wife. . . . That way I can appeal to the women on the jury too. . . .

Leslie adds, "You're right, you're right. Maybe tell them something about her background, how they met—" Karl interrupts Leslie and says to her, "I don't think so. It will open up too many holes in the defense." Directing his attention back to David, Karl says, "I think you're right. Something about his wife is good, but—"

In each statement, Karl uses "I think" to clearly distinguish his position from Leslie's. Leslie says the attorney is doing fine. Karl thinks the attorney is doing great. Leslie says that adding details about the wife's background is a good idea. Karl doesn't think so, but goes on to support the attorney's original idea with something he, Karl, thinks. In this way, Karl simultaneously differentiates his position from Leslie's and supports David's. Furthermore, Karl's tone of voice underscores that his is a confident assertion rather than a hesitant remark. Thus, Karl's strategy reinforces the attorney's position at the same time that it asserts his own difference from and superiority to the female paralegal, while Leslie's strategy emphasizes authority through connection to David.

Differences also emerged along the caretaking dimension of emotional labor. In terms of being pleasant, women were more likely to be what I call "nice," or affectively engaged, whereas men were more likely to be polite or affectively neutral. Lisa, for example, was the prototypical nice female paralegal. She was warm, friendly, and outgoing. Whenever I saw her in the office hallways, she was cheerful, smiling or laughing appreciatively at people's jokes. She made a point of asking coworkers how they were—attempting to draw them out. She tried to please people by buying flowers for them, remembering their birthdays, cheering them up when they were down, and being helpful. After our interview, she came back several times the following day to tell me additional personal stories that she thought might be "helpful." Bill, on the other hand, represented the ideal type of the polite male paralegal. He was always tactful, courteous, and considerate of other people's feelings, but never overly solicitous. Although he didn't smile much, he gave the appearance of being interested and concerned. I never saw him standing in the hallways to socialize with coworkers. His secretary told me that he ducked unobtrusively into his office most mornings without saying hello to her. "It's not that he's rude," she added quickly, "he's just reserved."

Being polite represents a more aloof version of being nice. The male paralegal is pleasant but distances himself from being nice. He does what Hochschild calls "surface acting," which involves acting as if one has a feeling through facial display, body movement, or tone of voice (1983: 37). Bill shows concern and interest through facial expression. He demonstrates consideration and tact through tone of voice. Another male paralegal, Daniel, describes his demeanor toward an attorney in this way:

I was waiting outside his door to talk to him while he was on the phone. As he talked, I began to imagine the face I wanted to present—calm, serious, competent. I watched my reflection in the plate-glass window and tried out various looks. As Mark said good bye and hung up the telephone, I entered with what I imagined to be the proper politesse, "Can I have a word with you Mark? It's about the American Bank case."

Greg, another male legal assistant, who was far more outgoing than either Bill or Daniel, greeted paralegals and secretaries with a booming hello. Whereas he was openly flirtatious with women paralegals and secretaries, with attorneys he was subdued. "I turn down the volume with them and put on my serious face."

Whereas men do "surface acting" by presenting a particular face or turning down the volume, women do what Hochschild calls "deep acting," that is, actually evoking the feeling itself (1983: 38). Lisa doesn't just smile, but "psyches" herself up to be cheerful and friendly to those around her. In describing herself, she says, "Everyone thinks I'm nice and cheerful all the time, but I'm not. On my bad days I try and think about how they're feeling and what I can do to make them feel better." When I asked Marsha, a twenty-eight-year-old single mother, how she coped with her boss's temper, she said, "I try and remember that he's stressed out about the trial. It's not me he's mad at—it's the craziness of the pre-trial schedule. So when he starts sniping at me, I don't let myself get upset. I try to be nice and considerate." Terry, another woman, said, "Whenever [the attorney] blows up, I try and calm down, think about what I can do, and what I can delegate. . . . If I'm still upset, I keep trying."

Women were also more likely to notice moods and feelings of the lawyers for whom they worked. As one woman paralegal said, "I always try to figure out his mood first thing in the morning—it determines what I do the rest of the day. You know, if he's in a bad mood, I try and hide out in my office." And another woman explained, "I can always tell Mary is going to be a bear to work with if she gives me flowers. She always gives me flowers before she gets stressed out and starts going crazy." By contrast, a male paralegal said, "If I want to know what kind of mood Michael is in, I ask Debbie. He's inscrutable, I just can't figure him out."

In addition to surface acting, male paralegals also distanced themselves from being nice through expressing contempt. Whereas most women said they liked the "people side" of the job, male paralegals were critical of "being nice," or as they called it, "taking shit." For example, Tony, a male paralegal, was openly contemptuous of Jane's behavior. He denigrated her for being "sugar sweet" and refusing to stand up for herself when the attorneys treated her badly. When Jane received a higher raise than Tony did, he was furious: "She doesn't even deserve the raise. She just pretends to be nicey-nice and sweet. She's really just a phoney and a wimp." He then went to the managing partner and complained politely about his raise, arguing that he was at least as qualified as Jane. He also threatened to quit if he didn't get the raise. He received the raise.

Men could get away with being polite instead of nice and bowing out of some of the caretaking, but women could not. Karen was a bright, competent paralegal whose behavior in many ways more closely resembled that of the men. She was somewhat aloof and businesslike in her presentation of self. She didn't smile much and expressed no interest in the personal problems of the attorneys she worked for. Nor did she do "interaction work" in meetings. She was regarded by the partner for whom she worked as "uncooperative" and was given a raise that reflected as much. When she inquired about what had happened, she was told that she had an "attitude problem." Concerned, Karen pressed to find out what precisely this meant: "If they think I'm not doing my job, I'd like to know about it, and if I've hurt someone's feelings, I'd like to know about that, too." However, neither her boss nor anyone else would tell her anything more specific. She eventually left the firm.

Women were aware that men were exempt from mothering the attorneys. They were also aware of the psychological consequences of the expectation that they provide mothering services. A thirty-four-year-old woman who had worked for both a private firm and Bonhomie Corporation said: "It's a lot of stress trying to figure these people out all the time. Their personalities are like that of small children, and we're like their mothers or their servants. 'Get me this, Get me that.' . . . It's disgusting." A thirty-two-year-old woman from the legal department at Bonhomie Corporation grumbled: "I hate that [expectation]. But with some attorneys, it's very significant that you be that way." Some women did not make the effort. Mary Ann, for example, said, "To [the attorney I work for], a paralegal is a mother. He could never understand why I didn't want to play 'Mom.' He didn't like that about me. A lot of attorneys are like that." Another woman said, "I just don't do it! [mother the attorneys] I have to produce billable hours just like the attorneys. I don't waste my time. . . ." A third woman described herself as "always fighting it [the expectation] off." Despite their complaints, most women found themselves engaged to some degree in doing this type of emotional labor. At one end of the continuum, 10 percent of women, like Karen and Mary Ann, refused to have any part in it. Next were the women, more than half of the group, who grudgingly went through the motions but complained. At the other end of the continuum, there were the women like Lisa, more than a third of the total, who were the epitome of niceness.

Why do some women feel compelled to perform this aspect of emotional labor and others do not? To answer this question, I draw from the theoretical account developed in Chapter 5. Structurally, at the most basic level, women paralegals must comply with "feeling rules" because of the gendered constraints they encounter in the occupation. However, they do not respond in a uniform way. At the level of behavior and identity, women perform different kinds of emotional labor as a way of doing gender, that is, a way of interacting that is consistent with their notions of gender-appropriate behavior. Some women remain safely and unambivalently within the boundaries of their feminized occupation by doing gender in accordance with the traditional female caregiving role, but others do gender by adopting a more distanced relation to the limits, performing the requisite feminized labor nonetheless. And finally, a small group of women cross over the boundaries, refusing to heed the limits. Like women lawyers who adhered to the male model, women in this last group do gender by being professional—in other words, by acting more like their male counterparts—and by downplaying any association with the traditional female role.

Despite this variation in behavior, these women share a common concern with relationships. For those who conform to the feminized socio-emotional requirements, ambivalently or not, a relational or feminine style of emotional labor serves to emphasize connection with others through language, reassurance, attentiveness to the moods and feelings of others, and "being nice." On the other hand, women who do not behave relationally remain psychologically preoccupied with these issues; even though their behavior approximates that of male paralegals, when relationships break down, they still express concern. Chodorow's theory of gender identity helps us to understand this concern. In her psychoanalytic understanding, women develop a sense of self as empathic and nurturant through the early mother-daughter relationship. As a consequence, feminine identity comes to be defined through attachment and relation to others. For some women paralegals, this sense of self is expressed through the performance of emotional labor, and for others, in their continuing preoccupation with relational issues.

Chodorow's theory alone, however, which does not address the link between occupational structure and personality, cannot explain why women behave relationally in some contexts and not in others. By theorizing a dynamic relationship between occupational structure, behavior, and gender identity, women can be understood to respond actively and creatively to the gendered limits set by their occupation, as they construct a style of emotional labor that is congruent with their notion of gender-appropriate behavior and informed by their sense of self as relational or feminine. In this dynamic account, gender shapes the structure of the occupation by setting limits on women's behavior. At the same time, women negotiate within and around these limits, reproducing gender in their interactions with others by being nice, reassuring, and attentive to the feelings of others, or simply through their preoccupation with relational issues.

This argument also applies to the behavior of male paralegals, who must also comply with emotional norms. However, as men in a feminized occupation they face different norms and expectations. Male paralegals are assumed to be more qualified for positions of authority within the occupation, more career oriented, and more intelligent. And they are often able to get away with doing different kinds of emotional labor than women (e.g., with being "polite" rather than "nice," and playing the role of "political adviser" rather than nurturing therapist). Furthermore, men also accrue a number of advantages by virtue of being able to socialize informally with male attorneys, which sometimes leads to more interesting work assignments, letters of recommendation for professional school, and personal recognition and affirmation for their work.

The contradictions inherent in doing gender in a female-dominated job explain in part why male paralegals choose to exclude themselves from women's social activities and why they express contempt for their "nicey-nice" female counterparts. They do gender in these ways to emphasize their differences as men and downplay any similarity to their women coworkers.

The concept of doing gender is further informed by the assumption that men have a sense of self as masculine. Chodorow's (1978) theory of gender identity suggests that masculine gender identity emerges through a definition of self as separate from the mother—as "not female." A masculine style of emotional labor emphasizes difference and self-assertion through emphatic language such as "I think" and through mechanisms such as contempt, politeness, and surface-acting, which distance men from the feminine aspects of the job. Moreover, men further emphasize difference by choosing to exclude themselves from all-female, informal social activities. While men accrue benefits structurally by engaging in such exclusionary practices, doing gender in this way also serves to affirm and enhance their gender identity as masculine.

Gendered Strategies of Resistance

In the Legal Department, there are two kinds of employees: the attorneys and non-attorneys. When you fill out all forms, vouchers, overtime slips and work requests, designate your status. Status determines priority.
Personnel Director, Bonhomie Corporation

When I first started working at the private firm I overheard one attorney ask another who I was. "Oh, her," he said. "She's just a paralegal."
Liz

Kill the lawyers.
Plaque on paralegal's desk

The reproduction of gender in corporate law firms and legal departments is not a smooth or uncontested process. Because the designation "non-attorney" connotes subordinate status, paralegals, like other support staff, such as secretaries, library assistants, case clerks and copy-machine operators, have fewer rights to entitlement and respect on the job than attorneys do, and many express dissatisfaction about this inequity. Female legal assistants, in particular, resent the gendered division of emotional labor. As a result, paralegals do not comply with feeling rules without some ambivalence, conflict, or resistance. This section describes litigation paralegals' dissatisfaction with the emotional dimension of their job, and examines the strategies they employ to resist and/or cope with the feeling rules implicit in their occupational life.

Paralegals reported feelings of strain, anger, ambivalence, and alienation about their jobs. On the average, they spent twice as much time in their interviews complaining about what they did not like about their work as describing what they did like. Mary Ann, a thirty-six-year-old legal assistant described in a single sentence what she liked: "The opportunity to research case law." Her typed, single-spaced interview transcript goes on for two pages listing her complaints:

Recently, I have decided that I want out. . . . I don't like much about it. Attorneys are stressful no matter where you work. It's always an adversarial relationship—that's the hardest thing.

Everything is done at the last minute. We're always putting out fires because no one had time to do them before. . . . [There has been] no time for attorneys to explain things, they just walk in, hand it to you and say, "Do it now!"

It's a caste system. At the firm, paralegals are clearly support staff, not equals. It's uncomfortable. The attorneys can't relate to you in a normal way. Sometimes you're just invisible to them. I find that stressful.

It's oppressive and stressful here. The firm is known for its slave mentality; that's why I want out.

Surveys done by regional paralegal organizations across the country[3] as well as Johnstone and Wenglinsky's sociological study also find that members of this occupation experience a high rate of dissatisfaction. Johnstone and Wenglinsky found, for example, that 47 percent disliked their current position because it was boring or because it was a dead-end job (1985: 84). In this study, legal assistants' dissatisfaction with the dead-end nature of the job was colored heavily by the demeaning character of their working relations with attorneys. A thirty-one-year-old woman who had previously been a primary-school teacher said: "Lots of jobs are dead-end, that's not what makes them so difficult. It's the people you work with who make the difference." A woman in her late twenties told me what she disliked most about her job: "It's a dead-end job. I mean, where do I go from here? Of course, that wouldn't be an issue if lawyers weren't such a pain to work with." And another woman described what she liked least about her job, "The work is boring, but the attitude of lawyers is the hardest thing you have to put up with in the law biz." In their view, it is not only the structure of the job that they dislike but the nature of working relations in law firms.

Dissatisfaction also stems from feelings of estrangement. In their interviews, paralegals often described their feelings as if they did not actually experience them. Sarah, for example, describes herself putting on her "reassuring routine" and "reassuring away." Other women talked about trying not to feel one emotion while they were actively inducing another. "When my boss snipes at me, I don't let myself get upset, I try and be nice. . . ." "Whenever he blows up, I try and calm down." Men described their feelings in a very mechanical way: "I erased the expression from my face" or "I turn down the volume." These examples underscore the difference between what Hochschild calls being and acting (1983: 182). It is one thing to be reassuring, but it is quite another to act as if you are reassuring. Putting on the act removes one from the actual emotion. When the act becomes part of the job, it no longer belongs to the individual; it is a service produced for the emotional stability of the lawyer. The job intrudes upon the self, separating feeling from self.

According to paralegals, the demands of emotional labor become even more taxing under conditions of "speed-up," such as before and during a trial. The frenetic pace, the ten-hour work days, the increasing number of tasks, and the lack of control become overwhelming. At the same time, the attorney becomes increasingly anxious, tense, and demanding of attention from the paralegal. In his article, "Stress and the Trial Attorney," psychologist Isaiah Zimmerman writes, "Back at the office, as tension builds, it's important for a lawyer to feel some support from people in the firm. . . . [There] is a strong need to be praised and to have someone to talk extensively to about a case" (1983: 38). In these situations, the paralegal who already feels overwhelmed by physical and mental demands, must respond to increasing emotional demands from the attorney. Some described themselves as going on "automatic pilot" or becoming a "zombie" during trial. One woman said, "I learned to bury my own feelings during trial. Later, I hardly had any feelings at all." Many paralegals reported feeling emotionally and physically exhausted shortly before, during, and even after a trial.

Over three-quarters of the paralegals interviewed described "burn-out" as the major occupational hazard for the litigation legal assistant. To deal with "burn-out," many invoked what was called the "two-year rule." Joe, a male legal assistant, described it in this way,

"After two years, you make a decision. Either you move out of litiga-tion into probate [a specialty considered less stressful], you take a job at another firm, or you check in at Napa [the state mental hospi-tal]." In actuality, not only do paralegals move with frequency within and between firms, but many eventually move out of the occupation altogether. The average tenure in the job for both field sites approx-imates the average for the occupation as a whole—five years (John-stone and Wenglinsky 1985).[4] Those who left became licensed as private investigators, opened their own businesses, or hired them-selves out to lawyers on a contract-by-contract basis. Despite the common assumption that the job is a stepping-stone to law school, only seven percent actually went on to professional school.[5]

Given that the levels of job dissatisfaction and turnover are so high, how do legal assistants maintain their sense of self-worth? In jobs that require emotional labor, Hochschild (1983) argues that workers con-stantly renegotiate the boundaries between self and work role to maintain self-respect. In both the private firm and in the legal depart-ment at Bonhomie Corporation, paralegals constructed a variety of strategies (Bourdieu 1979) to resist the "feeling rules" implicit in their occupational roles and, at the same time, resolve dilemmas about self-respect on the job.[6] The underlying purpose of resistance strategies lies in answering two questions: How can I make myself feel impor-tant in a job where I am required to be deferential and do caretaking at the same time that I am denigrated for doing it? And how can I maintain my core sense of gendered self under these conditions?

The remainder of this chapter describes the five coping and resis-tance strategies that paralegals employ to deal with these questions about emotional degradation on the job. These include (1) infan-tilization of the attorneys; (2) personalizing the attorney/paralegal re-lationship; (3) being "nice"; (4) defining oneself as an occupational transient; and (5) rationalization of one's career goals and lifestyle choices. Although these strategies were not always mutually exclu-sive, and paralegals sometimes utilized a combination of them, these forms of resistance were clearly gendered. Women tended to rely on the first three, whereas men more frequently manifest the latter two. After considering the underlying purpose and effectiveness of the different strategies, I explain why women and men paralegals adopt divergent strategies and argue that women confront a double bind in the performance of emotional labor that men do not.

The first strategy, employed primarily by women workers, is "infantilization of the attorney." This social-psychological strategy became evident when I sat in on "gripe" sessions that paralegals held when lawyers were not around. In these sessions, attorneys were frequently denigrated as egotistical jerks, petty tyrants, "drones," "dweebs," and workaholics with no social skills. But what came up with equal frequency was the tendency to describe an attorney as a "baby" or a child and to describe one's job as a paralegal as "babysitting." One woman paralegal was even referred to as Michael's [an attorney] "security blanket." "Michael is like Linus," his secretary said. "He needs [Debbie, a paralegal] to go everywhere [court, settlement conferences, depositions, etc.] with him—it makes him feel more secure." New, young associates fresh out of law school were most frequently called "baby attorneys." And they were considered the "biggest babies of all" because they often had to be trained not only in the basics of brief writing, local court rules, and firm politics, but in social etiquette, since many of them had never before held full-time jobs.

This strategy serves an interesting psychological function: it reverses the asymmetrical relationship between the attorney and the paralegal. The powerful attorney becomes the powerless, helpless, ineffectual, demanding baby, whereas the paralegal becomes the all-powerful, all-knowing, competent mother. In the short run, such a characterization makes legal assistants feel better about themselves and the work they do for attorneys. By making fun of their bosses, they can feel superior, knowledgeable, and competent. It also serves as an ironic twist on the attorneys' implicit assumption about "mothering." Rather than refusing to take care of them altogether, Marilyn, a thirty-four-year-old paralegal, said, "So they want me to be their mother? Fine! Then I'll treat them just like they are little kids."

The first move in this strategy is both cognitive and emotional. It involves a redefinition of the attorney-paralegal relationship and an emotional tone, contempt. These women do not like or respect the people they work for. The second move, which is behavioral, entailed actually treating the lawyers as if they were children. Paralegals accomplished this in a number of ways. Some talked to attorneys as they might talk to two-year-olds: "Did Jimmy forget his briefcase today?" "Did Stevie remember to wear matching socks to court today?" Others pinned or taped reminder notes on attorneys' overcoats, suit jackets, or books, or inside their brief bags: "Don't forget your meeting with Smith tomorrow." "Sign this voucher for your lunch money." "Read this case for the meeting tomorrow."

One paralegal told me she had gotten on the elevator one evening and saw the attorney she was working for wearing a note pinned to his coat that read, "Sign my overtime slip!" She stood behind him stifling a giggle because she had put the note on his coat herself, and he, in his absent-minded way, still had not noticed it. Others nagged their bosses for being "messy". One left a cartoon on an attorney's desk that depicted a man sitting at his desk in an office inundated with papers, books, and office supplies. The caption read, "Life is rough for the organizationally impaired."

These moves involved a careful balancing act on the part of paralegals. As long as the attorneys thought their comments or actions humorous or even useful, they were successful. Through their parody of mothering, paralegals continued to feel superior and contemptuous, and attorneys received the assistance and support they needed. However, paralegals who pushed the strategy too far were quickly reminded of their appropriate place in the law firm hierarchy. One attorney yelled at a legal assistant who formerly had been a first-grade teacher: "Stop talking to me like I'm a five year old." She immediately backed down, "Sorry, I used to be a schoolteacher. It's hard to lose that tone of voice." Nevertheless, she managed to retain her sense of dignity. As she said to me later, "What he doesn't know is that I didn't even talk to my first graders that way."

Another strategy utilized by female paralegals was to personalize their relationship with attorneys. By personalizing, I am referring to the tendency for paralegals to redefine their working relationships with attorneys as personal friendships. In contrast to the women who adopted the "babysitting" strategy, these women often said they liked the attorneys for whom they worked. Although they recognized that many attorneys were difficult, they thought the lawyers they worked for were "different." In recasting their working relations as personal ones, these women sought to make themselves feel "indispensable," "important," or "special." The actual extent of the personal relationship and the degree of emotional work done to accept its terms varied from relationship to relationship. As the following three cases illustrate, sometimes the strategy worked, and other times it broke down.

The first case involves Jenna, a twenty-nine-year-old paralegal, who works for John, a senior partner in the legal department at Bonhomie Corporation. At five o'clock one winter evening, as John was leaving the office, he told Jenna to do an urgent project for him. Jenna didn't realize how time-consuming the project was until she started working on it and ended up staying at the office all night to finish it. The next day, she bragged to many of her paralegal and secretary friends that she had stayed up all night to complete the work, sleeping for only a few hours on a couch in the attorney's office. Her continual bragging served to advertise the importance of her work to others in the office. It also hints at the closeness of her relationship with John. After all, she spent the night on the couch in his office.

The significance of this last detail is not lost on her audience. Some immediately responded, "You slept on his couch!" Jenna invariably giggled and said, "Yes, yes, I slept all night on the couch." Despite the obvious sexual overtones, John had not even been in his office that night. Nor did he and Jenna have any romantic involvement; in fact, they didn't even socialize together. Nevertheless, Jenna delighted in telling and retelling the story, and when anyone commented that it was a lot to expect on such short notice, she proudly exclaimed: "But I did it because I really like John." No one made her do it; she chose to do something nice for John, whom she liked. Thus, she characterized her fondness for her work in terms of interpersonal relationships with others.

The following day, John graciously thanked Jenna for finishing the project on time. However, he never apologized for asking her to drop everything at the last minute. Nor did he inquire whether it had been an inconvenience. When she told him that she had stayed up all night in the office to complete the work, he did not express any concern about her spending the night alone in a dark, deserted office building but said, "What would I do without you!" In acknowledging his dependence upon her, John's comment satisfied Jenna's need to be recognized as indispensable and important. She repeated it over and over to others in the office throughout the day. He and Jenna seemed to have reached a tacit agreement. She was willing to tolerate John's interruptions and his inconsiderate requests as long as the relationship was a "personal" one. On the other hand, John was willing to tolerate her personal innuendoes—he considered them "innocuous, but childish"—as long as "the work gets done."

The second case involved Debbie, an experienced paralegal who worked at the private firm. She had worked for several years for Michael, a highly successful litigator who had a reputation as a "magician" for getting what he wanted in settlement negotiations. The "magic" he used at the negotiation table carried over into his working relationships within the firm. He was accustomed to manipulating people through flattery, intimidation, or their own self-interest, but most of all, he was used to winning. This intense "bulldozer" style did not go over well with most of the paralegals and secretaries; he had gone through quite a number of secretaries and legal assistants in his tenure at the firm. Debbie was the only paralegal who had been willing to put up with his temper tantrums, his "hot one minute, cold the next" style, and his tendency to grill his assistants impatiently. Whenever anyone would comment that Michael was difficult to get along with, Debbie would say, "But you know, he's completely different at home. He's really not a mean person; he's only like that at the office." For Debbie, Michael's behavior could be justified by the fact that she and Michael had a more personal relationship. She knew his wife and children, and she believed that he wasn't really the "monster" that everyone at the office made him out to be.

Compared to Jenna, however, Debbie had to do even more emotion work to convince herself to accept the terms of the relationship. Michael was not nearly so gracious as John. Nor was he particularly attentive to Debbie's need for personal recognition. Her repeated justifications of Michael's abusive behavior in light of what he was really like often sounded unconvincing. In making these statements, she spoke with resignation and sighed frequently. Even her body language—with her shoulders slumped forward, her forehead creased in a frown, and her eyes carrying dark circles beneath them—conveyed the opposite of what she asserted. Moreover, her frequent complaints of fatigue suggested that she was overworked and unhappy.

By contrast, when Debbie talked about Michael's cases and big business deals, her voice lifted and her face brightened with a smile. As she told me about the most recent settlement agreement Michael had put together, her face became increasingly animated. Just as wives are expected to derive vicarious satisfaction from their husband's status, Debbie seemed to get satisfaction from Michael's accomplishments and from her role in helping such an important person. Michael, on the other hand, had a strong need to confide in her. Part of this need lay in the structure of final settlement negotiations. Many deals involve a seal of confidentiality, which dictates that the actual conditions and amounts of the settlement cannot be disclosed publicly. For an attorney whose success is measured by the number of "wins" and "losses," such a requirement precludes any external indicator of success. Confidentiality was particularly unbearable for Michael because he enjoyed bragging of his conquests and victories to other clients, colleagues, and employees. Because he couldn't boast publicly, he bragged to Debbie in confidence. This brought him the external recognition he sought at the same time that it made Debbie feel important.

There was yet another "hook" for Debbie in this working relationship. Michael often conveyed appreciation for her with gifts. He had his secretary remind him about "personal" things for Debbie, such as her birthday. The secretary would remind him, and he would send her out to buy an extravagant gift. In the popular stereotype, the secretary buys the birthday present for the boss's wife. In buying gifts for Debbie, the secretary symbolically confers status upon Debbie as Michael's "office wife." On a symbolic level, the relationship is confirmed as a personal one, in fact the most intimate of all, that of husband and wife.

This symbolic relationship does not hold up well outside the office. Debbie is not married to Michael, and she is invited to his home only as a guest. Though Michael confides in Debbie, his relationship with her is no less instrumental than his dealings with lawyers at the negotiating table. He describes his relationship with her in terms of a strategic calculation: "How can I get her to stay late? How can I get her to do overtime?" Although Debbie herself rarely complained about Michael, her carriage, her constant fatigue, and her unhappiness suggest that her emotion work was not succeeding fully.

In the third case, a young, inexperienced paralegal often socialized with her boss.[7] Naomi, whose husband was a lawyer, often went out to dinner with her boss, Ron, and his wife, Anne, who was a lawyer for another firm. Naomi liked Ron. She described him as "good-natured, funny, and easy to talk to." She also liked Anne. A year or so after Naomi had been working at the private firm, the two couples went out to dinner. Anne, who was looking for a new legal secretary at the time, lamented the difficulty of finding a "good one." Ron interrupted her lament, "Well of course it's hard to find a good one. I can't imagine why anyone would want that kind of job. I know some people keep them for years and years, but why would anyone want to do it?" Anne nodded vigorously in assent. Naomi, who felt uncomfortably aware of the small status differential between her own position and that of secretaries, said, "Some people like being secretaries." Ron, oblivious for the moment to Naomi's discomfort, continued his tirade: "No ambition, no smarts—but if they are smart, well, the smart ones always leave." After a moment's silence, Anne, who seemed to become aware of the awkwardness of the situation, quickly changed the topic.

Although the subject had been dropped and neither Anne nor Ron brought it up again, Naomi couldn't forget the hurt and the embarrassment. She felt betrayed:

I always thought they were my friends . . . and all along this is what they really thought.
Really thought what?
The implication is why would anyone want to be a paralegal, either. It's personally offensive to me. Such contempt lawyers have for non-lawyers. Oh, I know lawyers who are like that, but I always thought Ron was different, that's why I liked working for him. Maybe, I really did know that he

was like that—and I tried to convince myself that I was different: the special paralegal. If we were friends, then he must not think that about me, just other paralegals.

By personalizing the relationship, Naomi convinced herself that she was a special paralegal. By denying what Ron actually thought about secretaries and paralegals, she protected her sense of self-worth. However, once the denial was broken, Naomi could no longer accept the terms of the relationship. It was too damaging to her self-respect. "I've decided we can't be friends. I'd like that kind of working relationship, but it won't work, at least not in this kind of office."

Jenna, Debbie, and Naomi personalized work relationships to cope with emotional degradation. The first move in this strategy is both cognitive and emotional. It entails redefining the work relationship as friendship, and its emotional tone as personal instead of impersonal. The strategy seemed to work when attorneys also participated in this process. It made paralegals feel indispensable, important, or special. However, attorneys had different interests in pursuing this strategy than paralegals did. In his interview, John explicitly stated that he "put up with it" to get work done. And, Michael regarded Debbie as yet another player to manipulate to achieve his goals. As Judith Rollins (1985) has observed, personalizing relationships between employer and employee is a subtle form of psychological exploitation.[8] Treating workers as if they were friends when, in fact, they are not, obscures the asymmetrical nature of the relationship.

The third coping strategy often adopted by women is simply "being nice." This is similar to the personalizing strategy, in that it involves creating personal relationships, but it operates on a more general level. These women are not simply interested in creating exclusive friendships with their bosses, but in creating a pleasant and humane working environment. This strategy implicitly challenges the main assumptions underlying the adversarial relationship. Rather than regarding other workers as the "enemy, opposing counsel," they insist on being pleasant, kind, and thoughtful. In this light, the insistence on being nice can be seen as a protest or a refusal to accept the terms and conditions of adversarial practice. It can also be viewed as a means for making women feel important: by taking an active role in making the office a nice place, they are organizing the workplace in ways that feel comfortable to them.

These women attempted to please attorneys and other office workers by doing nice things, such as remembering birthdays with cards or flowers, throwing anniversary luncheons for various employees, and having baby showers. Others attempted to please attorneys by doing excessive amounts of overtime, running personal errands, and so forth. For example, during the holiday season Jenna did enormous amounts of overtime work (putting in more than twenty additional hours a week), spent her lunch hours helping an associate with his Christmas shopping, and baked cookies for everyone in her team [five attorneys, three secretaries and two paralegals]. Only one of the attorneys she worked for reciprocated by giving her a Christmas present, and she was devastated: "I tried so hard to please everyone, and they didn't seem to care." Similarly, Cindy, who was very polite and never said "no" to her ever-increasing work assignments, expressed a similar dissatisfaction:

No matter what I do, it's never enough. It's always "Cindy, do this," and "Cindy, do that." No one ever expresses any thanks for all the weekends I've spent at the office. They [attorneys] seem to think that since they spend so much time at the office, I should, too. They seem to forget that they get paid about ten times what I do.

These women workers seemed to think that if they were nice, the attorneys would eventually be nice back. In other words, in contrast to the one-sided objective of lawyers' strategic friendliness—the domination of another person—they expected caring behavior to be reciprocal. This was especially true of younger women who hadn't been paralegals for very long. However, as these examples illustrate, their relational style was often used against them. This is what I call the "tyranny of niceness": the nicer and more uncomplaining paralegals are, the more work gets dumped on them. And if paralegals are not nice, they are quickly typed by attorneys as troublemakers or as uncooperative. This is the double bind that emotional labor presents for women paralegals: if they are nice, they are exploited, and if they aren't, they are considered problematic.

Male paralegals had different styles of coping. One way of doing so was by defining oneself as an occupational transient: "I'm planning to go to law school [or business school or graduate school] after working as a legal assistant for a few years. This is a good way to get experience." For men, being a paralegal was a means to ends: money, experience, and a letter of recommendation to graduate or professional school. They were willing to tolerate the job because it was temporary. Although almost half of the men I interviewed said they planned to go to professional school, only two actually went. (One went to an MBA program, and another started law school but later dropped out.) This suggests that even if they did not go to professional or graduate school, it was important to define themselves in this way.[9]

Some of the men, however, had no interest in going to professional school. They described themselves in terms of their "real" interests and accomplishment. Over half told me that they were artists, writers, actors, or photographers; the job was "just for money." In fact, during the course of my interviews, several men insisted upon showing me their artistic work, which was prominently displayed on the walls of their offices or apartments. In another interview, a young gay man spent thirty minutes discussing the controversy over Robert Mapplethorpe's photography. For these men, being a paralegal was not part of their occupational identity: they were artists—not paralegals. As a consequence they did not take the job very seriously. Jonathan, a twenty-five-year-old paralegal said: "I don't let all the firm politics get to me. I don't care about those people [the attorneys]. It's not my life!" Another said, "I have seen the gamesmanship, and I do feel manipulated at times, but I don't take it that seriously." Like Goffman in *The Presentation of Self in Everyday Life*, these men viewed social interaction with attorneys as a carefully stage-managed affair. The performance was conveyed through the proper dramatic props: a Brooks Brothers' look-alike suit purchased at a local thrift store, the proper demeanor, and the proper tone of voice. Such an instrumental, pragmatic approach made life at the law firm bearable—"I'm just waiting till five o'clock so that I can go home and do my 'real' work"—and their real interests and accomplishments, which lay outside the office, made them feel important.

Another coping strategy utilized by male paralegals is rationalization of career and lifestyle choices. "Most attorneys hate their jobs," one paralegal told me. "They work long hours, do boring work, make a lot of money and have absolutely no social life—that's not for me. I may not have a lot of money, but at least I have fun!" When I asked another male paralegal why he decided not to go to law school, he said,

> I'm just not interested in that kind of lifestyle. . . .
> *What do you mean?*
> The workaholic attitude. Plus, I'm very skeptical about law at this point in my life. It really comes down to whoever has the most money wins. Lifestyle is important to me, so is my job, but I'm not willing to work sixty hours a week for the rest of my life. I have other interests besides my job.

Another reported that he once saw an attorney he worked for have a heart attack: "They don't pay me enough to get that stressed out. I just know how to set limits."

Such rationalizations served to legitimate the choices legal assistants make about choice of career and lifestyle: they preferred meaningful work and an active social life even if it meant less money. Of course, these choices meant a lot less money. The attorneys in this study earned two, three, sometimes even ten times what the average paralegal made. Some legal assistants admitted to feeling envious about this income differential. Tony said, "I'd like to have a lot of money, a car that doesn't break down all the time, no end-of-the-month scramble." Nonetheless, he was quick to add, he would "hate the kind of work attorneys do."

Attorneys seemed to sense the potential for envy and reacted with a defensive maneuver. John, a young associate recently out of law school, said to me: "It must be nice to have weekends off. Not only do you have weekends off, but you probably even make more money than I do on an hourly basis, because I work so many more hours than you do." And another male lawyer said to the paralegal who worked for him: "I resent the fact that you do the same kind of work I do without going to law school. You don't have to put in long hours or pay your dues like I do." In expressing their own envy or even hostility for the advantages of the paralegal's leisure time, they effectively denied that legal assistants had any reason to envy attorneys. They seemed to be saying, "I made the trade-off, and I am not so happy about it"; yet implicit in this was the message, "You made your choices, why envy me?"

Why did men and women adopt different strategies? For men, a dilemma is posed at the structural level by being male in a female-dominated occupation. In American society, men are expected to be career and goal oriented, hardworking, and financially successful (Connell 1987; Pleck 1981). As Williams (1989) found in her study on male nurses, men in non-traditional occupations are often under pressure to explain why they work in this job and not another one. The male paralegals I interviewed faced similar pressures from lawyers, colleagues and peers. In response to this assault on their masculinity, they struggled to maintain their self-esteem.

Other studies provide insight into the ways in which men may build up their self-esteem. Elliot Liebow (1967) describes in *Tally's Corner* how Black street corner men shelter their self-esteem behind a set of "shadow values." Street corner men who moved from one failed marriage to another had an explanation: they described themselves as oversexed, incapable of limiting their sexual desires to one woman. Failure in marriage became a virtue, the result of a manly "flaw," that of being too virile to be satisfied with just one woman. In her study on downward mobility, Katherine Newman describes how downwardly mobile executives also developed a "theory of manly flaws" (1989: 72). These men thought they had been laid off or dismissed because they were too smart, too aggressive, or too principled. These qualities were simply too threatening to their superiors. In this way, former managers transformed their failure into a virtue.

Male paralegals are not unemployed, but they are, in a sense, unusually employed. And like the men in Newman and Liebow's studies, they attempt to transform this "failure" into a "manly flaw." Some assert they're preparing for a career; the job is only temporary. Others keep the job to make money to enable them to pursue other, more appropriate, male occupational identities, such as the virtuous artist. Still others, transform their "failure" into a virtue through excessive rationalization: "I'm sacrificing financial well-being because

I'd rather have a social life." For men, these strategies entail locating the sources of one's identity and self esteem somewhere outside this strongly feminized occupation. At the same time, these strategies serve as ways of doing gender. By defining themselves as occupationally transient in a female-dominated occupation, emphasizing other more appropriate male occupational identities, or downplaying their loyalty to the firm, male paralegals emphasize their differences as men. In Chodorow's psychoanalytic understanding, such behavior serves to maintain their core sense of self as "not female." In this way, they make their work tolerable by defining what they do outside the office as important to themselves and others.[10] For these reasons, strategies that women utilized, such as personalizing work relationships, cannot work for men precisely because they entail locating one's identity in relationships at work within a feminized occupation.

Women confronted a different dilemma in this occupation. Because it was a female-dominated job, there was not the same kind of pressure to explain why they held these positions. It was presumed that women would hold them. For them, the problem lay in defining themselves through these work relationships. On the one hand, attorneys expected women to be personally engaged and to play "mother." Women, on the other, attempted to maintain their self-esteem by personalizing work relationships, by being nice or by "babysitting." These strategies all involve doing gender as traditional female caregivers. When these strategies worked, they also served to maintain what Chodorow (1978) terms women's core sense of self as relational.[11] By locating their identity within relationships at work, women defined themselves through their concern for and attachments to others. However, these strategies were not always successful. Babysitting involved a careful balancing act. If pushed too far, attorneys became critical of women legal workers. Personalizing work relationships was successful when women received some recognition for their efforts but quickly broke down when they could no longer deny that attorneys regarded them as subordinates. And finally, as a strategy, being nice fell through when women realized these relationships were not reciprocal.

When female paralegals gave up on defining themselves through relationships, or chose not to become affectively engaged, they encountered the "tyranny of niceness." In other words, they were sanctioned in some way whether they were nice or not. Similarly, women who attempted to adopt male strategies such as the occupational transient or defining one's self through their "real interests" found that they were not taken seriously. For example, Diana, who was an artist, was teased about her "dilettante interest in finger-painting." And although many attorneys knew that I was in graduate school, they could never remember what field I was in—"Social work, isn't it?" Nor could they ever recall that I was getting a Ph.D.—"What are you getting your master's in again?" Herein lies the double bind that emotional labor poses for women paralegals. If they define themselves through relationships, they are exploited as nurturing women; if they don't, they are considered problematic, "uncooperative," or alternately they are viewed as "dilettantes."

Conclusion

Paralegals play a crucial socio-emotional role in the reproduction of the labor process in the large, bureaucratic law firm. These legal workers function to support and maintain the emotional stability of the lawyers they work for, through deferential treatment and caretaking. By affirming lawyers' status, paralegals also reproduce gender relations in the law firm. Most attorneys who receive their nurturance are men, and the majority of legal assistants who provide these emotional services are women. Even when paralegals resist the "feeling rules" implicit in their occupational life, they reproduce their own emotional labor through individualized coping strategies such as "being nice" (for the women) and defining oneself as an occupational transient (for the men). Just as Burawoy's (1977) factory workers unwittingly reproduce the labor process by defying the factory time clock and working at their own pace, women reproduce the feminized socio-emotional requirements of paralegal work by being nice, personalizing relationships with attorneys, and "babysitting." On the other hand, by defining their identities somewhere outside the feminized occupation, men reinforce the notion that they are men, and hence, unsuited for this job.

These gender strategies underscore the qualitative difference in the emotional exploitation of women and men. Being a paralegal is not the same job for men as it is for women. Women, and not men, face a double bind in selecting coping mechanisms. If they are nice, they are overworked and unappreciated, but if they fail to be nice, they are viewed as uncooperative. Men, on the other hand, can get away with failing to be nice and can pass themselves off as attorneys, thus utilizing the informal "old boys" network to their advantage. Also, men could luxuriate in the privilege of defining themselves as occupationally transient and free from familial obligations. And finally, by virtue of being male they can and must distance themselves from the paralegal role. Male paralegals are doing a female-typed job that requires certain stereotypical feminine elements, such as caretaking and deference behaviors. Men can distance themselves from the role, as is expressed through contempt, excessive rationalizations, or repeated assertions of other, more appropriate male occupational identities. Women find it more difficult to distance themselves from being a paralegal; it is not a role they can pick up and drop at will. As Chodorow (1978) argues, gender identity provides a fundamentally deep-rooted sense of who we are. For women in this study, this identity is often tied to relations with others, and being a paralegal exploits precisely this capacity. As a consequence, on a very fundamental psychological level, emotional labor poses a double bind for women paralegals. As a woman, to distance oneself from the role of legal assistant means in some sense distancing oneself from one's feminine identity. On the other hand, to embrace the role means emotional exploitation of relational skills. Their ultimate form of resistance to this double bind is to leave the job, as many paralegals frequently do.

Chapter Seven

Conclusion

In this ethnographic study of litigation paralegals and trial attorneys at work, I have sought to ground and develop the claim that sex segregation in law firms is reproduced through a dynamic relationship between occupational structure, behavior, and identity. I have argued that gender shapes legal workers' practices at the same time that their practices constitute and reproduce hierarchical gendered relations. In addition, I have emphasized not only the structural characteristics of law firms and the roles of legal workers but also emotional labor as a site for the reproduction of gender asymmetry. My intent has not been to develop a set of universal generalizations or propositions regarding sex segregation, but rather to elucidate the dynamics of a neglected dimension—emotions—in socially and historically specific processes that sustain sex segregation. The Rambo litigator and the mothering paralegal are shorthand, normative expressions for this gendered emotional division of labor. When male trial lawyers lose their tempers or treat paralegals as adversaries, women legal assistants are expected to be nurturing and deferential in response. It is through these nonreciprocal emotional exchanges that the hierarchical structure of gendered relations is reproduced.

My focus on the gendering of organizations, occupations, and emotions brings the dynamics of power and exclusion in law firms into bold relief. Women across occupational categories face differential and sexist standards that men do not. In litigation, women lawyers face a number of obstacles that render it more difficult for them to be successful in their profession, while male paralegals luxuriate in "special" treatment. Women litigators, as token members of the legal profession, are excluded from the old-boy network, making it more difficult for them to bring clients into firms. They are subjected to sexual harassment and receive no institutional forms of support to aid the balance between family and career. They also encounter a constant double-bind in the performance of emotional labor—if they are intimidating and aggressive, they are dismissed as "shrill" and "unladylike," but if they are not aggressive, they are considered not tough enough to be good litigators. By contrast, male paralegals as token members of a feminized occupation simply do not encounter these problems and instead accrue a number of advantages by virtue of being male. They are assumed to be more qualified than female paralegals for positions of authority within their occupation and in fact are considered more intelligent, simply because they are men. Because their male status gives them the privilege of socializing informally with male attorneys, they are able to obtain more interesting work assignments as well as personal recognition and affirmation for their work. And finally, as men they are able to get away with doing different kinds of emotional labor than women paralegals do (e.g., playing the role of "political adviser" rather than nurturing mother). Thus, in contrast to Kanter's (1977) gender-neutral understanding of tokenism, *female* tokens are disadvantaged by the structure of the male-defined career, while *male* tokens benefit from favorable treatment because they are men—even in a female-dominated job.

These differentials in power are no different when women and men work in the same job. As I have argued, the same job is *not* the same job for male and female legal workers. Male paralegals and male attorneys make more money than their female counterparts. They are located in more powerful positions within their occupation—dramatically so in litigation, where the majority of partners who control the firm's management and finances are men. In addition, men incur higher status simply because they are male. They do not have to contend with sexual harassment at work, and they have more leeway than women do to express their feelings on the job.

Finally, I have emphasized throughout that the reproduction of gender asymmetry in law firms is not a static process, but a dynamic and contested one. While women encounter strong pressures to conform to gendered feeling rules, they do not passively acquiesce to these norms. For example, although women paralegals are required to "play mom," they move in and around this gendered expectation. Some women embody the norm of the mothering paralegal, while others refuse to play mom altogether, and still others go through the motions, cynically adopting "babysitting" strategies. Through such strategies they make fun of attorneys—the baby who can't take care of himself—and at the same time symbolically reverse the asymmetrical relationship between themselves and their bosses. Similarly, women litigators find a variety of ways to do gender in the male-defined context of the legal profession. A small minority of women conform to the male-defined norms of the profession. Others adopt the adversarial role in the courtroom and a more caring orientation in the office. And finally, others choose an alternative practice of law, which values an ethic of care and mutual respect.

The disjuncture between the gendered feeling rules for these jobs and women legal workers' actual behavior reveals not only the dynamics of power—i.e., the external pressures they face to conform—but the possibilities for resistance. In my understanding, the gendered structure of law firms is at once reproduced and destabilized through legal workers' practice. The dynamism of this account is located in my psychoanalytic understanding of subjectivity, particularly an object-relations approach. In my argument, legal workers' practices emerge from a socially and historically specific context, within which, individuals bring to bear their own unconscious interests, feelings, and identities, often remaking them in practice. For instance, some women lawyers express a relational sense of self in their interviews but redefine that identity in practice by adopting a male-defined professional stance and downplaying any association with the traditional female role. Other women litigators, on the other hand, redefine the practice of law to be congruent with their more relational and less adversarial understanding of justice.

This dynamic approach to the study of sex segregation has several important implications for sociology. First, rather than privileging either structure or agency in an explanation of the gendered division of labor, this study reconceptualizes the relationship between multiple levels of analysis by asserting a dynamic and interactive relationship between structure, behavior, and identity. Such an argument improves upon the weaknesses of both macro-level approaches, which deny the role of human agency, and actor-oriented approaches, which neglect the links between micro-level processes and larger institutional structures in historically grounded contexts. Furthermore, it makes an empirical contribution to Giddens's (1979) metatheoretical discussion on the "duality of structure" by showing not only that structure is both the medium and outcome of practice but that gender is integral to this process.

Second, my argument reconceptualizes theories of the labor process, specifically Burawoy's argument about manufacturing consent, by arguing that emotional labor is also a site of reproduction in the labor process. Unlike Burawoy's, my theoretical account demonstrates that gender is central to the reproduction of the labor process. Not only are the forms of emotional labor themselves gendered—i.e., the Rambo litigator and the mothering paralegal—but the labor process itself is gendered. In law firms, it is reproduced in such a way that male attorneys are superordinate and female paralegals are subordinate.

Finally, this account should help to clarify understanding about the link between gender identity and actual behavior in the workplace. Some feminist scholars have suggested that Chodorow's (1978) early argument provides an essentialized notion of gender identity, that is, a fixed and static notion of femininity (Fraser and Nicholson 1990). Still others argue that her focus on the reproduction of mothering cannot explain why some women choose to work in the paid labor force and some forgo motherhood altogether (Gerson 1985). By contrast, my account, which incorporates Chodorow's (1989a) more recent theoretical work, demonstrates that feminine identity varies both within and between occupational contexts. How women negotiate and renegotiate the meaning of being a woman and a lawyer, or a woman and a paralegal, varies a great deal. Moreover, having relational concerns and interests does not preclude working in the paid labor force—either in a feminized occupation or in a male-dominated profession. Many women paralegals and women lawyers in this study express relational concerns, yet they often redefine this identity as they "do gender." As this book has shown, women in contemporary law firms navigate between the limits of gender-appropriate behavior and their own feelings about being women, finding a variety of ways to do gender.

In addition to its theoretical contributions, this work suggests many questions for future research on the role of emotional labor in other occupations and professions. This study as well as others suggests that emotions are a significant feature of many jobs (Fineman 1993; Leidner 1993; Romero 1992; Hochschild 1983). Moreover, as our service sector continues to grow, more workers, particularly women, are subject to the demands of emotional labor (Smith 1989; Phillips 1990). Because of its informal and seemingly invisible nature, more research must be done to bring this hidden aspect of labor to light. Many questions require our attention: Is emotional labor gendered in other jobs? Under what conditions is it gendered? When does emotional labor take on racialized or classed dimensions? When is it exploitative, and when is it not? And finally, what role, if any, should emotions play in the workplace?

By focusing exclusively on gender as a principle of organization and an aspect of identity, I have neglected to consider how other forms of social identity may be mediated and reproduced in law firms. Like the majority of large elite corporate firms in the United States, the top tier of the law firms in this study is predominantly white and male, and the paralegal tier is predominantly white and female (Heinz and Laumann 1982; Johnstone and Wenglinksy 1985). As historians and sociologists have demonstrated, the legal profession is distinguished by a history of exclusionary practices that ensure that men from white, upper-middle-class Protestant backgrounds will make it into the corporate elite.[1] Historically, the consequence of these practices has been that both white women *and* people of color have been excluded from the elite ranks of the legal professions (Segal 1983; Auerbach 1976). While my theoretical account helps to explain how gender stratification is reproduced in law firms, it does not address the reproduction of racial and ethnic stratification.

Recent feminist scholarship suggests that we must avoid thinking of gender as the only grid organizing social life, because such an assumption ignores other experiences and identities, such as race and ethnicity (Collins 1990; Wharton 1991). This book began by problematizing what appeared to be a natural, yet salient, feature of law firms: the gendered division of labor. However, the racial division of labor is also a seemingly natural, salient feature of organizational life. What does it mean that racial and ethnic minorities are underrepresented in corporate law firms? If we are seriously committed to dismantling the natural, taken-for-granted features of inequality in law-firm work cultures, we must also think about how racial differences and other forms of differentiation are produced by organizational practices.

Implications for Social Change

This book has highlighted a number of serious problems that sex segregation poses for women working in litigation departments in large law firms. In feminized occupations such as paralegal and secretarial work, women receive much lower pay than men in male-dominated jobs. Disparities in wages are especially wide at the private firm I studied, where partners make eight times the salary of experienced women paralegals ($250,000 for partners, as opposed to $30,000 annually for paralegals). In addition, female-dominated jobs are on separate and unequal career ladders that offer far less opportunity for advancement than do male-dominated jobs. As paralegals, women have few opportunities for mobility within law firms and, unlike their male counterparts they receive little if any encouragement for advancement. On the other hand, women in male-dominated professions such as litigation fare better economically than paralegals and secretaries, though they make less money than men in the same job with comparable experience. Furthermore, women in these jobs are more likely than men to face a hostile and demeaning working environment.

The day-to-day harassment of women trial attorneys in the two law offices in this study ranges from teasing to social exclusion to overt hostility. These practices simultaneously serve to exaggerate gender differences and to disempower women in the workplace. By teasing women lawyers about their supposedly "innate ability to type," men suggest that they are not qualified to be lawyers because they are women and hence do not belong in this profession. By the same token, failure to include women in informal social gatherings reminds them that they are not recognized as part of the team, at the same time that it serves to exclude them from important political networks within firms—networks which could be beneficial to their careers. Finally, grotesque jokes such as the pig's foot in the elaborately wrapped gift box given to a woman lawyer, are suggestive forms of symbolic violence against women.

In addition to these hostile practices, women across occupational categories encounter sexual harassment.[2] This is not unique to the firms in this study. Surveys of women and the legal profession report that these practices continue to be widespread, particularly in private law firms (Rosenberg, Perlstadt and Phillips 1993; MacCorquodale and Jensen 1993). Sexualizing women workers is perhaps the most blatant way to exaggerate differences between women and men. Like other forms of boundary heightening, it is demeaning to women and, in the extreme, physically threatening. The secretary who overhears her boss tell a client to ask her to get up and get him a cup of coffee so he can "see what great legs she has" feels humiliated, powerless, and angry: "Part of me felt embarrassed and stupid, but another part wanted to take that pot of coffee and pour it over his head." Similarly, when a young woman associate slaps a partner who has been harassing her, it is she, not he, who becomes the object of derision. And in a more disturbing incident, a legal secretary is physically cornered against her desk by a partner who tells her that if she does not have sex with him, he will make sure that she never gets another job. What is most insidious about these practices is the fact that management in the two law offices in this study typically looks the other way when such incidents occur.

Finally, in addition to the assaults on women's bodies, the emotional demands of the job also intrude upon the psychological integrity of legal workers. Like men, women find emotional labor stressful when they experience a disjuncture between what they actually feel and the emotions they must induce for the job. Women litigators who see themselves as "nice people" complain about the requirement to act like "a jerk." Paralegals who do not feel like being nurturing and pleasant gripe about "playing mom." However, for women, producing a smile, a mood, or a feeling for the job is even more problematic because they confront a double bind that men do not. Women legal assistants who are nice are subjected to never-ending emotional demands from lawyers for whom they work, while those who are not nice are considered problematic and are sanctioned. Female attorneys who are pleasant and nice are not considered tough enough to be good litigators, but when they are tough and aggressive, they are criticized for being difficult, strident, or shrill. The constraints created by these double binds give women workers even less control over their emotional integrity than men have.

Emotional double-binds, sexual overtures, sexual innuendoes, teasing, and exclusionary practices are not isolated incidents but rather systematic and patterned forms of harassment. On a daily basis, these practices create a working environment that is at best indifferent to the experiences of women workers and at worst antagonistic and hostile. Moreover, the constant reiteration of gender difference through these practices serves to maintain and reproduce the gendered structural features of a sex-segregated workplace. By treating women as outsiders, excluding them from interactions beneficial to their careers and, in the extreme, sexually and physically intimidating them, men, consciously or not, systematically discourage and disempower women as workers. Furthermore, when firms fail to disrupt such practices, their laissez-faire policy suggests to men that harassment is acceptable and suggests to women that nothing will be done if they complain about it; it then becomes a "normal," taken-for-granted feature of the workplace.[3]

Given the nature of the problems women legal workers face, what can feminists and others who wish to challenge the gendered division of labor in law firms do? This book has sketched out an alternative explanation of sex segregation in the hope of providing a new starting point for changes in the organization of the workplace. In this account, I have emphasized the reciprocal and dynamic relationship between gender as a property of social structure and as an aspect of behavior and identity. Such an argument suggests that solutions to the problems associated with sex segregation must be implemented in both structure and individual practice.

At the structural level in feminized occupations, alternatives must be created to the low-paying, dead-end ghettos where women paralegals and secretaries work. One way to address this problem is to provide litigation training programs in the legal profession that give women workers credit for skills and knowledge they have already acquired on the job. The attorneys and support-staff workers I studied recognize that experienced paralegals and secretaries often know a great deal more than a new associate who has just graduated from law school. Furthermore, these legal workers participate informally in the training of new associates. For these reasons, it makes sense that paralegals and legal secretaries who wish to move up in the legal profession should not have to go through the same training as a college graduate who has no legal experience. By building alternative career ladders into the profession itself, women legal workers could apply their past experiences to obtain more challenging and better-paying jobs, which would break down boundaries between feminized and male-dominated occupations, reward women for the skills and knowledge they already possess, and provide incentives, rather than disincentives, for intrafirm mobility.

In addition to changing the structure of feminized occupations, the normative gendered expectations attached to these jobs must be altered. The emotional division of labor in paralegal work presents a double standard—one set of expectations exist for men and another for women. Whereas women are expected to be emotionally engaged, nurturing mothers, men can get away with being more distant and polite. This double standard and the constant reiteration of gender difference is disempowering to women: unlike men, they have very little room to be themselves on the job. Rethinking the workplace as a site where gender is less fixed—a setting that is open, rather than closed, to the contradictions and complexities of feminine identity—addresses some of these problems. On the most basic level, such a workplace demands respect for difference. As many paralegals and secretaries in this book report, a modicum of courtesy and respect on the part of individual attorneys would make their work lives much easier. As a collective practice, respect for difference among women could greatly alter the demeaning work culture in law firms.

Changes in the work culture must also be instituted in male-dominated professions such as litigation. Reward structures, performance evaluations, responses to harassment, and the myriad day-to-day actions and attitudes of male lawyers combine to create a web of social relations that debilitate women as lawyers, making the profession even more difficult for them to break into. In fact, studies suggest that many women are leaving the legal profession because of the discrimination and resistance they have encountered (Jacobs 1989; Lewin 1989; Kahler 1988; Liefland 1986). Leveling the playing field for women and men in law firms means making serious changes in these disempowering work cultures. Systematic efforts to educate men and women about what constitutes offensive behavior would be a good start. However, education alone is not enough without institutional support.

A more formal way to institutionalize changes in work culture is through law and social policy. As legal scholar Vicki Schultz (1992) observes, our current legal system does not adequately protect women from harassment that is *not* overtly sexual. For example, in a recent case, *Rabidue v. Osceola Refining Co.*, one federal court stated:

> [I]t cannot be seriously disputed that in some work environments, humor and language are rough hewn and vulgar. Sexual jokes, sexual conversations and girlie magazines may abound. Title VII was not meant to—or can—change this. Title VII is the federal court mainstay in the struggle for equal employment opportunity for female workers. . . . But . . . Title VII was [not] designed to bring about a magical transformation of social mores of American workers. (cited in Schultz 1992: 321)

Indeed, Title VII was not designed to legislate social mores among American workers. Nevertheless, it is precisely these unexamined beliefs and attitudes that often make the workplace inhospitable to women in non-traditional jobs. Expanding the scope of harassment to include the systematic forms of gender disparagement, exclusion, and hostility would provide women workers with a broader range of legal remedies to institutionalized sexism. As Schultz reminds us, when women bring a discrimination case to court, "a court must decide whether to affirm or alter the status quo. . . . When judges impose liability . . . they can prompt employers to restructure the workplaces in ways that empower women" (1992: 324).

On a final and more philosophical note, we must begin to rethink the adversarial model itself. The ethic of gamesmanship—that is, winning the client's case by any means whatsoever, within the letter of the law—encourages a calculated and strategic relationship between trial attorneys and their legal audiences. The focus on winning at almost any cost promotes a callous indifference to the needs and feelings of others, a view that is captured in the following excerpt from a poem published in the *National Law Journal*:

My basic goal would be, of course, my client's exculpation,
But also for myself, the other lawyer's subjugation.
So word would spread of nothing but complete humiliation
Awaits the fool who tries to take me on in litigation.

(White 1989: 13)

Although White's "Ode to Litigation" is intended as humor, its depiction of the consequences of gamesmanship—"nothing but complete humiliation awaits the fool who tries to take me on"—is not completely off the mark. As I have shown throughout this book, this kind of thinking not only influences relations with opposing counsel and other legal audiences but also carries over into working relations within law firms. Litigators treat paralegals as "emotional punching bags," "as if" they were adversaries, denying their intellectual and personal contributions to the job. At the same time, however, lawyers need legal assistants to nurture them, to pay attention to them, and to affirm their status as superordinates in the law-firm hierarchy.

The structure of this relationship parallels that of Hegel's (1977 [1807]) discussion of the master and the slave. For Hegel, the master denies and negates the slave's subjectivity in his quest for self-assertion, even as he needs the slave to recognize him as the master. This paradox of recognition and domination—that the master desires recognition from the very Other whom he negates—is also central to the attorney-paralegal relationship. In law firms, however, the relationship between subject and object is gendered. The paralegal is a woman, a "perfect mother," who selflessly tends to the needs of an attorney, a man. Like Hegel's slave, she becomes the Object, a feminized object, whose subjectivity is denied.

A way out of this paradox is presented by feminist scholar Jessica Benjamin's idea of "mutual recognition," that is, "the necessity of recognizing as well as being recognized by the other" (1988: 23). In her view, mutual recognition implies that we recognize the other as a separate person who is like us and yet, at the same time, distinct. Extending this conception to the practice of litigation entails the disruption of the power imbalance that underlies the attorney-paralegal relationship and the adversarial model itself. It compels us to imagine a workplace and a practice of law that is egalitarian, respectful of difference, and empowering, rather than disempowering.[4] Finally, it means rejecting the concept of deferential office wives who are required to mother their bosses, and recognizing them instead as subjects in their own right. Indeed, a first step in transforming the lives of women legal workers lies in moving beyond the fixed and static conceptions embodied in the male "fantasy of the perfect mother" and recognizing the diversity and complexity in women's experiences and identities.

Appendix One

Articulating the Self in Field Research

Recent methodological criticism suggests that the self in the research process should be fully articulated in research and writing,
not minimized or neglected (Krieger 1991; Stanley 1990). Susan
Krieger (1991), for example, argues that in detaching one's self from
the research process, social scientists distance themselves from their
research subjects, thereby rendering what they study more difficult
to see and understand. This theoretical/methodological appendix ex-
plores two issues in an attempt to more fully articulate the relationship between myself as a white, feminist sociologist and the research
process: my roles as a researcher and the "dilemma of ethnographic
authority" (Clifford 1988), the inequality inherent in the relationship
between the observer and the observed.

From conversations with colleagues and graduate students, I have
found that these issues were troublesome not only for me but for
others who do fieldwork and in-depth interviewing projects. My discussion here, which is an attempt to shed new light on these issues,
also has epistemological and pedagogical purposes. It has become
commonplace in field studies to include a detailed discussion of
one's relationship to the people in the field, especially when one is a
participant-observer (Stacey 1991; Stanley 1990; Van Mannen 1988).
Such writing serves as an important critique of positivistic methods,
which emphasize the passive, detached researcher stance.[1] In addition, this chapter, much like William Whyte's classic methodological
appendix to *Street Corner Society,* is intended to provide the reader
with a sense of how I, as a researcher, came to know and interact
with the people I studied, when I was successful in my interactions,
and when I made mistakes. It is my hope that such an appendix will

not only challenge the positivistic value on the erasure of self in the research process but demystify the process of fieldwork for the uninitiated, thereby serving as a teaching tool for graduate students and others who wish to learn more about doing fieldwork.

Insider, Outsider, Outsider Within

Anthropologist Lila Abu-Lughod argues that the ethnographer's knowledge of the field is positionally constructed and hence, always partial: "Standing on shifting ground makes it clear that every view is a view from somewhere and every act of speaking, a speaking from somewhere" (Abu-Lughod 1991: 141). Other feminist scholars also emphasize our roles in constructing "situated knowledges" (Haraway 1988; Harding 1991). Donna Haraway, for example, suggests that the only way to create a larger, more critical vision is "to be somewhere in particular." Taking these claims seriously means articulating our selves in the research process—delineating the "shifting ground" upon which we stand and considering how its shifts in position influence what we see and what we cannot see as ethnographers.

This essay highlights positionality in the relationship between ethnographers and the research process by examining two concepts typically utilized to define the relationship between social scientists and their subjects: *insider* and *outsider*. In the methodological literature, a researcher who shares the same gender and racial, ethnic, and social-class background as the subjects is considered to be an "insider," whereas a sociologist whose status differs from those of the subjects is an "outsider" (Merton 1972; Baca Zinn 1979). In addition to defining one's status in the field, each of these terms carries with it an implicit assumption about the political nature of the relationship between the observer and the observed. Insiders, for example, have argued that European Americans who study racial and ethnic minority communities reproduce a "neocolonial" relationship with their research subjects (Ladner 1971: 7). Proponents of research by outsiders deny this claim, asserting the value-neutral, detached, and dispassionate stance of a positivistic social science. These political concerns are closely related to a number of epistemological questions. Can an outsider, for instance, "know" or understand the culture of a group different from his or her own? On the other hand, can an insider be detached enough to produce an objective social scientific account? Which role produces "evidence" that will count as sociological knowledge?

These important political and epistemological questions have been discussed at length elsewhere.[2] By contrast, I ask whether the terms *insider* and *outsider* continue to be useful in conceptualizing the varied roles sociologists often enact in the field. Although these concepts continue to be used by social scientists, they are seldom examined critically[3] (e.g., Segura 1989; Kremer 1990). Drawing from my fieldwork experiences at Lyman, Lyman and Portia and Bonhomie Corporation, I would argue that ethnographers move back and forth in continuous tack between the statuses of insider, outsider, and what Patricia Hill Collins (1986) terms an "outsider within." In making this argument, I take issue not only with the dichotomous construction of the insider/outsider debate, but with feminist standpoint theorists (Smith 1974; Harding 1986, 1991; Hartsock 1983), who contend that women, by virtue of their different structural positions vis-à-vis men, have a privileged vantage point in understanding male supremacy. In contrast to these feminists, I make a more nuanced argument, which does not deny the centrality of race and gender as central social identities for the researcher or as "ways of knowing" but regards these identities as more or less salient with respect to other types of status.[4]

Historical Context

In the late 1960s and early 1970s, the distinction between insiders and outsiders became a hotly contested debate about who should be allowed to do social research, particularly on minority communities and populations (Bridges 1973: 392). Many scholars contended that poor and predominantly minority communities were exploited by the research practices of white social scientists. Joyce Ladner (1971), for example, argues that the relationship between the white researcher and African American subjects resembles that of a neocolonial relationship. Moreover, many scholars have shown that some research by white social scientists on minority families, particularly poor Black and Chicano families, systematically distorts and "pathologizes" any differences found between them and the idealized white, middle-class norm (Montiel 1970; Mirandé and Staples 1980). Because white social scientists failed to grasp the realities of African American life, early proponents of the insider view, particularly Black scholars, argued that whites should be excluded from doing research on Black communities (Wilson 1974).

Robert Merton's (1972) classic article, "Insiders and Outsiders: A Chapter in the History of the Sociology of Knowledge," is highly relevant to this debate. Merton criticizes Black scholars' claim to privileged forms of knowledge, characterizing them as elitist and exclusionary. On the other hand, he considers the outsider doctrine equally untenable, because it assumes that unprejudiced knowledge is accessible only to outsiders. Merton's solution is to transcend these distinct statuses. He concludes: "Insiders and outsiders in the domain of knowledge unite. You have nothing to lose but your claims. You have a world of understanding to win" (1972: 44).

Merton's article continues to stimulate considerable debate. Proponents of the outsider view uphold the positivist vision of an objective and neutral social science (e.g., Horowitz 1983; Sanchez Jankowski 1991). In their view, only an outsider will be detached enough to research and write about a community. Scholars who hold the insider position are critical of the so-called objective stance of positivism, arguing that social science is far from value-free and that an insider status often gives one advantageous access to a community or group. Denise Segura (1989), for example, argues that her status as a Chicana gave her access to a Mexican American community that would not have been available to an outsider. Catherine Riessman (1987) convincingly demonstrates that problems of interpretation arise when white women interview Latinas. More recently, the parameters of the debate have been extended to include gender as well as race and ethnicity (Oakley 1980; Kremer 1990). In "Learning When to Say No," Belinda Kremer (1990) puts forth the argument that feminists should keep research on women for themselves. Like feminist-standpoint theorists, these researchers claim they hold a privileged vantage point for understanding race and gender by virtue of their similar social identities.

Conceptual Problems

There are several problems with this debate as it is currently constructed. First, simply because a researcher shares the gender and ethnicity of her subjects does not automatically qualify one as an insider. By virtue of her academic training, the fieldworker has been trained to look at the world in a way that is different from the perspective utilized by people with no such academic background. In this sense, even an insider will be "estranged" from any community or group she studies. Furthermore, as Baca Zinn (1979) has observed, for many minority scholars this training has also meant upward mobility, so that the minority social scientist may no longer share the same class background of the people being studied, even if she shares their ethnic identity. On the other hand, being an outsider does not automatically signify complete detachment and objectivity. "Outsiders" can also be empathic and understanding and in some cases they are "adopted" temporarily by the community they study (Wood 1934). The history of anthropology and sociology abounds with examples of "honorary insiders" (Mead 1986; Warren 1988). And in sociology, some white men and women have produced thoughtful and insightful studies on minority populations (e.g., Blauner 1989; Miller 1986; Moore 1991).

In addition to the difficulty in conceptualizing a "true" insider or outsider, the dichotomy itself is false. It precludes the possibility of having any other distinctive status that may not fit neatly within either category. Patricia Hill Collins's (1986) conceptualization of the "outsider within" is illustrative in this respect. Such a marginal position simultaneously locates African American women within white families as domestics and outside of such families because they do not truly belong to them. Moreover, the static, dichotomous nature of these categories negates the likelihood that these distinctive statuses may be negotiated, understood, and reinterpreted in divergent ways at different times and in varying situations. For instance, Jennifer Hunt (1984) shows how she attempted to negotiate her status as female to gain acceptance in the gender-stratified world of police officers by adopting a liminal or marginal status, the role of an honorary male and the role of fieldworker "spy." Similarly, in her research on AIDS outreach workers, Kathryn Fox (1991) describes "floating" back and forth between the positions of researcher and committed activist while working in the field. These studies suggest not only that a variety of possible statuses exist for ethnographers but that such shifting positions have consequences for what we can 'know' and see as researchers.

In what follows, I suggest that fieldworkers move around continually among different statuses, changing status from insider to outsider to outsider within. I sidestep the insider-outsider debate by arguing that fieldworkers undertaking participant observation are neither insiders nor outsiders but rather, in the course of their research, assuming a role that is flexible, changing, and quite complex. While my gender and racial identity never changed, my achieved statuses, such as paralegal and graduate student, became more or less salient in various relationships and situations. Sometimes subjects responded to me as a paralegal and at others as a researcher. Further, there was not always a congruence between my identity and their perception of my role. For example, even at times when I self-consciously acted and identified myself as a graduate student doing sociology, I might be treated and perceived as a female paralegal by attorneys and by paralegals. Thus, not only do ethnographers enact varied roles, but these roles hold multiple meanings for different people.

Status as a Female Graduate Student

As a female graduate student in sociology, I was clearly an outsider in law firms. My training in sociology prepared me to problematize and question the activities and assumptions that most legal workers take for granted. On the basis of her first fieldwork experience, Shulamit Reinharz (1988) suggests that inexperienced fieldworkers may have problems maintaining their identity as sociologists because their professional identity is not yet fully developed. Although my professional training was not yet complete, I had developed a strong sense of identity as a Berkeley graduate student. Perhaps in response to what is often described as an anomic department (Duster 1987), a strong culture among graduate students has developed over the years that emphasizes non-hierarchical working groups, critical thinking, and leftist/feminist political activism. These values strongly shaped my views and behavior when I first entered the field.

In law firms, I made no secret of the fact that I was a graduate student doing a dissertation on occupational stress and legal workers. Although no one knew that I was doing participant observation, people did know I was conducting interviews with secretaries, paralegals, and attorneys and attending graduate school at the University of California at Berkeley. My graduate-student status usually came up in conversations with attorneys when they asked me where I went to college, and it came up in conversations with legal assistants and secretaries when they asked why I was working part-time. (I worked four days a week at the private firm until I began working fifty to sixty hours a week on a trial.)

Despite the fact that I had made this identity known and often acted in ways congruent with that identity, I was not regarded by attorneys as a graduate student. This conflict became most apparent when lawyers asked me to read and evaluate their written work. In such situations, I unwittingly played the role of the bright and critical graduate student. They asked for critical feedback, and I provided it. As I was to discover, this was not behavior appropriate to a female paralegal. Rather than providing the supportive comments expected of a female in a subordinate non-attorney position, I read their work with a highly critical eye. In so doing, I assumed a more egalitarian relationship and responded as if I were a peer. As I discuss in my ethnography, by acting this way, I violated one of the emotional norms for deference required of paralegals. Attorneys typically expressed surprise when I responded this way and were quick to remind me of my "actual" status. Their behavior suggests they did not perceive me as a graduate student or as a peer but as a paralegal, a subordinate in the law firm hierarchy.

Such conflicts are not so surprising. As I demonstrate in my research, occupational status is an important criterion for determining how one will be treated within the law-firm hierarchy. However, in formal interview situations where I very self-consciously adopted the role of graduate student, I sometimes found that I was not regarded by lawyers as a novice sociologist or even a graduate student. For example, in one interview, when a male attorney refused to be tape recorded, I promptly pulled out my note pad and prepared to take notes. In response to each question, the lawyer spoke very s-l-o-w-l-y. At first, I thought he was trying to be helpful and I explained that I used my own version of shorthand that enabled me to get his answers down verbatim. After that, he spoke more rapidly, but paused to spell words he thought I wouldn't know how to spell. When he was describing his law school experience, he said:

> When I lived in Cambridge, Cambridge, c-a-m-b-r-i-d-g-e.
> *Oh, that's okay, I know how to spell Cambridge.*
> Oh, good. . . . And, when I was in the moot court competition, moot court, m-o-o-t-. . . .
> *Yes, I know how to spell that.*
> Most people don't know what moot court is.
> *Ah.*
> As I was saying, when I was in the moot court competition. . . .

Here, I played the role of the interested graduate student, but the lawyer responded to me the same way—I was to learn later—he did to his secretary. Like many of the lawyers I worked with, this attorney operated on the assumption that people without law-school training could not possibly understand or possess knowledge about the field of law. His remark, "Most people don't know what moot court is," underscores this point. I also wondered whether his general attitude of condescension was sexist. In his eyes, I was not simply a non-attorney but a female non-attorney. The experiences of male paralegals, which I document in my study, show that even male paralegals without professional aspirations were assumed to be career-oriented and were taken more seriously by male attorneys. This particular lawyer was no exception to this general rule in his differential treatment of male and female paralegals.

In another attorney interview, my status as female researcher came to light quite explicitly. Bill, a young attorney, had been intrigued by my project and immediately agreed to be interviewed. It was one of my more successful interviews. Rapport was not difficult to establish, and he enthusiastically volunteered his views on the stress of doing litigation. He said several times during the interview that it really felt "cathartic to get all this shit off my chest."

During the course of the interview, he intimated that because of his wife's recurring health problems, their sex life had been less than satisfactory. At the time, I didn't probe for further details and let the issue pass. Marital sexual relations were not a part of my study and it seemed too personal a matter to investigate further. At the end of the interview the issue resurfaced in a different form.

> *What do you see yourself doing in five years?*
> That's hard, that's a hard one.
> *Well, what kind of fantasies do you have for your future?*
> I see myself as having a harmless, emphasis on the harmless, romantic interlude in Tahiti—that's the fantasy. [*Laughs.*] Are you really writing that down? [*Pauses.*] Another career, I would like interviewing people about their personal lives, like Studs Terkel. It must be a lot of fun to do what you're doing. [*Smiles, then laughs again.*] Okay, seriously, well, in five years, I guess I see myself working for a small firm or doing some kind of legal work with a bunch of people who have families and are congenial and do good law.

Initially, I felt that he clearly recognized me in the role of graduate student. He seemed very interested in the questions my research raised and responded thoughtfully throughout the interview. However, at the end of the interview, when he jokingly mentioned his "harmless-affair" fantasy, I realized I had been naive. Given that he had alluded to problems in his sex life earlier in the interview, the discussion of his sexual fantasy suggested that my status as an attractive female became more salient in his eyes than my status as graduate student. This interpretation is also supported by his repeated laughter, his knowing looks and smiles while answering the question. His behavior felt flirtatious and inappropriate, and what I had perceived to be good rapport in the interview I came to see in a different light.

Responses by paralegals and secretaries to my graduate-student status varied. Some regarded it with curiosity but not as my central identity: "You don't make money doing that, do you?" Some provided supportive and encouraging remarks: "Just go for it, all that education will get you somewhere." Still others expressed resentment. One male paralegal who had a reputation for being a grouch said, "Oh, back to school tomorrow. Must be nice to be on vacation all the time." (This was a reference to my part-time work schedule—four days in the office and one day off.)

Despite my self-conscious identification as a graduate student doing research, most attorneys refused to acknowledge this status. Instead, I was treated as a paralegal, or more specifically, a female paralegal, sometimes when conducting interviews for the purpose of my dissertation. Paralegals and secretaries responded in a less uniform way—some with curiosity, some with support and enthusiasm, and some with resentment. My role as a self-identified graduate student researcher shifted and changed depending upon the social relationship of the moment.

Status as Female Paralegal

As a covert participant observer, I not only recorded my observations daily in my field notes, but I worked as a paralegal. My shared occupational status with female legal assistants marked me as an insider. However, I qualified as insider in yet another way. I first began working as a paralegal in 1980 after I had graduated from college and before I had entered graduate school. I continued to do freelance and temporary paralegal work during graduate school, over summers and vacations, to pay for tuition and other school expenses. My previous work experience as a paralegal raises two related methodological questions: (1) Did this status, as insider proponents and feminist-standpoint theorists argue, give me greater understanding of the lives of women paralegals? And (2) Was I at risk of "going native" or overidentifying with paralegals?

Reinharz (1988) suggests that it is easier for novice sociologists to go native because their identity as a professional is still nascent. Although I had developed a strong identity as a graduate student, I found that I strongly identified with secretaries and paralegals, simply because I had spent part of my working life as a legal worker.

Most paralegals and secretaries assumed that I knew my way around law firms and around lawyers. For example, after an interview in which Theresa, a paralegal, described the difficulties of working with trial attorneys, she added, "But you know how it is." Such responses assumed a shared understanding of paralegal work. In fact, my paralegal experience often facilitated interviews, especially with hard-to-interview subjects. For instance, when I asked one woman what she found to be most stressful about her job as a paralegal, she said,

> Oh, lots of things.
> *What specifically?*
> Oh, you know, the attorneys.
> *What do they do that is stressful?*
> They just make work difficult.
> *Well, when I was working at Firm X, one of the lawyers I worked with just went crazy when we started working on a trial. He used to throw things around his office, stomp around the room and scream orders at me and his secretary. Do you think that's typical behavior?*
> Oh god, trials. I hate trials. My boss is even worse than that. He is such a perfectionist. You feel like you can't even breathe without asking his permission first. This one time. . . . [*transcript goes on for several pages*]

Thus, my previous experience gave a great deal of knowledge and insight into the working lives of legal assistants. In this sense, I did have certain privileged claims to knowledge. I knew what to ask and how to ask it. I also understood the law-firm support-staff discourse: "baby attorney" was a lawyer fresh out of law school; "summer jerks" referred to law students who came to work at law firms for the summer after their second year of law school. Such understanding facilitated communication with both male and female paralegals. As a consequence, I was more readily accepted by other paralegals than an outsider might have been.

The constant use and validation of my status as a paralegal meant that my graduate-student identity became more and more submerged. Although I never lost interest in my original sociological questions, I felt strongly pulled to the problems faced by paralegals. Over time, my discontent about work sounded more and more like theirs. While I complained in my field notes about "having to wait on these assholes all the time," other women legal assistants grumbled at work and in their interviews about having "to play mom all the time." Such strong feelings of identification with the role suggest that I was "going native." In their classic anthology on participant observation, sociologists George McCall and Jerry Simmons (1969) argue that one of the dangers of prolonged observation is that the fieldworker loses her detachment and fails to observe details and events that the relatively uninvolved researcher would notice. However, I found that while my sociological eye was submerged, it never disappeared completely. Addressing this issue in my field notes, I wrote:

There is a schizophrenic quality to my fieldwork. Sometimes I feel like I am a female paralegal working for a San Francisco financial district law firm. At others, I feel like Mata Hari—an undercover spy for the ASA. And still others, I am both. The internal conflict between these identities becomes most apparent when people confide in me. As a woman paralegal, I am concerned and sympathetic. As a graduate student, I am an instrumental and objective gatherer of "data." One voice asks, "What can I do to help?" A second one whispers, "Pay attention, this is great data!" A third voice cries out, "If this is 'naturalistic' observation, then fieldwork is crazy."

If anything, the conflict between these two statuses served as a painful reminder—I was not a paralegal, but a sociologist.

Status as a White Woman

In sociological research, race and ethnicity are typically treated as problematic in interracial fieldwork situations, such as whites studying African Americans or Chicanos and Latinos (Liebow 1967; Ladner 1971; Blauner and Wellman 1973; Riessman 1988). Few researchers, however, have considered the problems in interpretation that arise when white people study other whites. From the insider position in the debate, there is no conflict or problem in doing so. By contrast, in her recent book *White Women, Race Matters*, Ruth Frankenberg argues that "whiteness" must be problematized in the research process. In other words, we should not take whiteness for granted as a shared identity or social status. In my own research, where the majority of legal workers at both field sites were white, I quickly found that my own whiteness did not provide me with automatic entree as an insider. And in the few cases where I did work with African American women, I was not always an outsider, though I did not qualify as an insider either. Below, I comment briefly on how my "whiteness" influenced my status as an insider and an outsider.

On my first day on the job in the legal department of Bonhomie Corporation, part of my induction into the company included viewing videos on the company's affirmative action plan. After I had watched the video, one of the workers in the personnel department commented, "Well, you'll soon see one of the big problems here is that they hire lots of unqualified minorities because of affirmative action." I was surprised and, without thinking, angrily retorted that her comment was racist, adding that it seemed to violate the spirit of the videos I had just been watching. She was surprised by my response, but recovered quickly after glancing at my resume. "Oh, you went to Berkeley, didn't you?"

The personnel worker's choice to share her comment with me suggests that she assumed we would share a similar viewpoint on affirmative action. Since we had never met before, the only basis for her assumption appeared to lie in our similar racial identities. Because I was white, she assumed I would share her point of view on affirmative action. When I did not, she quickly looked for some other reason to explain and thereby dismiss my point of view. Thus, "whiteness" as a social category did not ensure a shared world view.

I encountered similar obstacles to shared understanding in my interactions with a particular group of white female paralegals who were dubbed the "nicey-nice" women by their white male counterparts. As a white woman and as a paralegal, I qualified as an insider with respect to this occupational and racial/ethnic group. Yet as a feminist who viewed their submissive behavior critically, I felt like an outsider. My critical distance becomes evident in the following example.

In Chapter 6 I described the experiences of Jenna, a paralegal, who stayed in the office all night to complete a last-minute project for her boss, John. Although John thanked her for completing his project "on time," he neither apologized for creating a personal inconvenience nor expressed any concern about her staying up all night alone in a deserted office building, which had recently been the scene of an attempted rape. When Jenna told me about the work she had done, I asked whether she felt that John had taken advantage of her time. She appeared to be surprised by my question and responded:

> But I did it, because I really like John.
> *I don't understand. How does "liking John" make it okay to do his last minute requests?*
> He's just really busy and I like helping him out.
> *Even when he asks you to stay all night in an office building we know isn't that safe?*
> But he didn't do that on purpose. He just needed the project done, and I did it. I like being able to help him out.

As my critical questions suggest, I found the excuses Jenna made for John's behavior hard to accept, especially given that most secretaries and paralegals whom I had interviewed described John as very difficult to work with. On a more personal level, I found Jenna's acquiescence to John's seemingly unreasonable requests to be problematic. Jenna actually seemed to enjoy being the taken-for-granted, deferential helpmate. In my view, the "nicey-nice" women like Jenna were emblematic of what feminist scholar Mary Daly (1978) calls "fembots," that is, women who uncritically accept the subordinate and submissive roles required of them in a male-dominated society.

As this example illustrates, my feminist politics precluded a shared understanding with white women like Jenna. Not only did I find their submissiveness difficult to accept, but I viewed their behavior critically—as collusion in their own subordination. My critical and judgmental response left me feeling that I had little in common with these women—a fact which the early 1970s feminist emphasis on sisterhood cannot explain. As recent scholarship by women of color reveals, this concept of sisterhood is inaccurate and idealistic (Thornton-Dill 1983; hooks 1984; Lorde 1984). There are differences between women in terms of race/ethnicity, social class background, sexual preference, religious background, and stance toward feminism. To assume that a woman researcher by virtue of her gender is an insider when she studies other women denies and obscures differences between women, differences that challenge the assertion of feminist-standpoint theorists that women share a similar "way of knowing."

In interracial interactions, my positioning 'inside' and 'outside' relationships varied. Early in my fieldwork at the private firm, my first field site, I mentioned to Danielle, an African American secretary, that the office reminded me of a big factory. She laughed at my analogy and promptly corrected me, saying:

A factory! Honey, this place is a fucking plantation. [She affects an old-timey dialect, in a Butterfly McQueen voice:] They's the massas and we's the slaves. At Christmas, they come out on the big porch and they give us all these bonuses and a big party, and we's spoze to shuffle around and be grateful for that. But all that money they got, they make it off our backs.

I laughed. Underlying her humor was an insightful sociological analysis of working relationships within the firm, one that I began to take seriously in my own theoretical work. Danielle's analogy served to racialize differences between us in "knowing." As an African American woman, she experienced work relationships in a very different way than I did, and the corrective she offered to my "factory" analogy underscored the differences between us and the sense in which, racially, I was an outsider.

At my second field site, I discovered that another African American secretary, Kimberly, had been given an unfavorable performance review by one of my office mates and coworkers, a woman paralegal referred to as Princess Di by secretaries who disliked her. Kimberly had a gruff exterior. Nevertheless, her work was excellent. Since Kimberly also worked for me, I wrote a memo to the personnel office contradicting Di's assessment, indicating the superior quality of the work Kimberly produced. Then, as company procedure required, I gave the memo to Kimberly to read and sign before I sent it on to Personnel. She expressed surprise that I had written the memo because, as she said to me, "You don't get anything out of this." I explained that this was a matter of principle and that I felt Di was behaving badly simply because Kimberly didn't treat her like "her royal highness." I added that my motives were not entirely altruistic. In general, I didn't like Princess Di or the way she treated

people, particularly her peers and subordinates. Kimberly laughed
and said,

Yeah, well I don't wait on anyone like they are some princess, especially
not some spoiled white bitch like her. But you're not like that.
What, a princess or a spoiled white bitch?
No, no. You're just different for a white girl. I just don't like people who
act like that. No, you're different, but then I always knew you were different.
I don't know what you mean.
You're a real person, you don't have any fancy, la-de-da airs. You got all
this college education, but you don't act like you think you're better than
anybody. When Alex's baby got sick, I heard you talking to her about it. You
made her feel a whole lot better. And doing this for me. . . . You treat
everybody like they're "just plain folks." Princess Di and the attorneys don't
like it much, but I do. . . . And, you've got a real good sense of style. Most
white girls don't know how to dress, but you're always wearing these bright
colors, you're different. Like that purple skirt you got on today, where did
you get that? . . . [We talk about various bargain basements where we like
to shop.] Now if you would just let me show you how to put on some make-
up, [laughs] you'd be real pretty too!

In supporting Kimberly's personnel case, I became accepted as an
ally against Princess Di. Her assertion that she liked the fact that I
treated people as "just plain folks" suggests we also shared values
about social etiquette. Still, her acknowledgment of "all that college
education" and the repeated phrase "different for a white girl"
served to underscore the differences in status between us. Her emphasis on the other ways I was "different for a white girl" served simultaneously to differentiate me from other white women in her
eyes and to distinguish me from Black women. I felt not so much an
insider, but in Collins's terminology, an "outsider within."
In these examples, I have attempted to problematize my ethnic
identity in relationship to African American as well as European
American women. As a white woman I was not always an insider in
relation to other white woman. If anything, in the conversations with
the personnel worker and with Jenna, I felt more like an outsider. In
situations with African American women, I sometimes felt like an
outsider (i.e., with Danielle) and sometimes like an outsider within

(i.e., with Kimberly). Here we can see how the ground shifts and changes in fieldwork, thereby shifting views and understandings.

I have shown how my status as a fieldworker, paralegal, and white woman sometimes allowed me access as an insider (e.g., a former paralegal), an outsider (e.g., a Berkeley graduate student, a feminist sociologist) and an outsider within (e.g., a white woman who seems "different for a white girl"). These findings demonstrate that the concepts of insider and outsider are not static and dichotomous categories, but fluid, layered, and changing. The shifting statuses I describe further suggest that this dichotomous construction must be reconceptualized if we are to account for the varied roles of fieldworkers. The richness and depth of naturalistic observation lies precisely in the fieldworker's ability to move and to be moved back and forth in a continuous tacking between the inside and outside of events. By fully articulating the self in the manner Krieger (1991) proposes, we better enable ourselves to capture the ever-changing multiplicity of views found in the workplace.

My argument also has implications for feminist-standpoint theory. In its earliest articulation, Dorothy Smith (1974) argued that women's divergent structural position vis-à-vis men produced a distinct consciousness or "way of knowing" the world. While my central social identity as a white women yielded a unique perspective on the workplace, this racial and gendered consciousness became more or less salient with respect to other types of status. In my interaction with "nicey-nice" white women paralegals, I found that my feminist politics served to differentiate our ways of seeing the workplace as white women. Further, in my encounter with the white female personnel department worker, my status as a Berkeley graduate student served to underscore our political differences with respect to affirmative action. These findings suggest that standpoint theory must be revised to account for the ways a particular woman's standpoint may shift or change depending upon status and/or varying situations. As Wendy Luttrell observes, more empirical work needs to be done "that either maps out women's diversity as knowers or describes the varied and changing conditions under which different women claim and construct knowledge" (1993: 506).

My shifting positions in the field also have consequences for the nature of sociological knowledge created through this study. As a white woman, a feminist, and a former paralegal, I had entree to the world of women paralegals that a male sociologist may not have had. As I have suggested, my multiple statuses, particularly as a former paralegal, made it easy to find interviewees—most women eagerly volunteered—and in some cases led to shared understanding about the difficulties of this work world. On the other hand, as a woman, I also faced a number of obstacles to my research. Male lawyers did not regard me as a peer, as they might have a white male researcher. As I have pointed out, most of them rejected my critical comments on their written work, and one assumed that I would have difficulty spelling. And, as I discuss in Chapter 6, they typically excluded me from informal, all-male socializing activities. In addition, some male attorneys may have been less forthcoming in their interviews with me than they would have been with another man. In an effort to please me, they may have presented themselves as more critical of the adversarial role. For example, in my interview with Bill, he flirted with me at the same time that he told me how great it was to talk about the stressful nature of his work. As a consequence, my writing about the work world of male litigators may appear to be flatter, less detailed, and perhaps even less interesting than my writing on women legal workers. However, given my subordinate positioning in relations with these men, such gaps in "knowing" are unavoidable. Indeed, this is what makes "situated knowledges" partial and incomplete.

Finally, this work raises questions for future methodological consideration. My account of the fieldworker's multiple and positional status resonates with recent postmodernist accounts, which maintain that subjectivity is "decentered" or "fragmented" (Flax 1990; Nicholson 1990). As Pauline Marie Rosenau (1992) observes, the postmodern individual is one who writes from the margins of society, one who is flexible, relaxed, and oriented to feelings and emotions. But do all fieldworkers write and research from the margins? Are all social scientists prone to multiple perceptions and statuses, or are some so ensconced in a "master status" that they cannot see or be seen in any other way? The fact that distinctive statuses such as race and gender may be negotiated, understood, and reinterpreted in divergent ways at different times and in varying situations suggests that even a master status can hold multiple and contradictory meanings. Thus, whether we write from the margins or from the mainstream, heeding varied and shifting meanings compels us to rethink sociological categories and to interrogate the implications such vantage points hold for the construction of sociological theory and method.

The Dilemma of Ethnographic Authority

Contemporary critical writing on ethnographic authority begins with the premise that ethnographers inescapably exercise textual and social authority over the people they study, particularly people who occupy subordinate social positions. James Clifford (1988), for example, suggests that ethnographic texts produce subjectivities in an unequal exchange between anthropologists and "natives." Sociologists also acknowledge the inequality in the relationship between the researcher and her subjects. In the early 1970s, Robert Blauner and David Wellman asserted that such research serves to maintain the subordination of racial minorities while maintaining the privileged status that (white) social scientists enjoy:

Exploitation exists whenever there is a markedly unequal exchange between two parties; and when this inequality is supported by a discrepancy in social power. In social research, subjects give up some time, some energy, some trust, but in the typical case get almost nothing from the transaction. As social scientists, we get grants which pay our salaries; the research thesis legitimates our professional status, then publications advance us along in income and rank, further widening the material and status gap between the subjects and ourselves (1973: 316).

Recently, feminist scholars have begun to pose a similar question about studying women. Sue Wise, for example, draws attention in particular to the inescapable power female researchers may hold in defining another woman's reality:

Another structural inequality in the research relationship is that the research products are produced by the researcher and it is her version of reality that is seen to have cognitive authority . . . No matter how we deny it we are still operating in an environment where the ethic prevails that those who publish research are the experts and those who are written about are not (1987: 76).

In my own fieldwork, I found that my feelings about the potential exploitation of my subjects varied over my time in the field. Ironically, the longer I was in the field and the more I became involved in my subjects' lives, the less I worried about this issue. But at the beginning I was acutely sensitive to the power I held over those I studied. It was clear to me what I would get out of the research—a dissertation to fulfill my Ph.D. requirements and, eventually, a book—but what would they get out of it? Every early personal confidence drove me wild with anxiety. People readily confided personal troubles to me. What was I to do with such personal information? Was I betraying them, even as I promised confidentiality?

The following excerpt from my field notes illustrates some of the guilt and anxiety I experienced when one of my subjects revealed personal fears about his career accomplishments as he approached the age of forty:

Today Stan and I drove down to [a suburb in the Bay area], to interview a potential witness for the upcoming trial. After reviewing the background of the witness and discussing the possible testimony we might uncover to bolster our case, the conversation took a more personal turn. Stan asked me what I would like to do if I wasn't in graduate school in sociology. I thought for a minute and said, "A rock-n-roll star." I explained it was a pretty far-fetched fantasy given that I am practically tone deaf, but I love to sing anyway.

Then I returned the question. This opened a long discussion about his frustrations about being an attorney, how much work it was and how little the psychological pay-off is. "You do a great job, and no one cares. The client doesn't understand the intricacies of law well enough to know how well you've done. And, other lawyers bite the bullet in envy." At one point, he said his wife had told him that he shouldn't feel he has to prove himself so much to people, that he should learn to like himself as he is. He added that it was a "sweet thought," but that's not how law works. "In the real world, you have to keep on proving yourself if you want to stay on top." Thinking of the academic world, I felt inclined to agree, but I also sensed some truth in what his wife said. His constant need to prove himself didn't appear to result simply from some external pressure, but an inner insecurity which compelled him to prove himself again and again. I nodded assent, but said nothing. We drove the last ten minutes of the trip in silence.

Initially, I felt pleased that he had confided in me, but now, as I write this, I feel guilty. This was a highly personal revelation for someone who is typically emotionally closed and distant. Stan does not strike me as the type of person who makes such personal disclosures easily. On the other hand, why did he tell me? Am I just the sympathetic female ear? Or was he just in a funk, and I just happened to be the closest available body?

Although the conversation had given me insight into the pressures trial lawyers face, I continued to feel somewhat uncomfortable after such disclosures were made. People trusted me. What was I doing with their trust? This was further exacerbated by the fact that although most people knew I was doing a dissertation on occupational stress and the legal profession, they did not know that I was doing participant observation. At least in interviews, the power relationship was somewhat apparent, but in fieldwork it went unacknowledged.

The power I had in defining the reality of others did not always go unacknowledged, however. Toward the end of my stint at the first field site, I ran into a situation where one of the attorneys clearly recognized that my critical and sociological understanding of working relations in the law firm was inconsistent with his own. At some point, Michael expressed interest in my dissertation prospectus. I naively assumed that he actually might find it interesting and provided a copy for him.[5] As I painfully discovered, he was highly offended by my "literature review." Below is a synopsis of events from my field notes:

He was really hurt because my prospectus, in his words, "portrays all these wonderful secretaries and paralegals who support these asshole attorneys." And how did I think he would respond, but to take it personally because [he raises his voice] "wasn't this really about me and Jane [his secretary] and Debbie [a paralegal]?" He added sneeringly, "And, it's so well-written and polished. All these footnotes and references. You must have spent a lot of time working on this."

I said that I was sorry that I had hurt his feelings, but that had not been my intention at all. I tried to explain that I was interested in how the structure of the legal profession necessitated certain kinds of behavior and I was interested in what the consequences were for people who were involved in such occupations. . . . I further explained that all interviews would be confi-

dential as were the names of the law firms where they worked. He continued to say how much I had hurt his feelings. . . . Then he started talking
about what a good interviewer I was. It's a "special skill." "Stan [an attor-
ney] calls six people and no one tells him anything. You call one person and
we get everything we need to know." He went on to say that it was a valu-
able, but dangerous skill because people feel so comfortable talking to me
that they might reveal a confidence they would later regret. (I think he was
talking about himself here.) I told him that yes I am a good interviewer and
people do enjoy talking to me, but my dissertation interviews are confiden-
tial. . . . And, to top it off, as I am leaving he tells me to never discuss our
conversation with my thesis adviser. (Is this a sign of his guilt or embarrassment?)

Over the weekend I brooded about Michael's behavior. Although
I had an inkling of why he was upset—he didn't like being an object
of study—I couldn't figure out how a fairly straightforward literature
review had produced this reaction. Moreover, I felt he had been
downright mean—the sneer about "it's so well-written" suggested
that he had not perceived me as a particularly intelligent or articulate person before he read the prospectus. In addition, his "orders"
about what I could or could not say to my thesis adviser struck me as
extremely controlling. His response strongly resembled adversarial
tactics—the intimidation, the attempt to control and direct the witness (me). The more I thought about it the angrier I became. After
talking to my thesis adviser and a number of other faculty members,
I decided that it was time to leave the field site and find a new one.
I had already accumulated voluminous field notes, and I was concerned that I might contaminate the field if I stayed any longer. At
the end of the weekend, I talked to the paralegal coordinator and
told her I would finish the projects I had begun, but I was planning
to quit.

[On Monday] when I came into the office, Michael did his best "charm"
routine, lots of big smiles, "how are you's" and so on. When everyone else
left the meeting, he said he had heard that I was angry with him. I said,
"That's right." He said he'd like to talk to me about it later in the day. . . .
    When I met with Michael, he said he wanted to "clear the air." He was
sorry if he had offended me and hoped we could be friendly. He repeated
several times that he really liked me—as if that were the issue. "You are
such a good paralegal." How could my feelings be hurt, he had said such

glowing things about my research skills. I explained why [his insinuation that I wasn't smart was insulting and giving me orders was offensive]. Rather than apologize again, he said, "Well, attorneys have feelings too." He tried to conclude on an upbeat note, saying he was willing to put this behind us, they really need me for the upcoming trial and everyone knows how much work I did interviewing all those witnesses [I interviewed almost forty witnesses in a three-month period.] I said that if I stayed, I would be very friendly and professional. I had no problems with that. However, I thought he should know that he was currently on my shit list. And [I added] people who are on my shit list have to do lots of penance to get off. He laughed in an overly hearty voice, but I knew he didn't like it.

    This encounter demonstrates at once the lawyer's recognition of my authority and my disruption of norms. By problematizing what he took for granted—the nature of working relationships in law firms—I had hurt his feelings, made him feel angry, and betrayed his trust. My critical view also violated my subordinate status as a woman paralegal, who is supposed to be nice and supportive of attorneys. My prospectus and my role as researcher demonstrated that I was critical, detached, and even instrumental. Not surprisingly, the attorney perceived this point of view as threatening.

    Secretaries and paralegals had an entirely different reaction to my research. When I casually mentioned my dissertation topic, people eagerly volunteered to be interviewed. One woman accosted me in the bathroom, providing a list of reasons why I should interview her. Others completely rejected the notion of confidentiality. As one secretary said repeatedly, "Use my real name. I want you to use my real name in your book." (This posed a stark contrast to the many lawyers who did not want to be tape-recorded in their interviews and worried a great deal about the issue of confidentiality.) Women legal workers also expressed curiosity about my written work. After I left the firm, a secretary I had interviewed asked to see my prospectus. I was reluctant and explained why, but since I had already done the interview and no longer worked in the firm where she did, I decided there was no risk of fireworks this time. She called me a week later and said, "No offense, Jennifer, but this thing is boring. How did Michael ever get riled up over this damn thing?"

    The difference between the secretary's response and the attorney's reflects their differential locations in the law-firm hierarchy. Unlike most lawyers, paralegals and secretaries not only saw my view as compatible with their own but also shared my vision of an alternative organization of the workplace.[6] In this sense, it might appear that I had resolved the dilemma of ethnographic authority—at least with secretaries and paralegals. Some feminists, for example, have suggested that ethnography and interviewing are particularly suited to feminist research because they represent egalitarian processes characterized by authenticity, reciprocity, and intersubjectivity between the researcher and her subjects (Duelli Klein 1983; Mies 1983; Reinharz 1983).[7] As Renate Duelli Klein argues, "a methodology that allows for studying women in an interactive process [e.g., participant observation,] . . . will end the exploitation of women as research subjects/objects" (1983: 93).

My success with paralegals and secretaries does not, however, resolve the dilemma of ethnographic authority. Fieldwork is far from egalitarian—I am still the person who benefits most from this research. Sociologist Judith Stacey (1988) argues that despite the seemingly egalitarian nature of ethnography, major contradictions exist. The personal relationship between the researcher and her subjects obscures power differences in knowledge and structural mobility and "places research subjects at grave risk of manipulation and betrayal by the ethnographer" (1988: 21–27). In addition, there is a contradiction between the desire for collaboration on the final research paper and the fact that the research ultimately belongs to the researcher.

Is there a solution to this "inescapable" problem of the authorial voice? Stacey's response is to despair a fully feminist ethnography: "There can be ethnographies that are partially feminist [and/or] accounts of culture enhanced by the application of feminist perspectives" (1988: 26). On the other hand, new ethnographers, in keeping with the postmodernist emphasis on narrative strategy and style, claim that they can best expose power relations embedded in traditional representations of other societies through new experimental writings. The essays in the influential volume *Writing Culture*, for instance, argue that standard narratives presented by ethnographers as definitive readings of culture actually obscure the provisional nature of anthropological interpretation: "The ethnographer does not recognize the provisional nature of [her] presentations. They are definitive" (Crapanzano, 1986: 51). By unmasking the process of textual production, the *Writing Culture* essayists raise important critical questions about researchers as authors who "invent" texts, while hiding behind an "objective," disembodied voice.

While new ethnographers compel us to think critically about ourselves as authors, their experimental writings do not necessarily disrupt the status quo. In their careful reading of Clifford's (1988) polyphonic representation of the Mashpee Indians, feminist scholars Frances Mascia-Lees, Patricia Sharpe, and Colleen Cohen (1989) suggest that Clifford's use of multiple voices (trial transcripts, interview transcripts, and other snippets of information) does not counter the powerful forces that continue to deny the Mashpee Indians access to their tribal lands. His carefully crafted academic text will certainly not be read by policy analysts, government officials, or laypeople interested in supporting the Mashpee Indians. This suggests that the problem of ethnographic authority might be weighed against another question: Who is the intended audience for social science research?

Sociologist Robert Bellah and his colleagues (1985) argue that social science is a public philosophy, engaging the public in dialogue about our culture's traditions, ideals and aspirations. Social science research

becomes a form of social self-understanding and self-interpretation. It brings the traditions, ideals and aspirations of society into juxtaposition with its present reality. It holds a mirror up to society. By probing the past as well as the present, by looking at "values" as much as "facts," such social science is able to make connections that are not obvious and ask difficult questions. (1985: 301)

In this view, the purpose of social science is not research for its own sake but rather research aimed at bringing sociological issues to a forum for public inquiry and discussion. Only by leaving the confines of the ivory tower and entering the public domain can research have an influence on women and men's lives. Such a stance is compatible with what feminist scholar Michelle Fine calls activist research because it positions "researchers as self-conscious, critical, participatory analysts, engaged but still distinct from our informants" (1992: 220). Such research is committed to the study of social change or of the move toward change, or it is provocative of change.

Such a strategy by no means resolves the dilemma of ethnographic authority, though it does compel us to weigh the social costs of forgoing research altogether against the costs borne by the subjects of a study. What is more worthwhile? To do a study that raises important questions about the sources of stress in the workplace and run the risk of offending the sensibilities of some of its participants, or, in the interests of offending no one, consider dropping socially important questions, or at the extreme, suspending study altogether? Although I strongly believe in protecting the confidentiality of subjects and in treating them with respect, I realize that not all people I study—particularly those in power—will like my presentation of their work world. However, sociology as public philosophy is not intended to please the people we study but rather to address the social and political conditions of their lives. In this way, sociology seeks to enhance the lives of those we study by bringing issues and questions to public attention and calling for social change.

Appendix Two

Lawyer Jokes

The lawyer jokes catalogued here were collected from secretaries, paralegals, attorneys, and other legal workers during the fifteen months I was conducting my research (1988–1989). The jokes told most often are listed first, with frequency of retelling indicated by a number in parentheses. At the end of the list are lawyer jokes I have heard more recently, during discussions of my research in both academic and non-academic settings.

1. *Question*: How can you tell when a lawyer is lying?

   Answer: His lips are moving. (13)

2. *Question*: Why don't lawyers get eaten by sharks?

   Answer: Professional courtesy. (12)

3. *Question*: Why did research scientists substitute lawyers for rats in their laboratory experiments?

   Answer: There are more of them, scientists don't become emotionally attached to them, and there are just some things that white rats won't do. (9)

4. *Question*: What is the difference between a dead lawyer in the road and a dead skunk [or rattlesnake]?

   Answer: There are skid marks by the skunk. (7)

5. *Question*: Why can't a lawyer be circumcised?

   Answer: Because there's no end to those pricks. (4)

6. *Question*: What's a criminal lawyer?

   Answer: Redundant. (3)

7. *Question*: What's black and brown and looks good on a lawyer?

   Answer: A Doberman pinscher. (3)

8. *Question*:   If you find a lawyer buried up to his neck in sand, what do you do?

   Answer: Find more sand. (2)

9. *Question*:   What did the lawyer name his daughter?

   Answer: Sue. (1)

10. *Question*:   Why don't lawyers have hemorrhoids?

    Answer: Because they are perfect assholes. (1)

11. *Question*:   How many lawyers does it take to screw in a light bulb?

    Answer: Two. One to screw it in and one to sue the manufacturer. (1)

12. *Question*:   What are 500 lawyers at the bottom of the river?

    Answer: A good start. (1)

Recent Lawyer Jokes

Question: What's the difference between a lawyer and a flounder?

Answer: One is a scum-sucking bottom-dweller; the other is a fish.

Question: What's the difference between a lawyer and a bucket of shit?

Answer: The bucket.

Question: What do lawyers and sperm have in common?

Answer: One in a million makes a human.

Question: How do you get a lawyer out of a tree?

Answer: Cut the rope.

God decided to take the devil to court and settle their differences once and for all. When the devil heard this, he was greatly amused. "And where," he said, "do you think you will find a lawyer?"

Notes

Chapter One

1. According to Jacob's analysis of census data, more than two-thirds of American women in the paid labor force worked in jobs that were 70 percent or more female (1989: 1). Also see England (1992) and Reskin and Roos (1990).

2. Theories of sex segregation do not always fall neatly into these two categories. Hartmann's (1976) early work on "the partnership between patriarchy and capital," for example, suggests that capitalism as a structure of social relations determines positions within the economic division of labor, while patriarchy as a form of solidarity among men enables both capitalists and working-class men to control women's labor power. However, her account is not a successful attempt to link structure and agency. Though working-class and capitalist men have agency to control women's labor power, women, as workers, are granted no agency whatsoever. They are merely passive actors in this process.

3. In Hochschild's (1983) conceptualization, emotional labor differs from emotion work. Although both involve the management of one's emotions, the former is related to labor in the paid work force, while the latter is utilized in one's private life. For example, trying not to appear disappointed in a social situation with friends, when in fact one is disappointed, is emotion work, not emotional labor. If such behavior were called for in a work situation, however, then according to Hochschild's distinction it would constitute emotional labor. Throughout the book I use the term *emotional labor* rather than *emotion work* when referring to the workplace.

4. Hochschild's (1983) groundbreaking study on gender and emotional labor was the first to articulate the commercialization of feelings in the workplace. For more recent research on work and emotions, see Rollins

(1985) and Romero (1992) on domestic workers; Diamond (1988) on nurses' aides; Leidner (1993) on hamburger counter clerks and insurance sales agents; and Fineman's (1993) anthology on emotions in organizations.

5. Willmott (1990) also criticizes Burawoy's account for its lack of attention to the subjectivity of the worker.

6. Socialization theories have also been criticized because they tend to view gender as a role to be adopted and relinquished as the situation demands, neglecting the fact that gender is an ascribed social status marked by power relations (Lopata and Thorne 1978; Stacey and Thorne 1985).

7. There are a variety of schools of thought or traditions within psychoanalytic theory. My account relies on an object-relations theory reading of psychoanalysis rather than on drive theory or a Lacanian interpretation. Drive theory, for example, tends to reduce all human motivation to pleasure-seeking impulses. For further criticisms of drive theory, see Chodorow (1985). On the other hand, traditional Lacanian accounts also provide an inadequate theory of agency because they assume that subjectivity is the effect of a pre-given linguistic structure. For an excellent critique of Lacan, see Elliott (1992).

8. A number of social theorists and feminist scholars view psychoanalysis as a potentially emancipatory theory (see Habermas 1971, Benjamin 1988, Chodorow 1989b, and Elliott 1992), while others see it as a way to explain the function and integration of traditional gender roles in society (Parsons 1964).

9. Psychoanalytic sociology embraces work from divergent sociological traditions, ranging from Parsonian functionalism (Parsons 1964) to feminist theory (Chodorow 1978; Benjamin 1988) to the Marxist work of the Frankfurt school (Horkheimer 1972 [1936]) As Denise Segura and I (1993) have recently argued, these perspectives share two main elements: a focus on unconscious mental processes and the assumption of an active subject.

10. For examples of key expositions in object-relations theory, see Fairbairn (1952) and Winnicott (1958).

11. Some critics have objected to Chodorow's use of psychoanalytic theory, while others have suggested that the gender differences she describes, such as her conceptualization of women as relational, falsely universalize the experiences of women (Lorber 1980; Joseph 1981). Other criticisms of her work include inattention to racial and ethnic differences between women (Joseph 1981); neglect of the role fathers play in parenting (Johnson 1988; Benjamin 1988); assumption that two-parent, heterosexual families are best suited for parenting (Flax 1981); and lack of attention to gay or lesbian sexual identity (Bart 1984; Rich 1980). For responses to these criticisms and others, see Chodorow (1980; 1989a; 1989b).

12. We make a similar argument about psychoanalytic thinking and so-

cial specificity in our article on gender personality in Chicano families. See Segura and Pierce (1993).

13. Only a few other sociological studies have incorporated psychoanalytic insights into the study of women and paid work. For example, Pringle's (1988) book, *Secretaries Talk,* utilizes psychoanalytic feminist insights to study the relationship between bosses and secretaries. Rather than integrating these insights with theories of the labor process, as I attempt to do, Pringle relies upon a Foucauldian framework. Williams's (1989) work on female marines and male nurses also relies on Chodorow's theory of gender identity to explain gender difference; however, she focuses only on the micro level of analysis (see Chapter 6).

14. In addition to scholarly studies on stress and litigation, there are numerous journalistic accounts. See Beckhusen 1989; Brill 1986; Ciotti 1988; Hulstuk 1989; Kanter 1989; Lefer 1986; Marcus 1987; Margolick 1989, 1990b, 1990c; and Rohrlich 1990.

15. There are two ethnographies on lawyers: Smigel's (1969) classic study, which was conducted in the late 1950s and John Flood's (1991) more recent research. Neither focuses on the relations between attorneys and other legal workers in law firms.

16. Nelson (1988) describes large firms as those employing one hundred or more lawyers.

17. To protect the confidentiality of the law firms as well as the people interviewed for this study, all individual and institutional names have been changed to pseudonyms unless otherwise specified.

18. Despite minor differences in job description and occupational status between legal secretaries and paralegals, their experiences in this study were similar, especially for male tokens, as was the emotional labor required of the jobs. Because so little research has been done on paralegals and a number of excellent studies have already been conducted on secretaries (for example, Benet 1973; Kanter 1977; Pringle 1988; Statham 1988), I focus primarily on the experiences of legal assistants and use the findings from my interviews with secretaries to supplement their accounts. This is not to say, however, that there are no differences between paralegal and secretarial work experiences. Secretaries are much more likely to be sexualized as women workers, whereas paralegals are more apt to be regarded as mothers and confidantes. See Pierce (1995) for a further discussion of these issues.

Chapter Two

1. Hurst (1950) and Friedman (1973) provide general surveys of American legal history. Auerbach (1976) provides an interesting history of the

stratification within the legal profession, though the development of large firms is not the book's main focus. Nelson (1988) describes the recent emergence of large firms but does not detail history before the 1960s. In addition, there are a number of accounts of specific firms written by partners or commissioned historians. For examples, see Taft (1938), Swaine (1946), Dean (1957), Earle (1963), and Koegel (1953).

2. Although Murphree's (1981) dissertation on legal secretaries provides a descriptive account of the historical changes in the large firm and considers the entry of women as clerical workers, it does not conceptualize the large law firm's past or contemporary structure as gendered.

3. In her study of contemporary law offices, Spangler (1986) also finds that in-house legal departments and large law firms have similar organizational structures.

4. Training and administrative time, e.g., time spent supervising support staff or associates, is not included in billable time. At both my field sites, billable time was recorded down to the tenth of the hour. Lawyers were expected to turn in their time sheets on a daily basis to the accounting department so that the firm could track the time billed for each client. At most firms, paralegals, but not secretaries, also keep track of billable hours.

5. Organizations are also structured by racial hierarchies. Although private law firms catering to corporate clientele tend to have predominantly white work forces (Epstein 1983; Segal 1983; Auerbach 1976), my research shows that with the exception of a few hires at the top levels, minorities tend to be concentrated in lower-level positions, such as janitorial work.

6. There is a third "invisible" tier of workers in the law firm—the janitorial workers who come into the office at night to clean and maintain the premises. At Lyman, Lyman and Portia and at Bonhomie Corporation, these workers were either women and men of color or recent immigrants to the United States. Their presence adds a racial dimension to the gendered structure of the law firm.

7. Instead of partners, Bonhomie Corporation has senior counsel positions. Lawyers who put in seven to eight years of service and show promise may be promoted to senior counsel. Senior counsel function much as partners do in the private firm.

8. At Lyman, Lyman and Portia, the only two paralegals of color were an African American man and an Asian American woman.

9. Legal assistants of color included: two Asian American women, one African American woman, and one Chicana.

10. These salaries reflect the averages for the San Francisco Bay area. In 1989, the top salary for associates was $62,000 (Abrahamson 1989a, 1989b;

Freinkel 1989). In 1988, the average starting salary nationwide for in-house counsel was $35,682 (Langer 1988). According to the *San Francisco Association for Legal Assistants 1989 Survey*, the average salary for paralegals in the Bay area ran from $22,000 to $40,000. In their study of in-house legal-departments in California, C. B. Estrin and Associates found that legal assistants averaged $23,000 to $65,000 (Hickey 1989).

11. Some San Francisco firms house their paralegals and case clerks in separate, less expensive, and much less glamorous office space. In one firm, legal assistant offices are located in an entirely separate office building, in an expansive room filled with a maze of gray cubicles.

12. Thanks to Mary Beth Kelsey for reminding me of Foucault's provocative image.

13. Although another legal worker intervened in the situation to defend her friend, Dana was so disturbed by the incident that she left her job. Although the partner had been caught in the act, he was never sanctioned in any way by the firm for his behavior. I argue (see Chapter 7) that by sweeping such incidents "under the rug," law firms normalize sexual harassment in the workplace.

14. In this study, women secretaries were more likely to encounter sexual harassment than were women paralegals. Whereas legal secretaries were often treated as potential sex objects, paralegals were more likely to be regarded as "mothers" and "therapists." See Pierce (1995) for a further discussion of this "division of labor."

15. At first glance, these restrictions resemble the characteristics of a "caste-like bureaucracy," which has strict interdictions on both mobility and social interaction (Berreman 1960). However, as I suggest below, gender plays a crucial role in facilitating limited mobility and social interaction.

16. According to *Baron's Profile of American Colleges*, elite colleges are defined as "most competitive in terms of student admissions" (1980: x). Prestige schools are designated as "highly competitive or very competitive" by this criteria (1980: x–xiii).

17. I am distinguishing here between office romances as consensual relationships and sexual harassment, which is not consensual. Sexual harassment was not uncommon in both law firms. For a more detailed discussion of harassments, see chapter 5.

18. For other accounts detailing the influence of the Cravath system, see Hurt (1950); Smigel (1969); Friedman (1973); Hoffman (1976); Auerbach (1976); Larson (1977) and Nelson (1988).

19. As Davies points out, the feminization of clerical work did not happen overnight. The demand for clerical workers was so great in the early twentieth century that both men and women poured into these jobs

(Davies 1982: 53). However, these jobs became increasingly female-dominated throughout the first half of the century, and today, 97 percent of all typists are women (Reskin and Roos 1990: 26).

20. Attorneys hired in Wall Street firms have been almost entirely male until quite recently. The first woman lawyer to work in a Wall Street firm, Catherine Noyes Lee, daughter of U.S. Court of Appeals judge Walter Noyes, was hired in 1924 by the firm Cadwalader, Wickersham and Taft (Morello 1986: 201–02). Lee's hire did not create a new demographic trend. In the late 1950s, Smigel (1969) found that there were only eighteen women lawyers on Wall Street.

21. Because women were not allowed to attend many law schools, two special women's law schools were created—the Portia School of Law in Boston and the Washington College of Law in the District of Columbia (Chester 1985).

22. In 1920, none of the women lawyers included in this percentage worked on Wall Street (Epstein 1983, table 1.1). Wall Street did not hire a woman lawyer until 1924 (Morello 1986). See note 20.

23. For further discussion of these programs and the shifts they brought about in the practice of law, see Reich (1964); Katz (1982); Burstein (1986); Friedman (1985); Nelson (1988).

24. The rise in in-house legal departments has been discussed by sociologists and other commentators on the legal profession. See Bellis and Morrison (1989); Roy (1989); Nelson (1988); Spangler (1986); Banks (1983); Chayes (1983); Bernstein (1978).

25. Sociologists distinguish professionals from other workers on the basis of their specialized knowledge and its connection to their exclusive control over profession (Bloom 1971; Friedson 1971). Semi-professionals, on the other hand, apply knowledge derived from the profession rather than creating it (Simpson and Simpson 1969; Etzioni 1969). More recently, sociologists have debated the extent to which professionals actually have autonomy (e.g., Derber 1982; Spangler 1986; Nelson 1988).

26. Because legal assistants are not disaggregated by U.S. Census data, Johnstone and Wenglinsky arrived at these percentages by comparing a number of paralegal surveys done across the country (1985: 69, 105).

27. The *San Francisco Association for Legal Assistants Survey 1989* reports that 88 percent of paralegals who responded to the survey are women (Hickey 1989).

28. Leidner (1993) also argues that jobholders themselves participate in creating sex-typed idioms about their work. In her view, workers interpret their jobs as appropriate to a specific gender "even under the most unlikely conditions" (1993: 194).

Chapter Three

1. For a summary of popular reasons for disliking lawyers, see Josephson's (1988) article "Unloved Lawyers: Why People Don't Like them." Also, see Goldberg (1987); Margolick (1988); Miner (1988); Sontag (1988); and Hall (1989). For a catalogue of lawyer jokes obtained in this study, see Appendix 2.

2. According to a survey conducted by the *National Law Journal*, the top three reasons for disliking lawyers were that they (1) "are too interested in making money"; (2) "manipulate the legal system without any concern for right and wrong"; and (3) "file too many unnecessary lawsuits" (1986: S-3).

3. Special thanks to Laurence Rose, Lou Natali, and the National Institute of Trial Advocacy for allowing me to attend and observe NITA's three-week training seminar on trial advocacy.

4. Studies on the legal profession have typically focused on the tension between professionalism and bureaucracy. For examples, see Smigel (1969); Carlin (1961); Spangler (1986); and Nelson (1988).

5. In contrast to the adversarial system, the inquisitorial model in Germany is a judge-driven system. It is considered to be less adversarial and less controlled by combative attorneys (Schwartz 1979).

6. Blumberg (1967) describes lawyers as practicing a "confidence game." However, in his account it is the client who is the "mark" and the attorney and other people in the court who collude in "taking him out." In my usage, litigators "con" not only their clients but also juries, judges, and opposing counsel.

7. Francis Wellman (1854–1942) was one of the great nineteenth-century trial lawyers who made his reputation in New York courtrooms in the 1880s and 1890s as an assistant district attorney. He became widely known for his spectacular coups in the cross-examination of witnesses (Wellman 1986 [1903]).

8. This conception of courtroom drama infuses popular culture. Television shows are filled with actors who play lawyers in such courtroom dramas as *Perry Mason, L.A. Law, Matlock,* and *Civil Wars.*

9. Leidner (1991), for example, shows that the predominance of men in sales leads salesmen to construe the work they do as "manly."

10. In *The Fundamentals of Trial Technique*, Mauet describes two approaches to cross-examination. In the first, the purpose is to elicit favorable testimony by getting the witness to agree with the facts that support one's case. The second approach, the destructive cross-examination, "involves asking questions which will discredit the witness or his testimony" (1980: 240).

11. Properly formed leading questions are allowed in cross-examination but *not* in direct examination. Mauet defines a leading question as "one which suggests the answer" and provides examples such as "Mr. Doe, on December 13, 1977, you owned a car, didn't you?" (1980: 247). In his view, control comes by asking "precisely phrased leading questions that never give the witness an opening to hurt you" (1980: 243).

12. Spangler (1986) and Abramson (1986) make similar observations about the relationship between in-house legal counsel and the members of other departments in the same company.

13. Most jurisdictions have statutory criteria under which certain jurors are automatically disqualified, such as age, criminal record, residency, and citizenship. Jurors may also be challenged for cause if they possess a state of mind that would prevent them from giving a fair trial. A peremptory challenge, on the other hand, does not require the party to identify any cause or reason for the challenge; attorneys usually have only a limited number of these (Mauet 1980: 28).

14. A sympathetic witness is one who by virtue of personal circumstances or characteristics will automatically have the sympathy of the jury (Ring 1987). Widows are a good example.

15. Leidner makes a similar observation about the insurance salesmen she studied who used a "mix of deference and ruthlessness" to make their sales pitches (1991: 169–70).

Chapter Four

1. Murphree's (1984) study on legal secretaries addresses these issues peripherally. Although she does not focus on paralegals, she observes that legal assistants, much like secretaries, are expected to provide emotional support for their bosses.

2. Similarly, Kanter (1977) and Rollins (1985) discuss the centrality of a "personal relationship" in secretarial work and in domestic work.

3. After reviewing more than one hundred ads, I found one atypical ad in *The Recorder* for a paralegal who "had the patience of Job and a sense of humor" (June 13, 1988: 40).

4. One female paralegal told me, "I can think of better things to do with a jump rope" and demonstrated by holding an imaginary noose around an attorney's neck and pretending to tighten it.

5. In contrast to feminist scholarship that conflates the roles of wife and mother, Johnson (1988) argues that these two roles are analytically distinct. One does not have to be a wife to be a mother and vice versa. Further,

Johnson suggests that wives play the subordinate role in the family, whereas mothers not only provide emotional caretaking but have some semblance of power. She argues that the former role, not the latter, is the source of women's subordinate status in society. For Johnson, it is only in the context of male domination that mothering (i.e., genuine reciprocal caring) becomes distorted. Her distinction informs my analysis of the litigator-paralegal relationship. For example, paralegal work done in the context of a male superordinate–female subordinate relationship means that caretaking will be non-reciprocal, and hence, associated with subordinate status. However, as Johnson suggests this does not mean that caretaking is always associated with subordinate status or that mothering is bad. Such caretaking is non-reciprocal because it is embedded in a relationship of inequality.

6. Rollins (1985) makes a similar argument about the deference required in domestic work, but she does not use the concept of emotional labor.

7. Rollins (1985) examines the racial and gendered form that deference takes between Black domestic workers and their white employers.

8. My findings do suggest that deference in law firms sometimes assumes a racialized character as well. For example, a white women paralegal who worked with an African American secretary complained that the secretary was not friendly enough. See my discussion of Princess Di and Kimberly in the section in Appendix 1 titled "Insider, Outsider, Outsider Within."

9. Hughes (1958) argues that in making mistakes, workers unwittingly reveal norms underlying a given social situation.

10. Some legal assistants oppose regulation, but not for the same reason that attorneys do. They believe state regulation will decrease rather than increase their autonomy (Whalen 1988; Chernowsky 1988).

Chapter Five

1. In her more recent work with Lyn Brown, *Meeting at the Crossroads*, Gilligan modifies her earlier position, arguing that adolescent girls sometimes use many moral voices rather than only one. While the variation Brown and Gilligan document is consistent with the findings in this chapter, I see my theoretical account as distinctive. I am concerned with a specific set of theoretical questions regarding the reproduction of gender at micro- and macro- levels of analysis, but Brown and Gilligan's work, though interesting and evocative, is primarily descriptive.

2. By 1990, this figure had risen from 19 to 22 percent (Epstein 1993: 426).

3. According to the National Association for Law Placement, male law school graduates in 1986 made an average of $1,207 more than female graduates (Salaman 1988: 18).

4. Epstein also draws this conclusion in the epilogue to the 1993 edition of her book *Women and Law*.

5. See Rhode (1989) for a detailed review of changes in law that have affected women's paid labor-force employment.

6. The extent of sexual harassment within the profession has been reported by academic studies (Rosenberg, Perlstadt and Phillips 1993; MacCorquodale and Jensen 1993) as well as by studies conducted by the legal profession itself (Butler 1989; Lewin 1989; Margolick 1990a).

7. Although none of the men I interviewed experienced sexual harassment, several reported that they knew of men in other firms who had been harassed by male partners.

8. The Bohemian Grove is an exclusive all-male retreat in the San Francisco Bay Area. For a discussion of the cohesiveness of upper-class retreats such as the Bohemian Grove, see Domhoff (1974).

9. Officially, the law firm expressed a public condemnation in its daily newsletter of the individual or individuals who sent Chris the "gift." An unsuccessful investigation was launched to identify the culprit, and though staff members proffered various theories about who might have done it, no one was ever identified.

10. Sanctions are typically court rules for the enforcement of deposition discovery where a party has sent out interrogatories or noticed a deposition and the other side has failed to respond (*Federal Rules of Civil Procedure* 37(d)). Judges can also issue sanctions or fines for contempt of court and other violations of civil procedure. Issuing sanctions is a matter for the judge's discretion.

11. These percentages were calculated by adding together the number of women trial lawyers in each law firm and dividing the total by the number of women who fell into each category. The total number of women litigators in both firms was nineteen. Five women (approximately 26 percent) fell into the first category, "Resisting and Reshaping the Adversarial Role." Eleven women (58 percent) fell into the second category, "Splitting the Roles"; and three women (16 percent) fell into the third. I utilized the same method to determine the percentages of male attorneys in each category.

12. Only a few of the women I interviewed in this category identified themselves as feminists. Most opted for what Stacey (1991) terms a postfeminist description of their political identity which takes the form, "I believe in equal opportunity, but I am not a feminist. . . ."

13. This is similar to what Jessica Benjamin calls "mutual recognition" or

"the necessity of recognizing as well as being recognized by the other" (1988: 23), which I discuss further in Chapter 7.

Chapter Six

1. For Kanter, tokenism occurs in situations where dominants outnumber tokens in a ratio of up to 85:15 (1977: 209).

2. This male paralegal eventually left the law firm, but he did not go on to law school.

3. See Larson and Templeton (1980, 1981); Stibelman (1988b); and San Francisco Association of Legal Assistants Survey (1989).

4. According to the U.S. Department of Labor, the average tenure for *all careers* is 6.6 years. Barbers had the highest tenure, 24.8 years; fast-food workers the lowest, one year. Lawyers averaged 10.1 years, and secretaries, 7.5 years (August 1989). Paralegals rank higher than fast-food workers, but still fall below the average listed for all careers.

5. One male paralegal went to an MBA program and another went to night law school but later dropped out. One woman paralegal went to law school and recently completed her degree.

6. I use "strategy" in Bourdieu's (1979) sense of the term to emphasize that a strategy is not simply a purposive pursuit of goals, as Coleman (1986) suggests, but rather the active deployment of object oriented "line of action" that obeys regularities and forms systematic patterns even though it does not necessarily flow from preplanned objectives.

7. Only two of the women I interviewed socialized with their bosses. Both had husbands whose professional stature was comparable to that of their boss.

8. Rollins (1985) terms this form of exploitation "maternalism" when it occurs between women in the domestic worker–employer relationship.

9. These men defined themselves as occupational transients not only in their interviews but also to other people in the law firm.

10. This sentence paraphrases sociologist Everett Hughes's argument about how men make "their work glorious, and hence, tolerable to themselves and others" (1951: 342). Though I find Hughes's insight useful, our theoretical perspectives diverge. Hughes's work falls squarely within the symbolic interactionist tradition, whereas mine is more eclectic, drawing from feminist psychoanalytic theory, symbolic interaction, and theories of the labor process.

11. In her study of service workers, Leidner argues that women are unlikely to affirm their identity through their work for two reasons (1993: 210). First, femininity, unlike masculinity, is not typically seen as something

that can be achieved through paid work. Second, because most female-typed jobs involve servility and deference, they are not likely to provide women with personal satisfaction. By contrast, my research suggests that women legal workers do try to define themselves through their work but are often frustrated because they encounter a double bind.

Chapter Seven

1. For a historical account of the legal profession's exclusionary character, see Auerbach (1976). Sociological studies draw similar conclusions about the racial and ethnic composition of elite corporate law firms; see Heinz and Laumann (1982); Smigel (1969); and Carlin (1962).

2. Women lawyers reported more incidences of sexual harassment than women paralegals did in this study. These findings support evidence from other studies that suggest that women in non-traditional occupations are particularly likely to experience sexual harassment (Gutek and Morasch 1982). However, legal secretaries in this study also reported a high incidence of sexual harassment (Pringle 1988.) In contrast to Gutek and Morasch, my findings suggest that women in both non-traditional jobs and *some* traditional jobs in law firms encounter a high degree of sexual harassment, for complex reasons. In traditional jobs, there appears to be a sexual and emotional division of labor. Secretarial work is often more sexualized than is paralegal work. Legal secretaries typically face expectations to be attractive and "sexy," whereas paralegals are expected to play the nurturing role of mothers (see Pierce 1995). On the other hand, in a male-dominated job such as litigation, the sexualization of women is not part of the formal or informal job description. Despite the glamorized depictions of women lawyers in television shows such as *L.A. Law*, one's personal appearance is not the overriding personal attribute taken into account in hiring decisions. Further, both attractive and unattractive women attorneys are subjected to sexual innuendoes and harassment. I would argue that sexualization in this job appears to be a means for men to intimidate women who are perceived as encroaching on male turf.

3. Whether the normalization of sexual harassment continues may be called into question by a recent decision against law firm Baker & McKenzie. In September 1994, a jury awarded legal secretary Rena Weeks $7.1 million in punitive damages for sexual harassment she experienced while working in the Palo Alto offices of Baker & McKenzie. The award against the firm and one of its partners is considered the largest amount ever awarded in a sexual harassment case (Chiang 1994). Some have called this the wake-up call to law firms to rectify mistreatment of women employees

(Pristin 1994). However, in October the judge cut punitive damages in half, ruling that the original amount was "excessive" (Hoover and Chiang 1994). And in December, Baker & McKenzie filed a notice that it will appeal (Burress 1994). As of this writing (February 1995), this case is still being litigated. Whether the case will be indicative of a future trend is open to further investigation.

4. Menkel-Meadow (1985) suggests that existing alternatives to the traditional adversarial model may already be found in the practice of mediation or alternative dispute resolution (ADR). However, Harrington and Rifkin (1989) report that ADR has become another feminized occupational ghetto associated with low pay, low prestige, and paraprofessional status. Seventy percent of its practitioners are female. As a feminized semi-profession on the margins of the legal profession, it seems unlikely that ADR will change the adversarial model.

Appendix One

1. For other critiques of the positivistic stance in fieldwork, see Krieger 1991; Reinharz 1988; and Rabinow 1977.

2. For a discussion of these political and epistemological questions, see Ladner 1973; Blauner and Wellman 1973; Merton 1972 and Wilson 1974.

3. Patricia Hill Collins's (1986) work is an exception to this point. See my discussion of her work below.

4. This notion of "salience" draws from Nancy Chodorow's (1989c) research on women psychoanalysts, where she found that generational differences were more salient than gender in describing the experiences of these women.

5. The section of Chapter 1 presenting a theoretical overview of this book is a significantly revised version of my prospectus.

6. This response has been confirmed numerous times when I give talks about my research. Secretaries and former secretaries inevitably volunteer that my research provides an accurate depiction of their workplace lives.

7. Other feminist scholars disagree with this view, arguing that quantitative methods are also compatible with feminist ends. See Jayaratne and Stewart (1991); Cancian (1992).

References

Abrahamson, Alan. "Orick Goes With the Trend, Raises Starting Pay to $60,000." *San Francisco Banner*, 6 March 1989a: 2.

———. "Market Drives Entry Pay Past $60,000." *San Francisco Banner*, 8 March 1989b: 1.

Abrams, Philip. *Historical Sociology.* Ithaca, N.Y.: Cornell University Press, 1982.

Abramson, Jill. "For Women Lawyers, An Uphill Struggle." *New York Times Magazine*, 6 March 1988: 36–37.

Abramson, Jill, and Barbara Franklin. *Where Are They Now: The Women of Harvard Law 1974.* Garden City, New York: Doubleday, 1986.

Abu-Lughod, Lila. "Writing Against Culture." In Richard Fox, ed., *Recapturing Anthropology: Working in the Present.* Santa Fe, N.M.: School of American Research, University of Washington Press, 1991.

Acker, Joan. "Hierarchies, Jobs, Bodies: A Theory of Gendered Organizations." *Gender & Society* 4, no. 2 (June 1990): 139–58.

———. *Doing Comparable Worth.* Philadelphia, Penna.: Temple University Press, 1989.

Alameda County Bar Association Bulletin. February 1990.

American Bar Association. *Model Code of Professional Responsibility and Code of Judicial Conduct.* Chicago, Ill.: National Center for Professional Responsibility and the American Bar Association, 1982.

Auerbach, Jerold. *Unequal Justice: Lawyers and Social Change in Modern America.* London: Oxford University Press, 1976.

Baca Zinn, Maxine. "Field Research in Minority Communities: Ethical, Methodological and Political Observations by an Insider." *Social Problems* 27, no. 2 (December 1979): 209–19.

Banks, Robert. "Companies Struggle to Control Legal Costs," *Harvard Business Review* (March/April 1983): 168–70.

Baron, James, and William Bielby. "Bringing the Firms Back In: Stratification, Segmentation and the Organization of Work." *American Sociological Review* 45 (1980): 737–65.

Bart, Pauline. "Review of Chodorow's Reproduction of Mothering." In Joyce Treblicott, ed., *Mothering: Essays in Feminist Theory*. Totowa, N.J.: Rowman and Allenheld, 1984.

Bay, Monica. "Poll: Sex Bias Pervades State's Legal Profession." *The Recorder*, 13 September 1989: 1.

Becker, Gary. *A Treatise on the Family*. Enlarged edition. Cambridge, Mass.: Harvard University Press, 1991 [1981].

Beckhusen, Lesah. "Lawyers Must Look Within." *San Francisco Banner*, 17 March 1989: 7.

Bellah, Robert, and Richard Madsen, William Sullivan, Ann Swidler and Steven Tipton. *Habits of the Heart: Individualism and Commitment in American Life*. Berkeley and Los Angeles: University of California Press, 1985.

Bellis, Jonathan, and Rees Morrison. "In-House Lawyers Facing Third Stage of Evolution." *National Law Journal*, 18 September 1989: 18.

Benet, Mary. *The Secretarial Ghetto*. New York: McGraw Hill, 1973.

Benjamin, Jessica. *The Bonds of Love: Psychoanalysis, Feminism and the Problem of Domination*. New York: Pantheon Books, 1989.

Benson, Susan. "Women in Retail Sales Work: The Continuing Dilemma of Service." In Karen Sacks and Dorothy Remy, eds., *My Troubles Are Going To Have the Trouble With Me: Everyday Trials and Triumphs for Women Workers*. New Brunswick, N.J.: Rutgers University Press, 1984.

Berg, David. "Cross-Examination." *Litigation: Journal of the Section of Litigation, American Bar Association* 14, no. 1 (Fall 1987): 25–30.

Bernstein, Peter. "The Wall Street Lawyers are Thriving on Change." *Fortune*, 13 March 1978: 104–12.

Berreman, Gerald. "Caste in India and the United States." *American Journal of Sociology* 66 (1960): 120–27.

Bibby, John, Thomas Mann, and Norman Ornstein. *Vital Statistics on Congress*. Washington D.C.: American Enterprise Institute, 1982.

Bielby, William, and James Baron. "A Woman's Place is with Other Women: Sex Segregation with Organizations." In Barbara Reskin and Heidi Hartmann, eds., *Women's Work, Men's Work: Sex Segregation on the Job*. Washington D.C.: National Academy Press, 1986.

Blauner, Bob. *Black Lives, White Lives: Three Decades of Race Relations in the United States*. Berkeley and Los Angeles: University of California Press, 1989.

Blauner, Robert, and David Wellman. "Toward the Decolonization of Social Research." In Joyce Ladner, ed., *The Death of White Sociology*. New York: Random House, 1973.

Blinder, Martin. "Picking Juries." *Trial Diplomacy* 1, no. 1 (Spring 1978): 8–13.

Bloom, Samuel. "The Medical Center as a Social System." In Robert Coombs and Clark Vincent, eds., *Psychosocial Aspects of Medical Training*. Springfield, Ill.: Thomas, 1971.

Blumberg, Abraham. "The Practice of Law as Confidence Game: Organizational Co-optation of a Profession." *Law and Society Review* 1, no. 2 (June 1967): 15–39.

Bourdieu, Pierre. "The Sense of Honor." In his *Algeria 1960*. Cambridge: Cambridge University Press, 1979.

———. *Outline of a Theory of Practice*. New York: Cambridge University Press, 1977a.

———. "Cultural Reproduction and Social Reproduction." In Jerome Karabel and Allen Halsey, eds., *Power and Ideology in Education*. New York: Oxford University Press, 1977b.

Braverman, Harry. *Labor and Monopoly Capital: The Degradation of Work in the Twentieth Century*. New York: Monthly Review Press, 1974.

Brazil, Wayne. "The Attorney as Victim: Toward More Candor about the Psychological Price Tag of Litigation Practice." *The Journal of the Legal Profession* 3 (1978): 107–17.

Bridges, Lee. "Race Relations Research: From Colonization to Neo-Colonialism? Some Random Thoughts." *Race* 14, no. 3 (January 1973): 341–441.

Bridges, W. P. "The Sexual Segregation of Occupations: Theories of Labor Stratification in Industry." *American Journal of Sociology* (1982) 88: 270–95.

Brill, Steven. "Labor Pains." *National Law Journal*, January/February 1986: 1.

Brown, Lyn, and Carol Gilligan. *Meeting at the Crossroads: Women's Psychology and Girls' Development*. Cambridge, Mass.: Harvard University Press, 1992.

Buchan, John. "The Judicial Temperament." In his *Homilies and Recreations*. Third edition. London: Hodder and Stoughton, 1939.

Bulmer, Martin, ed. *Social Research Ethics*. London: Macmillan, 1982.

Burawoy, Michael. *Manufacturing Consent: Changes in the Labor Process Under Monopoly Capitalism*. Chicago: University of Chicago Press, 1979.

Burress, Charles. "Largest Law Firm Will Appeal $3.5 Million Harassment Award," *San Fransisco Chronicle*, 22 December 1994: A23.

Burstein, Paul. *Discrimination, Jobs and Politics: The Struggle for Equal Opportunity in the United States Since the New Deal.* Chicago: University of Chicago Press, 1986.

Butler, Katy. "Women Lawyers Still Complain of Bias." *San Francisco Chronicle*, 4 December 1989: A3.

Cancian, Francesca. "Feminist Science: Methodologies That Challenge Inequality." *Gender & Society* 6, no. 4 (December 1992): 623–42.

Carlin, Jerome. *Lawyers on Their Own.* New Brunswick, N.J.: Rutgers University Press, 1962.

Carter, Walter. "A Well Known Lawyer Honored." *American Lawyer*, March 1901: 104.

Cartwright, John. 1977. "Jury Selection," *Trial* 28 (December 1977): 13.

Chayes, Antonia, Bruce Greenwald, and Maxine Winig. "Managing Your Lawyers," *Harvard Business Review* (January/February 1983): 84–91.

Cheatham, Elliott. *Cases and Materials on the Legal Profession.* Second edition. Brooklyn: Foundation Press, 1955.

Chernowsky, Fran. "Paralegal Regulation: No Panacea." *California Alliance of Paralegals Association, Recap.*, Winter 1988: 3.

Chester, Ronald. *Unequal Access: Women Lawyers in a Changing America.* South Hadley, Mass.: Bergin and Garvey, 1985.

Chiang, Harriet. "Judge Halves $7.1 Million Award in Harassment Case," *San Fransisco Chronicle*, 29 November 1994: A15.

———. "More Trouble For Women Lawyers." *San Francisco Chronicle*, 9 April 1990: 1.

Chodorow, Nancy, and Susan Contratto. "The Fantasy of the Perfect Mother." In Barrie Thorne with Marilyn Yalom, eds., *Rethinking the Family: Some Feminist Questions.* New York: Longman, 1982.

Chodorow, Nancy. *Feminism and Psychoanalytic Theory.* New Haven, Conn.: Yale University Press, 1989a.

———. "Introduction." In Nancy Chodorow, ed., *Feminism and Psychoanalytic Theory.* New Haven, Conn.: Yale University Press, 1989b.

———. "Seventies Questions for Thirties Women: Gender and Generation in a Study of Early Women Psychoanalysts." In Nancy Chodorow, ed., *Feminism and Psychoanalytic Theory.* New Haven, Conn.: Yale University Press, 1989c.

———. "Beyond Drive Theory: Object Relations Theory and the Limits of Radical Individualism." *Theory and Society* 14, no. 3 (May 1985): 271–319.

———. *The Reproduction of Mothering: Psychoanalysis and the Sociology of Gender*. Berkeley and Los Angeles: University of California Press, 1978.

Ciotti, Paul. "Lawyer's Life: High Pay, Low Satisfaction." *San Francisco Chronicle and Examiner*, 16 October 1988: 15.

Clifford, James, and George Marcus, eds. *Writing Culture: The Poetics and Politics of Ethnography*. Berkeley and Los Angeles: University of California Press, 1986.

Clifford, James. *The Predicament of Culture*. Cambridge, Mass.: Harvard University Press, 1988.

Cockburn, Cynthia. *Machinery of Dominance: Women, Men, and Technical Know-How*. London: Pluto Press, 1985.

———. *Brothers: Male Dominance and Technological Change*. London and Sydney: Pluto Press, 1983.

Coleman, James. "Social Theory, Social Research and a Theory of Action." *American Journal of Sociology* 91, no. 6 (May 1986): 1309–35.

Collins, Patricia Hill. *Black Feminist Thought*. Cambridge, Mass.: Unwin Hyman, 1990.

———. "Learning From the Outsider Within." *Social Problems* 33, no. 6 (December 1986): 14–29.

Connell, Robert. "A Whole New World: Remaking Masculinity in the Context of the Environmental Movement," *Gender & Society* 4, no. 4 (December 1990): 452–78.

———. *Gender and Power: Society, the Person and Sexual Politics*. Stanford: Stanford University Press, 1987.

Coser, Rose Laub. "Laughter Among Colleagues." *Psychiatry* 23 (February 1960): 81–90.

Crapanzano, Vincent. "Hermes' Dilemma: The Masking of Subversion in Ethnographic Description." In James Clifford and George Marcus, eds. *Writing Culture: The Poetics and Politics of Ethnography*. Berkeley and Los Angeles: University of California Press, 1986.

Daly, Mary. *Gyn/Ecology: The Metaethics of Radical Feminism*. Boston: Beacon Press, 1978.

Davies, Margery. *Woman's Place is at the Typewriter: Office Work and Office Workers 1870–1930*. Philadelphia: Temple University Press, 1982.

De Beauvoir, Simone. *The Second Sex*. New York: Knopf, 1976 [1958].

Dean, Arthur. *William Nelson Cromwell, 1854–1948: An American Pioneer in Corporation, Comparative and International Law*. New York: Ad Press, privately printed, 1957.

Derber, Charles, ed. *Professionals as Workers: Mental Labor in Advanced Capitalism*. Boston, Mass.: G. K. Hall, 1982.

Diamond, Timothy. "Social Policy and Everyday Life in Nursing Homes: A

Critical Ethnography." In Anne Statham, Eleanor Miller, and Hans Mauksch, eds., *The Worth of Women's Work*. Albany: State University of New York Press, 1988.

Dombroff, Mark. "Winning Is Everything!" *National Law Journal*, 25 September 1989: 13.

Domhoff, William. *The Bohemian Grove and Other Retreats: A Study in Ruling Class Cohesiveness*. New York: Harper and Row, 1974.

Douglas, Jack. "Living Morality versus Bureaucratic Fiat." In Karl Klockars and Finbarr O'Connor, eds., *Deviance and Decency: The Ethics of Research with Human Subjects*. Beverly Hills, Calif.: Sage, 1979.

Duelli Klein, Renate. "How to Do What We Want to Do: Thoughts about Feminist Methodology." In Gloria Bowles and Renate Duelli Klein, eds., *Theories of Women's Studies*. London: Routledge and Kegan Paul, 1983.

Duster, Troy. "Some Thoughts on Graduate Education" *American Sociologist* (Spring 1987): 83–87.

Earle, Walter. *Mr. Sherman and Mr. Sterling and How They Grew: Being Annals of Their Law Firms*. New Haven, Conn.: Yale University Press, 1963.

Elliott, Anthony. *Social Theory and Psychoanalysis in Transition: Self and Society From Freud to Kristeva*. Oxford: Basil Blackwell, 1992

England, Paula. *Comparable Worth: Theories and Evidence*. New York: Aldine, 1992.

Epstein, Cynthia Fuchs. *Women in Law*. Third edition. Urbana: University of Illinois Press, 1993.

———. *Women in Law*. Second edition. New York: Anchor Books, 1983.

———. *Woman's Place: Options and Limits in Professional Careers*. Berkeley and Los Angeles: University of California Press, 1970.

Etzioni, Amitai. *The Semi-Professions and Their Organization: Teachers, Nurses, Social Workers*. New York: Free Press, 1969.

Fairbairn, W. R. D. *An Object Relational Theory of Personality*. New York: Basic Books, 1952.

Fernandez-Kelly, Patricia. *For We Are Sold, I and My People: Women and Industry in Mexico's Frontier*. Albany: SUNY Press, 1983.

Fine, Michelle. *Disruptive Voices: The Possibilities of Feminist Research*. Ann Arbor: University of Michigan Press, 1992.

Fineman, Stephen, ed. *Emotions in Organizations*. Newbury Park, Calif.: Sage, 1993.

Fishman, Pamela. "Interaction: The Work Woman Do," *Social Problems* 25, no. 4 (April 1978): 397–406.

Flax, Jane. *Thinking Fragments: Psychoanalysis, Feminism and Postmod-*

ernism in the Contemporary West. Berkeley and Los Angeles: University of California Press, 1990.

———. "The Family in Contemporary Feminist Thought." In Jean Bethke Elshtain, ed., *The Family in Political Thought.* Amherst: University of Massachusetts Press, 1981.

Flood, John. "Doing Business: The Management of Uncertainty in Lawyers' Work." *Law & Society Review* 25, no. 1 (1991): 47–91.

Foster, Dean, and Ellen Raider. "Bringing Cultural Sensitivity to the Bargaining Table." *San Francisco Banner,* 17 October 1988: 14.

Foucault, Michel. *Discipline and Punish: The Birth of the Prison.* New York: Pantheon Books, 1977.

Fox, Kathryn. "The Politics of Prevention." In Michael Burawoy et al., *Ethnography Unbound.* Berkeley and Los Angeles: University of California Press, 1990.

Fox, Priscilla. "Good-bye to Game Playing." *Juris Doctor,* January 1978: 37–42.

Frank, Cheryl. "Leaving the Law: Are Reasons Gender-Based?" *American Bar Association Journal,* December 1985: 34–35.

Frankenberg, Ruth. *White Women, Race Matters: The Social Construction of Whiteness.* Minneapolis: University of Minnesota Press, 1993.

Fraser, Nancy, and Linda Nicholson. "Social Criticism Without Philosophy: An Encounter between Feminism and Postmodernism." In Linda Nicholson, ed., *Feminism/Postmodernism.* New York: Routledge, 1990.

Freinkel, Susan. "Wilson, Sonsini Boosts 1st-Year Pay to $62,000." *The Recorder,* 22 February 1989: 3.

Friedman, Lawrence. *Total Justice.* New York: Russell Sage Foundation, 1985.

———. *A History of American Law.* New York: Simon and Schuster, 1973.

Friedson, Eliot. *The Profession of Medicine.* New York: Dodd, Mead, 1970.

Galanter, Marc. "Mega Law and Mega-Lawyering in the Contemporary United States." In Robert Dingwall and Philip Lewis, eds., *The Sociology of the Professions: Lawyers, Doctors and Others.* New York: St. Martin's Press, 1983a.

———. "Reading the Landscape of Disputes: What We Know and Don't Know (and Think We Know) about Our Allegedly Contentious and Litigious Society. *U.C.L.A. Law Review* 31 (1983b): 4–71.

Game, Ann, and Rosemary Pringle. *Gender at Work.* Sydney: Allen and Unwin, 1983.

Garfinkel, Harold. "Conditions of Successful Degradation Ceremonies." *American Journal of Sociology* 61, no. 11 (March 1956): 420–24.

Gerson, Kathleen. *Hard Choices: How Women Decide About Work, Career and Motherhood.* Berkeley and Los Angeles: University of California Press, 1985.

Giddens, Anthony. *Central Problems in Social Theory: Action, Structure and Contradiction in Social Analysis.* Berkeley and Los Angeles: University of California Press, 1979.

Gillette, Paul. "Burn-Out: The Essential Element is Loss of Enthusiasm." *California Lawyer,* October 1982: 48–51.

Gilligan, Carol. *In A Different Voice: Psychological Theory and Women's Development.* Cambridge, Mass.: Harvard University Press, 1982.

Glenn, Evelyn Nakano. "A Belated Industry Revised: Domestic Service among Japanese-American Women." In Anne Statham, Eleanor Miller, and Hans Mauksch, eds., *The Worth of Women's Work.* Albany: State University of New York Press, 1988.

Goffman, Erving. *The Presentation of Self in Everyday Life.* Garden City, N.Y.: Doubleday, 1959.

————. "The Nature of Deference and Demeanor." *American Anthropologist* 58, no. 3 (June 1956): 473–502.

Goldberg, D. "Playing Hardball." *American Bar Association Journal,* 1 July 1987: 48.

Goode, William. "Theoretical Limits of Professionalization." In Amitai Etzioni, ed., *The Semi-Professions and Their Organization.* New York: Free Press, 1969.

Goodman-Plater, Valery. "State Level Paralegal Certification: Everybody Wins." *California Alliance of Paralegals Association, Recap,* Summer 1988: 2–3.

Gould, Brian. "'Burn-out': Law and Disorder." *National Law Journal,* 30 April 1984a: 13.

————. "Attorney 'Burn-out': Law and Disorder." *National Law Journal,* 7 May 1984b: 14.

Granat, Richard, and Dana Saewitz. "Paralegals Move Up to Management." *National Law Journal,* 30 January 1989: 19.

Gutek, Barbara, and Bruce Morasch. "Sex Ratios, Sex-Role Spillover and Sexual Harassment of Women at Work" *Journal of Social Issues* 38, no. 4 (1982): 55–74.

Habermas, Jurgen. *Knowledge and Human Interests.* Trans. by Jeremy Shapiro. Boston: Beacon Press, 1971.

Hall, Elaine. "Waitering/Waitressing: Engendering the Work of Table Servers." *Gender & Society* 7, no. 3 (September 1993): 329–46.

Hall, Michael. "Lawyers Told to Emulate Polite Cabbies." *San Francisco Banner,* 6 March 1989: 3.

————. "Paralegal Advocates See Firms in Future." *San Francisco Banner*, 12 September 1988: 4.

Haraway, Donna. "Situated Knowledges: The Science Question in Feminism as a Site of Discourse on the Privilege of Partial Perspective." *Feminist Studies* 14, no. 3 (1988): 575–99.

Harding, Sandra. *Whose Science, Whose Knowledge?* Ithaca, N.Y.: Cornell University Press, 1991.

————. *The Science Question in Feminism.* Ithaca, N.Y.: Cornell University Press, 1986.

Harragan, Betty. *Games Mother Never Taught You: Corporate Gamesmanship for Women.* New York: Warner Books, 1977.

Harrington, Christine, and Janet Rifkin. *The Gender Organization of Mediation: Implications for the Feminization of Legal Practice.* Madison:Institute for Legal Studies, University of Wisconsin Law School, 1989.

Hartmann, Heidi. "Internal Labor Markets and Gender." In Clair Brown and Joseph Pechman, eds., *Gender in the Workplace.* Washington, D.C.: Brookings Institute, 1987.

————. "Capitalism, Patriarchy and Job Segregation by Sex." In Martha Blaxall and Barbara Reagan, eds., *Women and the Workplace.* Chicago: University of Chicago Press, 1976.

Hartsock, Nancy. 1983. "The Feminist Standpoint: Developing the Ground for a Specifically Feminist Historical Materialism." In Sandra Harding and Merrill Hintikka, eds., *Discovering Reality: Feminist Perspectives on Epistemology, Metaphysics, Methodology and the Philosophy of Science.* Dordecht, Holland: Reidel, 1983.

Hazard, Geoffrey. "Male Culture Still Dominates the Profession." *National Law Journal*, 19 December 1988: 13.

Hedstrom, Margaret. "Beyond Feminisation: Clerical Workers in the United States from the 1920s through the 1960s." In Gregory Anderson, ed., *The White Blouse Revolution: Female Office Workers Since 1870.* Manchester, England: Manchester University Press, 1988.

Hegel, G. W. F. *The Phenomenology of Spirit.* Trans. by A. V. Miller. Oxford: Clarendon Press, 1977 [1807].

Heinz, John, and Edward Laumann. *Chicago Lawyers: The Social Structure of the Bar.* New York: Russell Sage Foundation and the American Bar Foundation, 1982.

Henley, Nancy. *Body Politics: Power, Sex and Non-Verbal Communication.* Englewood Cliffs, N.J.: Prentice Hall, 1977.

Hickey, Shannon. "Paralegals Find Fertile Ground for Career Growth in Corporations." *The Recorder*, 27 September 1989: 2–3.

Hobson, Wayne. "Symbol of the New Profession: Emergence of the Large

Law Firm, 1870–1915." In Gerald Gewalt, ed., *The New High Priests: Lawyers in Post–Civil War America*. Westport, Conn.: Greenwood Press, 1984.

Hochschild, Arlie. *The Managed Heart: Commercialization of Human Feeling*. Berkeley and Los Angeles: University of California Press, 1983.

———. "Inside the Clockwork of Male Careers." In Florence Howe, ed., *Women and the Power to Change*. New York: McGraw Hill, 1975.

Hoffman, Paul. *Lions in the Street: The Inside Story of the Great Wall Street Law Firms*. New York: Saturday Review Press, 1973.

Holmes, Deborah. *Structural Causes of Dissatisfaction Among Large-Firm Attorneys: A Feminist Perspective*. Madison: Institute for Legal Studies, University of Wisconsin Law School, 1988.

hooks, bell. 1984. *Feminist Theory: From Margin to Center*. Boston, Mass.: South End Press, 1984.

Hoover, Ken, and Harriet Chiang. "Harassment Award Totals $7.1 Million," *San Fransisco Chronicle,* 9 September 1994: A1.

Horkheimer, Max. "Authority and the Family." In his *Critical Theory*. New York: Herder & Herder, 1972 [1936].

Horowitz, Ruth. *Honor and the American Dream: Culture and Identity in a Chicano Community*. New Brunswick, N.J.: Rutgers University Press, 1983.

Hossfeld, Karen. "Divisions of Labor, Divisions of Lives: Immigrant Women in the Silicon Valley." Ph.D. diss., Department of Sociology, University of California, Santa Cruz, 1987.

Hughes, Everett. *Men and Their Work*. Glencoe, Ill.: Free Press, 1958.

———. "Work and Self." In *The Sociological Eye: The Selected Papers of Everett C. Hughes*. New Brunswick, N.J.: Transaction, 1951.

Hulstuk, Martin. "Rising Tide of Lawyers Who Quit." *San Francisco Chronicle*, 2 October 1989: 1.

Hunt, Jennifer. *Psychoanalytic Aspects of Fieldwork*. Newbury Park, Calif.: Sage, Qualitative Research Methods Series no. 18, 1989.

———. "The Development of Rapport Through the Negotiation of Gender in Fieldwork Among Police." *Human Organization* 43, no. 4 (Winter 1984): 283–96.

Hurst, James. *The Growth of American Law: The Lawmakers*. Boston: Little Brown, 1950.

Irving, Clifford. *Trial*. New York: Dell, 1990.

Jack, Dana, and Rand Jack. *Moral Visions and Professional Decisions: The Changing Values of Women and Men Lawyers*. New York: Cambridge University Press, 1989.

———. "Women Lawyers: Archetypes and Alternatives." In Carol Gilligan,

J. Ward, and J. Taylor, eds., *Mapping the Moral Domain: A Contribution of Women's Thinking to Psychological Theory and Education.* Cambridge, Mass.: Harvard University Graduate School of Education, 1988.

Jacobs, Jerry. *Revolving Doors: Sex Segregation and Women's Careers.* Stanford, Calif.: Stanford University Press, 1989.

Jayaratne, Toby Epstein, and Abigail Stewart. "Quantitative and Qualitative Methods in the Social Sciences: Current Feminist Issues and Practical Strategies." In Mary Fonow and Judith Cook, eds., *Beyond Methodology: Feminist Scholarship as Lived Research.* Bloomington: University of Indiana Press, 1991.

Jensen, Rita. "Is Dough a Problem at Pillsbury?" *National Law Journal,* 3 April 1989: 3.

Johnson, Miriam. *Strong Mothers, Weak Wives: The Search for Gender Equality.* Berkeley and Los Angeles: University of California Press, 1988.

Johnstone, Quintin, and Dan Hopson, Jr. *Lawyers and Their Work: An Analysis of the Legal Profession in the United States and England.* Indianapolis: Bobbs-Merrill, 1967.

Johnstone, Quintin, and Martin Wenglinsky. *Paralegals: Progress and Prospects of a Satellite Occupation.* Westport, Conn.: Greenwood Press, 1985.

Jordan, Hallye. "ABA Head Urges Peer Pressure." *San Francisco Banner,* 22 March 1989: 3.

Joseph, Gloria. "Black Mothers and Daughters." In Gloria Joseph and Jill Lewis eds., *Common Differences: Conflicts in Black and White Feminist Perspectives.* New York: Anchor Press/Doubleday, 1981.

Josephson, Michael. "Unloved Lawyers: Why Don't People Like Them?" *The Good Lawyer,* Winter 1988: 1–2.

Kahler, Kathryn. "More Female Lawyers Leaving Jobs." *San Francisco Examiner,* 18 December 1988: A24.

Kanter, Arnie. "We Did It To Ourselves." *National Law Journal,* 17 April 1989: 13.

Kanter, Rosabeth Moss. "Reflections on Women and the Legal Profession: A Sociological Perspective." *Harvard Women's Law Journal* 1, no. 1 (Spring 1978): 1–22.

———. *Men and Women of the Corporation.* New York: Basic Books, 1977.

Katz, Jack. *Poor People's Lawyers in Transition.* New Brunswick, N.J.: Rutgers University Press, 1982.

Knights, David, and Hugh Willmott. *Gender and the Labour Process.* Aldershot: Gower Publishing Company, 1986.

Knights, David. "Subjectivity, Power and the Labour Process." In David Knights and Hugh Willmott, eds., *Labour Process Theory*, pp. 297–335. Basingstoke: The Macmillan Press, 1990.

Koegel, Otto. *Walter S. Carter: Collector of Young Masters or the Progenitor of Many Law Firms*. New York: Round Table Press, 1953.

Kremer, Belinda. "Learning When to Say No: Keeping Feminist Research for Ourselves," *Women's Studies International* 13, no. 5 (1990): 463–67.

Krieger, Susan. *Social Science and the Self: Personal Essays on an Art Form*. New Brunswick, N.J.: Rutgers University Press, 1991.

Krier, James, and Richard Stewart. *Environmental Law and Policy: Readings, Materials and Notes*. Second edition. Indianapolis: Bobbs-Merrill, 1978.

Ladner, Joyce. *Tomorrow's Tomorrow: The Black Woman*. Garden City, N.Y.: Doubleday, 1971.

Lakoff, Robin. *Language and Woman's Place*. New York: Harper & Row, 1975.

Langer, Abbott. "House Counsel Average Pay Nears $77,000." *San Francisco Banner*, September 1988: 5.

Larbalestrier, Deborah. *Paralegal Practice and Procedure: A Practical Guide for the Legal Assistant*. Second edition. Englewood Cliffs, N.J.: Prentice Hall, 1986.

Larson, J., and Templeton, D. "Job Satisfaction of Legal Assistants." *Legal Assistant Update '80*, 1980.

———. "Legal Assistants and Job Satisfaction: A Further Analysis." *Legal Assistant Update '81*, 1981.

Larson, Magali Sarfatti. *The Rise of Professionalism: A Sociological Analysis*. Berkeley and Los Angeles: University of California Press, 1977.

Lefer, Gary. "Attorneys Are Among Most Severely Stressed Groups." *New York Law Journal*, 29 September 1986: 23.

Leidner, Robin. *Fast Food, Fast Talk: Service Work and the Routinization of Everyday Life*. Berkeley and Los Angeles: University of California Press, 1993.

———. "Serving Hamburgers and Selling Insurance: Gender, Work and Identity in Interactive Service Jobs." *Gender & Society* 5, no. 2 (June 1991): 154–77.

Lewin, Tamar. "Women Say They Face Obstacles as Lawyers." *New York Times*, 4 December 1989: A21.

Lieberman, Jethro. *The Litigious Society*. New York: Basic Books, 1981.

Liebow, Elliot. *Tally's Corner: A Study of Negro Street Corner Men*. Boston: Little Brown, 1967.

Liefland, Linda. "Career Patterns of Male and Female Lawyers." *Buffalo Law Review* 35 (Spring 1986): 601–31.

Lockwood, David. *The Blackcoated Worker: A Study in Class Consciousness.* London: George Allen and Unwin, 1958.

Loden, Marilyn. "A Machismo That Drives Women Out." *New York Times,* 9 February 1986: 2F.

Lopate, Helen, and Barrie Thorne. "On the Term 'Sex Roles.'" *Signs: Journal of Women in Culture and Society* 3 (1978): 718–21.

Lorber, Judith, Rose Laub Coser, Alice Rossi, and Nancy Chodorow. "On *The Reproduction of Mothering*: A Methodological Debate." *Signs: Journal of Women in Culture and Society* 6, no. 3 (Spring 1981): 482–500.

Lorde, Audre. *Sister Outsider: Essays and Speeches.* Trumansburg, New York: The Crossing Press, 1984.

Luban, David. *Lawyers and Justice: An Ethical Study.* Princeton, N.J.: Princeton University Press, 1988.

Luttrell, Wendy. "'The Teachers, They All Had Their Pets': Concepts of Gender, Knowledge, and Power." *Signs: Journal of Women in Culture and Society* 18, no. 3 (Spring 1993): 505–46.

Lyman, Peter. "Be Reasonable: Anger and Technical Reason in Middle-Class Culture." Paper presented at Society for Study of Social Problems panel on Social Control and Everyday Life. San Francisco, September 4, 1984.

———. "The Fraternal Bond As a Joking Relationship: A Case Study of Sexist Jokes in Male Group Bonding." In Michael Kimmel, ed., *Changing Men: New Directions in Research on Men and Masculinity.* Newbury Park, Calif.: Sage Publications, 1987.

Lyson, Thomas. "Race and Sex Segregation in the Occupational Structures of Southern Employers." *Social Science Quarterly* 66 (1985): 281–95.

MacCorquodale, Patricia and Gary Jensen. "Women in the Law: Partners of Tokens?" *Gender & Society* 7, no. 4 (December 1993): 582–93.

Machung, Anne. "Word Processing: Forward for Business, Backward for Women." In Karen Sacks and Dorothy Remy, eds., *My Troubles Are Going To Have the Trouble with Me: Everyday Trials and Triumphs for Women Workers.* New Brunswick, N.J.: Rutgers University Press, 1984.

Mahler, Margaret, Fred Pine, and Anni Bergman. *The Psychological Birth of the Human Infant.* New York: Basic Books, 1975.

Manikas, William. "A Paralegal Is Not a Lawyer in a Wheelchair." *Manpower,* October 1975: 11–14.

Mann, Elizabeth. "Women Practitioners Face Conflict Between Pregnancy, Trial Appearances." *San Francisco Recorder,* 31 January 1989: 1.

Marcus, Ruth. "The High Price of Boredom." *San Francisco Chronicle*, 28 June 1987: p 1.

Margolick, David. "Curbing Sexual Harassment in the Legal World." *New York Times*, 9 November 1990a: B11.

————. "At the Bar: When a Law Firm Hires a Psychiatrist for Treatment of Its Institutional Psyche." *New York Times*, 18 May 1990b: A32.

————. "At the Bar: More Lawyers are Less Happy at Their Work, a Survey Finds." *New York Times*, 17 August 1990c: A32.

————. "Lawyers Just Want to Have Fun." *San Francisco Chronicle and Examiner*, 8 October 1989: A2.

————. "At the Bar: Rambos Invade the Courtroom." *New York Times*, 5 August 1988: B5.

Marini, Margaret, and Mary Brinton. "Sex Typing in Occupational Socialization." In Barbara Reskin, ed., *Sex Segregation in the Workplace*. Washington, D.C.: National Academy of Sciences, 1984.

Mascia-Lees, Frances, Patricia Sharpe, and Colleen Cohen. "The Post Modernist Turn in Anthropology: Cautions From a Feminist Perspective." *Signs: Journal of Women in Culture and Society* 15, no. 1 (Autumn 1989): 7–33.

Mauet, Thomas. *Fundamentals of Trial Techniques*. Boston, Mass.: Little Brown, 1980.

McCall, George, and J. L. Simmons, eds.. *Issues in Participant Observation: A Text and Reader*. Reading, Mass.: Addison-Wesley, 1969.

McElhaney, James. *McElhaney's Trial Notebook*. Second edition. Chicago: Section of Litigation, American Bar Association, 1987.

Mead, Margaret. "Field Work in the Pacific Islands." In Peggy Golde, ed., *Women in the Field: Anthropological Experiences*. Berkeley and Los Angeles: University of California Press, 1986.

Menkel-Meadow, Carrie. "Feminization of the Legal Profession: The Comparative Sociology of Women Lawyers." In Richard Abel and Philip Lewis, eds., *Lawyers in Society*. Volume III: *Comparative Theories*. Berkeley and Los Angeles: University of California Press, 1989.

————. "Portia in a Different Voice: Speculations on a Women's Lawyering Process." *Berkeley Women's Law Review* 1, no. 1 (Fall 1985): 39–63.

Merton, Robert. "Insiders and Outsiders: A Chapter in the History of the Sociology of Knowledge." *American Journal of Sociology* 78, no. 1 (July 1972): 9–47.

Messner, Michael. " Masculinities and Athletic Careers." *Gender & Society* 3, no. 1 (March 1989): 71–88.

Meyberg, Leonard. "Not a Pocketbook Issue: Unregulated Legal Technicians Put Indigent Clients at Risk." *The Recorder*, 6 August 1989: 6.

Michael, Jerome. "The Basic Rules of Pleading." *The Record: New York City Bar Association* 5 (1950): 175–99.

Mies, Maria. "Towards a Methodology for Feminist Research." In Gloria Bowles and Renate Duelli Klein, eds., *Theories of Women's Studies*. London: Routledge and Kegan Paul, 1983.

Milkman, Ruth. *Gender at Work: The Dynamics of Job Segregation During World War II*. Urbana: University of Illinois Press, 1987.

Miller, Eleanor. *Street Woman*. Philadelphia: Temple University Press, 1986.

Mills, Albert, and Peta Tancred, eds. *Gendering Organizational Analysis*. Newbury Park, Calif.: Sage Publications, 1992.

Mills, C. Wright. *The Power Elite*. New York: Oxford University Press, 1956.

———. *White Collar: The American Middle-Classes*. London: Oxford University Press, 1951.

Miner, Roger. "Lawyers Owe One Another." *National Law Journal*, 19 December 1988: 13–14.

Montiel, Miguel. "The Social Science Myth of the Mexican American Family." *El Grito: A Journal of Contemporary Mexican American Thought* 3, no. 4 (Summer 1970): 56–63.

Moore, Joan. *Going Down to the Barrio: Homeboys and Homegirls in Change*. Philadelphia, Penna.: Temple University Press, 1991.

Moraga, Cherrie, and Gloria Anzaldua. *This Bridge Called My Back: Writings by Radical Women of Color*. Watertown, Mass.: Persephone Press, 1981.

Morello, Karen. *The Invisible Bar: The Woman Lawyer in American, 1638 to the Present*. New York: Random House, 1986.

Mortimer, John. *Rumpole of the Bailey*. Harmondsworth: Penguin Books, 1978.

Murphree, Mary. "Brave New Office: The Changing World of the Legal Secretary." In Karen Sacks and Dorothy Remy, eds., *My Troubles Are Going to Have the Trouble with Me: Everyday Trials and Triumphs of Women Workers*. New Brunswick, N.J.: Rutgers University Press, 1984.

———. "Rationalization and Satisfaction in Clerical Work: A Case Study of Legal Secretaries." Ph.D. diss., Department of Sociology, Columbia University, 1981.

National Law Journal. "What America Really Thinks About Lawyers." October 1986: 1.

Nelson, Robert. *Partners with Power: The Social Transformation of the Large Law Firm*. Berkeley and Los Angeles: University of California Press, 1988.

————. "Ideology, Practice, and Professional Autonomy: Social Values and Client Relationships in Large Law Firms." *Stanford Law Review* 37 (January 1985): 503–51.

Newman, Katherine. *Falling From Grace: The Experiences of Downward Mobility in the American Middle-Class.* New York: Vintage Books, 1988.

Nicholson, Linda, ed. *Feminism/Postmodernism.* New York: Routledge, 1990.

O'Neil, Suzanne. "Associates Can Attract Clients, Too." *National Law Journal,* 16 January 1989: 17.

Oakley, Ann. "Interviewing Women: A Contradiction in Terms." In Helen Roberts, ed., *Doing Feminist Research.* London: Routledge and Kegan Paul, 1981.

Oppenheimer, Valerie. *The Female Labor Force in the United States: Demographic and Economic Factors Governing Its Growth and Changing Composition.* Westport, Conn.: Greenview Press, 1970.

Parsons, Talcott. *Social Structure and Personality.* New York: Free Press, 1964.

Perlman, Peter. "Jury Selection." *The Docket: Newsletter of the National Institute for Trial Advocacy,* Spring 1988: 1.

Philips, Anne, and Barbara Taylor. "Sex and Skill." In Feminist Review, ed., *Waged Work: A Reader.* London: Virago Press, 1986.

Phillips, Kevin. *The Politics of Rich and Poor: Wealth and the American Electorate in the Reagan Aftermath.* New York: Random House, 1990.

Pierce, Jennifer. "Sexy Secretaries and Mothering Paralegals: Sexualization and Desexualization in Women's Work." Paper, Department of Sociology, University of Minnesota, 1995.

Pleck, Joseph. *The Myth of Masculinity.* Cambridge: MIT Press, 1981.

Podomore, David, and Anne Spencer. "Gender in the Labour Process—the Case of Women and Men Lawyers." In David Knights and Hugh Wilmott, eds., *Gender and the Labour Process.* Hampshire, England: Gower Publishing Company, 1986.

Post, Robert. "On the Popular Image of the Lawyer: Reflections in a Dark Glass." *California Law Review* 75, no. 1 (January 1987): 379–89.

Pringle, Rosemary. *Secretaries Talk: Sexuality, Power and Work.* Sydney: Allen and Unwin, 1988.

Pristin, Terry. "Firms Wake Up to Problem of Sex Harassment," *New York Times,* 14 October 1994: B18.

Prokop, Donna. "Increased Enrollments Include More Women." *San Francisco Banner,* 17 March 1989: 5.

Punch, Maurice. *The Politics and Ethics of Fieldwork.* Beverly Hills: Sage Publications, Qualitative Research Methods Series no. 3, 1986.

Rabinow, Paul. *Reflections on Fieldwork in Morocco.* Berkeley and Los Angeles: University of California Press, 1977.

Reich, Charles. "The New Property." *Yale Law Journal* 73 (April 1964): 733–87.

Reinharz, Shulamit. *On Becoming a Social Scientist.* 2d printing. New Brunswick, N.J.: Transaction Press, 1988.

———. "Experiential Analysis: A Contribution to Feminist Research." In Gloria Bowles and Renate Duelli Klein, eds., *Theories of Women's Studies.* London: Routledge and Kegan Paul, 1983.

Reskin, Barbara, and Patricia Roos. *Job Queues, Gender Queues: Explaining Women's Inroads into Male Occupations.* Philadelphia: Temple University Press, 1990.

———. "Status Hierarchies and Sex Segregation." In Christine Bose and Glenna Spitze, eds., *Ingredients for Women's Policy.* Albany: State University of New York Press, 1987.

Rhode, Deborah. *Justice and Gender: Sex Discrimination and the Law.* Cambridge, Mass.: Harvard University Press, 1989.

———. "Perspectives on Professional Women." *Stanford Law Review* 40 (May 1988): 1163–1207.

Rice, Susan. "Two Organizations Provide Training, In-House or Out." *San Francisco Banner,* 24 May 1989: 6.

Rich, Adrienne. "Compulsory Heterosexuality and Lesbian Existence." *Signs: Journal of Women in Culture and Society* 5, no. 4 (1980): 631–60.

Riessman, Catherine. "When Gender Is Not Enough: Women Interviewing Women." *Gender & Society* 1, no. 2 (June 1987): 172–207.

Ring, Leonard. "Cross-examining the Sympathetic Witness." *Litigation: Journal of the Section of Litigation, American Bar Association* 14, no. 1 (Fall 1987): 35–39.

———. "Voir Dire: Some Thoughtful Notes on the Selection Process." *Trial* 19 (July 1983): 72–75.

Rinzler, Carole. "Women Lawyers: Trading Clout for Fulfillment." *Vogue Magazine,* February 1986: 232.

Rohrlich, Ted. "Sobering Study: More Lawyers Associate with the Bar." *Oakland Tribune,* 6 December 1990: B8.

Rollins, Judith. *Between Women: Domestics and Their Employers.* Philadelphia: Temple University Press, 1985.

Romero, Mary. *Maid in the U.S.A.* New York: Routledge, 1992

Rosenau, Marie. *Post-Modernism and the Social Sciences: Insights, Inroads and Intrusions.* Princeton University Press, 1992.

Rosenberg, Janet, Harry Perlstadt, and William Phillips. "Now We That Are Here: Discrimination, Disparagement and Harassment at Work and the Experience of Women Lawyers." *Gender & Society* 7, no. 3 (September 1993): 415–33.

Roy, Paul. 1989. "In-House Law Departments: Strategies for Success." *National Law Journal*, 5 June 1989: 19.

Salaman, Linda. "Progress for Women? Yes, But. . ." *American Bar Association Journal*, 1 April 1988: 18.

Sanchez-Jankowski, Martin. *Islands in the Street: Gangs and American Urban Life.* Berkeley and Los Angeles: University of California Press, 1991.

Sattel, Jack. "The Inexpressive Male: Tragedy or Sexual Politics?" In Rachel Kahn-Hut, Arlene Daniels, and Richard Colvard, eds., *Women and Work: Problems and Perspectives.* New York: Oxford University Press, 1982.

Sayler, R. "Rambo Litigation: Why Hardball Tactics Don't Work." *American Bar Association Journal*, 1 March 1988: 79.

Schultz, Muriel. "The Semantic Derogation of Women." In Barrie Thorne and Nancy Henley, eds., *Language and Sex: Differences and Domination.* Rowley, Mass.: Newbury House, 1975.

Schultz, Vicki. "Women 'Before' the Law: Judicial Stories about Women, Work and Sex Segregation on the Job." In Judith Butler and Joan Scott, eds., *Feminist Theorize the Political.* New York: Routledge, 1992.

Schwartz, Murray. *Lawyers and the Legal Profession: Cases and Materials.* Indianapolis, Bobbs-Merrill, 1979.

Scott, Joan. "Gender as a Useful Category of Historical Analysis." *American Historical Review* 91, no. 5 (December 1986): 1053–75.

Segal, Geraldine. *Blacks in the Law: Philadelphia and the Nation.* Philadelphia: University of Pennsylvania Press, 1983.

Segura, Denise, and Jennifer Pierce. "Chicana/o Family Structure and Gender Personality: Chodorow, Familism and Psychoanalytic Sociology Revisited." *Signs: Journal of Women in Culture and Society* 19, no. 1 (Autumn 1993): 62–91.

Segura, Denise. "Chicanas and Mexican Immigrant Women at Work." *Gender & Society* 3, no. 1 (March 1989): 37–52.

Shipp, E. R. "Paralegals Show Strength in Numbers." *San Francisco Banner*, 30 August 1989: 3.

Sikes, Bette, Clara Carson, and Patricia Gorai, eds. *The 1971 Lawyer Statistical Report.* Chicago: American Bar Foundation, 1972.

Simpson, Richard, and Ida Harper Simpson. "Women and Bureaucracy in the Semi-Professions." In Amitai Etzioni, ed., *The Semi-Professions and Their Organization: Teachers, Nurses, Social Workers.* New York: Free Press, 1969.

Smigel, Erwin. *The Wall Street Lawyer: Professional or Organizational Man?* Second edition. New York: Free Press, 1969.

Smith, Dorothy. "Women's Perspective as Radical Critique of Sociology." *Sociological Inquiry* 44, no. 1 (1974): 7–13.

Smith, Joan. "The Paradox of Women's Poverty: Wage-Earning Women and Economic Transformation." In D. Stanley Eitzen and Maxine Baca Zinn, eds., *The Reshaping of America: Social Consequences and the Changing Economy.* New York: Prentice Hall, 1989.

Sokoloff, Natalie. *Between Money and Love: The Dialectics of Women's Home and Market Work.* New York: Praeger, 1980.

Sontag, Sherry. "Skirmishing Escalates Between Drexel, SEC" *National Law Journal,* 17 October 1988: 3.

Spangler, Eve, Marsha Gordon, and Ronald Pipkin. "Token Women: An Empirical Test of Kanter's Hypothesis." *American Journal of Sociology* 84, no. 1 (July 1978): 160–70.

Spangler, Eve. *Lawyers for Hire: Salaried Professionals at Work.* New Haven: Yale University Press, 1986.

Spence, Gary. *With Justice For None.* New York: Times Books, 1989.

Spencer, Anne, and David Podomore. "Women Lawyers—Marginal Members of a Male Dominated Profession." In Anne Spencer and David Podomore, eds., *In a Man's World: Essays on Women in Male Dominated Professions.* London: Tavistock Publications, 1987.

Stacey, Judith, and Barrie Thorne. "The Missing Feminist Revolution in Sociology." *Social Problems* 32 (1985): 301–16.

Stacey, Judith. *Brave New Families.* New York: Basic Books, 1991.

———. "Can There Be a Feminist Ethnography?" *Women's Studies International Forum* 11, no. 1 (1988): 21–27.

Stanley, Liz, ed. *Feminist Praxis: Research, Theory and Epistemology in Feminist Sociology.* London: Routledge, 1990

Staples, Robert and Alfredo Mirandé. "Racial and Cultural Variation Among American Families: A Decennial Review of Literature on Minority Families." *Journal of Marriage and Family* 42, no. 4 (November 1980): 887–903.

Statham, Anne. "Woman Working for Women: The Manager and her Secretary." In Anne Statham, Eleanor Miller, and Hans Mauksch, eds., *The Worth of Women's Work.* Albany: State University of New York Press, 1988.

Stibelman, Arleen. "Tips for Keeping Clients Happy." *San Francisco Banner,* 26 September 1988a: 9.

———. "Paralegal Group Releases Salary Survey." *San Francisco Banner,* 5 October 1988b: 5.

Strachan, Nell. "A Map for Women on the Road to Success." *American Bar Association Journal*, May 1984: 94–96.

Swaine, Robert. *The Cravath Firm and Its Predecessors, 1819–1947.* New York: Ad Press, privately printed, 1946.

Taft, Henry. *A Century and a Half at the New York Bar.* New York: privately printed, 1938.

Thornton-Dill, Bonnie. "Race, Class and Gender: An All Inclusive Sisterhood?" *Feminist Studies* 9, no. 1(1983): 131–48.

Turow, Scott. "Crossing the Star." *Litigation: Journal of the Section of Litigation, American Bar Association* 14, no. 1 (Fall 1987): 40–42.

Van Mannen, John. *Tales of the Field: On Writing Ethnography.* Chicago: University of Chicago Press, 1988.

Wagner, Ward. *The Art of Advocacy: Jury Selection.* New York, N.Y.: Matthew Bender, 1981.

Warren, Carol. *Gender Issues in Field Research.* Newbury Park, Calif.: Sage Publications, Qualitative Research Methods Series no. 9, 1988.

Warwick, Donald. "Tearoom Trade: Means and Ends in Social Research." In Martin Bulmer, ed., *Social Research Ethics*, pp. 38–58. London: Macmillan, 1982.

Weber, Max. "Bureaucracy." In Hans Gerth and C. Wright Mills, eds., *From Max Weber: Essays in Sociology.* New York: Oxford University Press, 1946 [1922].

Weitzman, Lenore. "Sex-Role Socialization." In Jo Freeman, ed., *Women: A Feminist Perspective.* Palo Alto, Calif.: Mayfield, 1975.

Wellman, Francis. *The Art of Cross-Examination: With the Cross-Examinations of Important Witnesses in Some Celebrated Cases.* Fourth edition. New York: Collier, 1986 [1903].

West, Candace, and Don Zimmerman. "Doing Gender." *Gender & Society* 1, no. 2 (June 1987): 125–51.

Whalen, Joe. "Paralegal Regulation: Consider the Alternatives." *San Francisco Association for Legal Assistants, At Issue*, September 1988: 1.

Wharton, Amy. "Structure and Agency in Socialist Feminist Theory." *Gender & Society* 5, no. 3 (September 1991): 373–89.

White, [no first name listed]. "Ode to Litigation." *National Law Journal*, 13 February 1989: 13.

Whyte, William. *Street Corner Society: The Social Structure of an Italian Slum.* Fourth edition. Chicago: University of Chicago Press, 1993 [1943].

Wickser, Philip. "Law Schools, Bar Examiners and Bar Associations: Cooperation vs. Insulation." *American Law Review* 7 (1933): 729.

Williams, Christine. *Gender Differences at Work: Women and Men in Non-*

traditional Occupations. Berkeley and Los Angeles: University of California Press, 1989.

————, ed. *Doing "Women's Work": Men in Nontraditional Occupations.* Newbury Park, Calif.: Sage Publications, 1993.

Willis, Paul. *Learning to Labour: How Working Class Kids Get Working Class Jobs.* Farnborough, England: Saxon House, 1977.

Willmott, Hugh. "Subjectivity and the Dialectics of Praxis: Opening Up the Core of Labour Process Analysis." In David Knights and Hugh Willmott, eds., *Labour Process Theory.* Basingstoke: Macmillan, 1990.

Wilson, William Julius. "The New Black Sociology: Reflections on the 'Insiders' and 'Outsiders' Controversy." In James Blackwell and Morris Janowitz, eds., *Black Sociologists: Historical and Contemporary Perspectives.* Chicago: University of Chicago Press, 1974.

Winnicott, D. W. *Collected Papers: From Pediatrics to Psychoanalysis.* London: Hogarth, 1958.

Wise, Sue. "A Framework for Discussing Ethical Issues in Feminist Research: A Review of the Literature." In Vivienne Griffiths et al., eds., *Writing Feminist Biographies 2: Using Life Histories.* Studies in Sexual Politics, no. 19. Department of Sociology, University of Manchester, 1987.

Wolfe, Susan. *The Last Billable Hour: A Novel.* New York: St. Martin's Press, 1989.

Wood, Margaret. *The Stranger: A Study in Social Relationships.* New York: Columbia University Press, 1934.

Ziegler, Dee. "Testifying Can be Deadly, Witness Says." *San Francisco Banner,* 18 January 1989: 6.

Zimmer, Lyn. "Tokenism and Women in the Workplace: The Limits of a Gender-Neutral Theory." *Social Problems* 35, no. 1 (February 1988): 64–77.

Zimmerman, Don, and Candace West. "Sex Roles, Interruptions, and Silences in Communication." In Barrie Thorne and Nancy Henley, eds., *Language and Sex.* Rowley, Mass.: Newbury House, 1974.

Zimmerman, Isaiah. "Stress and the Trial Lawyer." *Litigation: Journal of the Section of Litigation, American Bar Association* 9 (Summer 1983): 37–42.

Index

Abu-Lughod, Lila, 190
Acker, Joan, 8, 28, 30
activist research, 213–14
adversarial model, 13, 23–24, 52–54, 59, 61, 86, 91, 104–5, 120–28, 130–32, 135–38, 140–42, 159, 168, 178, 186–87, 206, 223n5, 229n4
affective engagement, 147–48, 152, 173, 184
affective neutrality, 147, 152, 184
affirmative action, 111, 201
agency, 4–5, 14, 178–79, 218n7
aggression: as rule-governed, 65. *See also* intimidation
alternative dispute resolution (ADR), 229n4
American Bar Association, 54, 61
American Bar Association Commission on Women, 106
American Bar Association Journal, 106
American Bar Association's Model Code of Professional Responsibility, 53
anger, 62, 108, 134, 148–49, 158, 65
artists, 150, 170, 172, 174
associates, 28–30, 32–33, 36, 40, 45, 49, 96, 102
attorneys. *See* trial lawyers
Auerbach, Jerome, 26, 38–39, 41, 43, 180

Baker & McKenzie, 228–29n3
Bellah, Robert, 213
Benjamin, Jessica, 11, 52, 65, 59, 187, 226–27n13
Bielby, Denise, 4, 144
billable hours, 28, 220n4
Blauner, Robert, 200, 207
Blumberg, Abraham, 223n6

boss-secretary relationship, 28, 86, 219n13
Bourdieu, Pierre, 5, 111, 161, 227n6
Brown, Lyn, 225n1
Burawoy, Michael, 6–8, 9–10, 13, 60, 73, 174, 179

career ladders, 181, 184
career women, 133
"caretaking," 2–3, 13, 31, 98–102, 147–48, 157, 174, 176–77, 182, 184, 186. *See also* emotional labor
Chiang, Harriet, 110
Choate, Rufus, 71
Chodorow, Nancy, 10–13, 52, 59, 98, 138–40, 156–57, 173, 175, 179, 218n11, 229n4
clerical workers, 1, 28, 31, 37, 42, 44, 46, 48
clients, 34, 41, 51–52, 56, 59, 69, 80–81, 110, 112, 113, 122
Clifford, James, 189, 207, 213
Cockburn, Cynthia, 5, 8
Cohen, Colleen, 213
Collins, Patricia Hill, 181, 193, 204
Connell, Robert, 59–60, 132, 172
Contratto, Susan, 98
corporate capitalism, 38
Coser, Rose Laub, 119
Crapanzano, Vincent, 213
Cravath, Paul D., 39–40
Cravath model, 38, 39–42, 43
cross-examination, 55, 57, 61, 63, 65–67, 76–77, 223n7

Daly, Mary, 202
Davies, Margery, 42, 48, 221–22n19
de Beauvoir, Simone, 91

253

Compositor: ComCom
Text: Caledonia
Display: Caledonia
Printer and Binder: Haddon Craftsmen